THE TRIALS OF MUMIA ABU-JAMAL

THE TRIALS OF MUMIA ABU-JAMAL

A Biography in 25 Voices

EDITED BY
TODD STEVEN BURROUGHS

DIASPORIC AFRICA PRESS
NEW YORK

This book is a publication of
Diasporic Africa Press
New York | www.dafricapress.com

Copyright © Diasporic Africa Press 2022

All rights reserved. No part of this publication may be reproduced or distributed in any form or by any means, or stored in a database or retrieval system, without the prior written permission of the publisher.

Library of Congress Control Number: 2021950338
ISBN-13 978-1-937306-74-8 (pbk.: alk paper)
ISBN-13 978-1-937306-75-5 (ebook)

Special discounts are available for bulk purchases of this book. For more information, please contact us at support@dafricapress.com.

Diasporic Africa Press uses environmentally friendly book materials, including recycled text paper that is composed of at least 30 percent post-consumer waste, whenever possible.

For my friends and mentors Don Rojas, Herb Boyd and Ollie A. Johnson III, who taught me many, many things about our worldwide struggle and always listened

And for Glen Ford (November 5, 1949-July 28, 2021) and Askia Muhammad (March 1947–February 17, 2022), two very public and strong print and radio journalistic supporters of Mumia Abu-Jamal who journeyed to the Realm of the Ancestors while this work was in process

TABLE OF CONTENTS

Foreword—Zayid Muhammad..i
Introduction—Todd Steven Burroughs...v
Mumia Abu-Jamal FAQ: The Voice of the Voiceless
—The Campaign to Bring Mumia Home..xv
NOW 1
   Introduction by YahNé Ndgo 3
   Mumia Abu-Jamal Explained in (Roughly) Four Dates, 2020-2021:
   a Zoom/YouTube Oral History 7
THEN 37
   Introduction by Johanna Fernandez and Linn Washington, Jr. 39
     1969-1970 41
         A Way To Fight Back: The Black Panther Party In
         Philadelphia—Reginald Schell/Dick Custer................................... 43
         Excerpts Of The FBI Files Of Mumia Abu-Jamal............................. 66
         Mumia Abu-Jamal's Black Panther Party Days: "Do Something,
         Nigger, Even If You Only Spit!" (full chapter excerpt from the
         forthcoming Talking Drums and Raised Fists: Mumia Abu-Jamal, A
         Biography Of A Voice) –Todd Steven Burroughs 75
     1971-1979 91
         Mumia, Me And the MOVE Organization
         —Linn Washington, Jr. 93
     1981-1983 107
         The Good-Old Frame-Up: How Police, Prosecution and the Courts
         Turned Mumia Abu-Jamal Into a "Murderer"
         —Michael Schiffmann 115
     1995 141
         Deathwatch—Joe Davidson.. 147
         Mumia Abu-Jamal and The "Death Row Phenomenon"
         —Stanford Law Journal excerpt by Daniel P. Blank 161

1996-2019 163
    Updated Version of Mumia's All-Or-Nothing-Gamble
    —David Lindorff.. 165
    Gun Test Shows Key Witnesses Lied at Abu-Jamal Trial: Sidewalk
    'Murder' Scene Should Have Displayed Bullet Impacts But There
    Were None—David Lindorff and Linn Washington, Jr.................... 199
2020 231
    A Giant Has Fallen: Frances Goldin Presente!
    —Noelle Hanrahan.. 233
    The Invisible Scholar? Mumia Abu-Jamal's Impact on Africana
    Studies—Kelly Harris.. 237
    Mumia Speaks: Heartened by Black Lives Matter, Imprisoned
    Activist Mumia Abu-Jamal is Still Fighting The Good
    Fight—Which Now Includes a Deadly Pandemic
    —Kevin L. Clark.. 247
    "The Power of Truth is Final": Publisher's Note for Vol. 3 of
    Abu-Jamal/Stephen Vittoria's Murder, Incorporated—Jennifer Black
    and Miranda Hanrahan Beach.. 253
Post-Script: An Open Letter to Pennsylvania Governor Tom Wolf
—Julia Wright.. 259
About the Contributors 263

FOREWORD
ZAYID MUHAMMAD

This is for those whose eyes have not yet seen what we've seen. This is for those whose eyes have not seen what the rest of the world has seen. This is for those who still can't believe that the government and the state of Pennsylvania can actually be actively trying to eliminate a courageous dissident and a dissident journalist.

For those of u who believe that this government, that this country, is not capable of that...

Think again.

Nearly 100 years ago, they framed and killed two leftists, Italian immigrants Sacco and Vanzetti.

Shortly before that, they put another leftist unionist artist and activist before a firing squad named Joe Hill, the same Joe Hill immortalized by the robust barrel-chested baritone of Paul Robeson, who would find himself chained to his passport in the madness of the congressional fascist '50s of McCarthy.

Huey Newton and Angela Davis survived possible dates with the gas chambers in the modern era, but their lesser-known comrades Ajamu Nassor and Ziyon Yisrael were each executed in Mike Pence's Indiana in the '90s for surviving and defending themselves from an unannounced police attack on their homes.

This is for those of u who had conveniently forgotten what u know u saw when Pennsylvania state law put Mumia back in court in 1995 before Judge Albert Sabo, the same racist judge who took the point for his frame-up. You know u saw Sabo deny every motion by Mumia's attorneys. You know u saw him have a witness, Veronica Jones, arrested on the stand for coming forward to recant her coerced testimony in the trial that he oversaw. You know what u saw, but insisted to yourself that this was just too out of the ordinary to be believed. Even after evidence later revealed Sabo's pathological deep-seated 'n' word contempt for Mumia... "I'm going to help them fry the nigger"... yes, that kind of lynch thirsty racist contempt,... too many of u stood by and believed that this just can't be!...

It was, and it is...

Yet so many of you genuinely don't know what really is involved in this incredible case about this incredible man because of a big white elephant in the room that no one is really talking about at all... the Corporate American media order which has so skillfully kept u from knowing. They would rather participate in the silencing of this fearless searing voice because he has devoted his entire life, since he was a teenager, to exposing the racist abuses of this very corporate order!...

So for those of u who didn't see Mumia banned from the court in his own trial for his very life; for those of u who don't believe or didn't know that each of the eyewitnesses in his trial had been coerced for their manufactured testimony;

For those of u who didn't know that J. Patrick O'Connor already revealed in another important book, *The Framing of Mumia Abu-Jamal*, that the actual killer of Officer Daniel Faulkner was Kenneth Freeman, who himself was killed incredibly under cover of a flaming and smoking of Osage Avenue sky when Move was bombed on May 13, 1985;

For those of u who didn't know that Black jurors were systematically kept from being on the jury and that the state of Pennsylvania was so blatant in the process that they even had a video showing prosecutors how to keep Black jurors off of juries even though that is supposed to be against the law;

For those of u who didn't know that every cop involved in the crime scene, all 15 of them, would be implicated for corruption;

For those of u who didn't know, the lead cop on the scene was withheld from testifying in Mumia's case because he was about to face his own case 'as a defendant' on federal charges;

For those of u who didn't know that they wanted Mumia dead so bad that when he had Hep C, treatable Hep C (deadly if not treated, however), that they were willing to let 10,000 other Pennsylvania prisoners similarly diagnosed with the disease die from not receiving the treatment right along with Mumia,... *10,000!*... ;

For those of u who would rather question and challenge the current so-called liberal reformer D.A. Larry Krasner for "finding" and turning over six boxes of "lost" files that include within them in writing one of the witnesses against Mumia, one Robert Chobert, making it very plain to then D.A. Joe McGill "Where is my money?",... money for testifying against Mumia;

For those of u in so much disbelief and who rather instead believe that this must all be a bad episode of *The Twilight Zone*; America, and the hypocrisy of its Democracy, Malcolm's language, is The Twilight Zone; For those of u stuck in that space, for those of u who just didn't know, this volume is for u!

After almost 40 years of trying to get the real evidence in this case heard, which includes Mumia surviving two death warrants, several major medical crises, including that Hep C just mentioned that eerily sounds like the pathetic mishandling of our current COVID Crisis, the time has come for a court somewhere in these united states (I am not going to capitalize it until Black Lives Matter) to allow the real evidence, the wrongly withheld evidence, and all the overtly racist procedural and prosecutorial misconduct, and all the legal "exceptionalism," the time has come for all of this to be properly put on the record, for all of this to be openly and properly heard and treated in order for this man, this brave lone voice for the voiceless in the north american wilderness, to finally have a fair hearing in the name of simple justice!

The time for that is now!

We are thankful for the editor, Dr. Todd Steven Burroughs, who also gave us another rich tome, *Warrior Princess: A People's Biography of Ida B. Wells*, on another dissident journalist and suffragist, and who, assisting Dr. Jared Ball of Morgan State University, co-edited a hugely important volume of scholars, *A Lie of Reinvention: Correcting Manning Marable's Malcolm X*, taking apart Marable's attack on Malcolm X, helping set that record straight. We are thankful to all of the contributors, virtually all of whom have joined us on the streets and in packing the courts for the humanity of Mumia and the humanity of our struggle, in our people's push to have the truth finally told and for Mumia to finally get free...

In this very historical moment that we all share, we are now not only at the crossroads for Mumia's case and for Mumia's life; We are at the crossroads for the very immediate future of this country... When at the crossroads, there is but one way to go... Forward...

INTRODUCTION

TODD STEVEN BURROUGHS

Carving out your own space in life can be a lonely endeavor because you have to figure out your own signposts. The Tweet from Sirius XM broadcaster Karen Hunter was very direct: I had Tweeted folks about Mumia Abu-Jamal being interviewed in the November/December 2020 issue of *Essence*. This was right after NFL activist Colin Kaepernick publicly came out in support of Abu-Jamal, so a lot of activist energy was in the air. Hunter answered: "When are you coming on the show?"

My response was equally direct: "Me or the Mumia Movement?" And I recommended the people I knew most involved for decades: Johanna Fernandez, who organized the press conference that contained Kaepernick, and Zayid Muhammad, an activist and poet who had been involved with the political prisoner movement for decades. My thinking was: *activists should activate. The Male Principle and the Female Principle.*

I let the Free Mumia listserv know that Hunter had reached out and what I had said. "ATTENTION JOHANNA AND ZAYID: In response to my Tweet about Mumia and *Essence*, Karen Hunter of XM Radio is on Twitter asking me, @BringMumiaHome and @MumiaAbuJamal when are 'we' coming on the show. I'm bowing out, telling her to contact you and Zayid Muhammad to talk about Mumia, Maroon and COVID and linked both of you on Twitter! FYI!" I had cc'd Zayid Muhammad, so he knew I had mentioned him.

Fernandez told me to connect them. I told her I already had on Twitter. Muhammad responded to me, cc'ing the listserv: "Todd, You have serious work coming out on Mumia!", referring to this very book and my forthcoming Abu-Jamal journalistic biography. "These more commercial talk types are more 'comfortable' going to those they know, or think they know. They tend to keep their airspace 'small' or, in their minds, 'exclusive'. Don't dismiss going on because of us. It's more important for us to get our PPs (political prisoners) stories told in as many audiences as we can... She is not likely to call us. She is one of my many press contacts for several organizations i do press for, incl P.O.P. [the People's Organization for Progress]. She is even a friend of a prominent P.O.P. member. Never has reached out to any of us... We kick doors open... We don't close them... All weapons on the table..."[1]

I was humbled by the love and respect behind that particular email. So I responded thusly to him and to the listserv: "I'm hearing you. But as a biographer, I speak *about* Mumia. This is a critical time to speak *for* Mumia and the other struggling-to-survive PP—the people on the frontlines *for* them—to come forward! This is the right move for me for now, but I appreciate your kind words."

I don't know if Hunter ever responded to Fernandez. A day later, I got this email from Julia Wright of France, a mainstay of the listerv and the "Free Mumia" movement.

> *Hey Todd,*
>
> *From a veteran journalist in the struggle, here is my take on that issue—just my 2 cents for all they're worth.*
>
> *As a biographer, you are writing* ABOUT *Mumia and therefore would refrain from speaking* FOR *him, you say—if I get you.*
>
> *To my mind, there is a very porous line between the two: when you attempt in all "neutrality" to write about your bio subject and get at the truth about him, you help bring to the table facts in his defense because of your very attempt at objectivity. When we advocate for Mumia, we bring forth facts that create a different objective narrative, an alternative truth.*
>
> *The two viewpoints bleed into each other.*
>
> *One example.*
>
> *The 800-page FBI file on Mumia establishes a set of facts - the opponents' established narrative - but those very facts come to Mumia's defense, establishing the political racism at the root of their targeting of him.*
>
> *On the other hand, Colin Kaepernick's fierce, historical advocacy for Mumia breaking FOP silence for the first time in years,*

INTRODUCTION

creating a tsunami in the media, has highlighted and given new relevance to objective facts buried in "cold case" indifference.

So, there is dialectical give and take between the two ways of approaching Mumia ... Or so I would think.

These are such exhilarating times; our ideas are in effervescence!

Right on!
Julia[2]

And that's how this book's Introduction started before the on-the-way-to-death-virus tide of March 2021. Mumia Abu-Jamal was diagnosed with COVID, and the "Free Mumia" movement—via its listserv and Zoom—sprang into action, maintaining an almost hourly presence in email inboxes for the entire month. As an Abu-Jamal biographer, I suddenly was involved again with active biographing—observing how effective the activists were using the technology—social media, Zoom calls, and YouTube. *The Jamal Journal,* the print newspaper that I remember from the 1990s campaigns, was revived online and in print. "Free Mumia" events on Zoom had been established by the time of Abu-Jamal's diagnosis, and now they became an important national and international platform for those who could not gather in Philadelphia for protests demanding Abu-Jamal get the proper treatment.

The observation—the *about*—eventually and inevitably spilled over into the activism—the *for*—as I shared transcripts, gave suggestions and forwarded social media posts. My Gmail inbox proved the activists worked nonstop over the month of March to put increased pressure on Philadelphia D.A. Larry Krasner to push the Department of Corrections and his fellow Democrat, Pennsylvania Governor Tom Wolf, to give Abu-Jamal the compassionate release so feared by the Faulkner forces.

When word spread that WHYY-FM—Abu-Jamal's old NPR station, back then WUHY—was preparing an advance obit, a standard operating procedure for major mainstream news media, many on the MAJ listserv were incensed because they felt NPR's inquisitive, journalistic energy could be better spent discussing instead why two elderly Pennsylvania Black political prisoners (translation: Black Panther Party) in state lockup with COVID—Abu-Jamal and Russell "Maroon" Shoatz—should or should not be given compassionate release.

A recovering Abu-Jamal shot a loving arrow to three targets: his wife; a consistent member of The Family Africa now known worldwide, and to his many supporters.

> *Dear sisters, brothers, comrades, and friends and family on a MOVE!*
>
> *How can I thank you? These, my words, can hardly measure the flood of love that you have radiated on my behalf recently. I am almost—almost—without words, but I'll try.*
>
> *Thank you, Wadiya.*
>
> *Thank you, Pam Africa. Your support from Philadelphia to France, from points across the nation and literally around the globe, have pulled me from a prison cell and placed me in a hospital room to be treated for a condition I didn't know I had.*
>
> *In the age of pandemic—now, indeed, deeply doubted pandemic—as of January 2021, over 300,000 prisoners have tested positive for COVID-19.*
>
> *Imagine that: in a cell, trying to breathe with a weight pressing on your chest. Imagine an elder man or woman, or even a young person, because yes, we are also in an age of mass incarceration, which day-by-day increases its infliction upon the elderly struggling, unsuccessfully, to breathe, to walk, to be.*
>
> *I thank you all for reaching out, and I urge you all, let our mission be abolition. I love you all. Thank you again, from the bottom of my heart.*
>
> *From imprisoned nation, this is Mumia Abu-Jamal.*[3]

After 26 years, it's strange to know that there is now an unmovable-but-flexible actual deadline for Abu-Jamal, the writer and the written. I have had to deal with the revelation that five to ten years from now, Mumia Abu-Jamal may no longer be freshly recorded or in new print, no more "From Imprisoned Nation, this is Mumia *Abu*-Jamal." I know that even though he beat COVID, a 68-year-old senior citizen with a heart condition, previously-known diabetes, a bad skin condition and liver cirrhosis from his untreated Hepatitis C days, does not add up to living another two decades or so. A case, a life and a struggle so protracted that it seemed never-ending at times suddenly had a *medical* death warrant issued—one signed by time itself, one that could not be rescinded. The activists are right: the best treatment is freedom. But one day soon, in or out of Imprisoned Nation, the *about* is going to win.

This dual distinction that Wright, the daughter of 20TH-century Black writing legend Richard Wright, placed in my brain's foreground is really important to discuss from a macro perspective in 2021. We have had a collection of Black public intellectuals who write for the white, liberal public for a generation now. The decolonized writing of a Hubert Henry Harrison, the writer-editor-speaker-thinker who set the foundation for the Garvey movement, or a teenaged Black Panther named Wes in Philadelphia, is considered passé. *Not Ready For* (MSNBC) *Primetime*. An army of Black, Brown, and Other Ivy League degree holders who have been trained how to sound radical but call for standard, "progressive" reforms. Standing for everything Democratic, liberal and moderate and against only the most egregious parts of hegemony, they are all over the airwaves like *Doctor Who's* Daleks, loudly exterminating other lines of thought. As far as I know, only one of them in the last decade has ever put their job on the line for a radical cause, and that was Marc Lamont Hill, who was almost booted from Temple University for boldly standing up for the Palestinians at the United Nations. What made him different is that he knew that to stand for Palestine meant he had to stand against the Israeli government and its apartheid practices. Like Abu-Jamal promoting MOVE on-air circa 1980, Hill lost his CNN commenting job for his tone and content. It is not surprising that Hill is a co-author of a 2011 book with Mumia, *The Classroom and the Cell: Conversations on Black Life in America,* because he understood the yin/yang so many 21ST century pretenders just ignore: an activist is judged by his enemies and how they have tried to publicly crush you.

Abu-Jamal carries levels of distinction, but, in my slightly informed opinion, not in the way too many activists have said for the last 27 or so years. He was a Black Panther, yes, but so were thousands of young Black people who have not spent 40 years in prison. He reported on police brutality, but that's no big deal either because so did others in Black media in Philadelphia, then and now. He was followed by the FBI the way hundreds were in the Movement. Did the state of Pennsylvania threaten to "fry the nigger?" Yes, but Pennsylvania had that reputation before and kept it after Mumia's 1982 trial and 1983 sentencing. So Mumia is *not* special in any of the above. The Leftist romance around him should not obscure the situation's most common spots. What makes Mumia Abu-Jamal distinctive, then? From my point of view as a *journalistic* biographer, it's the radio commentaries, the Op-Eds (the print versions), the mini and maxi-essays and the constant battle waged by the state against them.

I have had a *long* relationship with many in this book because I have written about Mumia Abu-Jamal for about half my life now, with strong historic leanings in the *for* category. So I definitely understand Wright's idea of the porous division. (I remember how sad I was to find out, way too late, about a *for* book in 1996 called *In Defense of Mumia*, edited by S.E. Anderson and Tony Medina. This book is the first to do such a wide-ranging, multi-author MAJ anthology since then.) If you just chose to write about the legal injustices inflicted on Mumia, as Linn Washington Jr. has done for 40 years, it reads more like representation than reporting. If you just write about the violation of his First Amendment rights, as I have for 26 years now, it reads like representation more than reporting. Mumia Abu-Jamal is an American revolutionary, and that means that a) the state will be merciless and b) the supporters will be small but devout. The wheat and the chaff showed themselves in 2011 when he was taken off of Death Row and put in the general population, his date to die before his COVID diagnosis as blurred as ours. The international, well-funded anti-death penalty movement moved on to other, less articulate and less openly radical people, leaving just a relatively small, but no-less-dedicated MAJ band—but clearly bigger than it was in the beginning, back in the 1980s when MOVE was bombed, and Abu-Jamal was in solitary because he wouldn't cut off his dreadlocks. So writing about the Pennsylvania prison journalist, whether one chooses to be "objective" or not, is to stick your toe into a nonlinear whirling pool of potential lost causes, risking post-revolutionary oppression and depression.

What has always fascinated me about the "Free Mumia" movement is its unflagging passion for someone they are powerless to move, but not powerless to keep healthy. It takes bucketloads to spend 30 years of your life taking collect calls from someone in prison and record, edit and distribute them for posterity, as Noelle Hanrahan has done via Prison Radio. (Hanrahan's passion has now extended to the printed word, with the formation of Prison Radio Publishing, the publisher of Abu-Jamal's and Stephen Vittoria's three-volume radical masterpiece on the dirty doings of the American empire.) It takes passion for finding out Mumia Abu-Jamal is sick and then making sure the world knows, as Johanna Fernandez, Pam Africa and Hanrahan have done. And it takes the most burning commitment—the steadiest, most serious love—to fight to get advocates for Abu-Jamal the way Pam and Romana Africa and the rest of The Family Africa have done. To be an advocate for Abu-Jamal—to be in the ditch with Betsey Piette, Wright, and others—is to spend much of your life with/for him.

All involved are clear on objectives. All have gathered thousands of documents, newspaper and magazine articles, audio, video. But we have different prisms, with different questions coming out of differing goals. They're trying to get a cat out of the joint while I attempt to assess a world-historical, self-described 20TH and 21ST century revolutionary figure. So while I, now in the *about* category, struggle with, for example, critical-biographer questions *(Was Mumia idiotic, if not naïve, to turn down an offer by some in the Black community in late 1981-early 1982 to fundraise for a high-quality Black lawyer? Was his trial strategy and behavior reckless? Was his 2001 affidavit, his first extended version of what happened at 13TH and Locust on December 9, 1981, a desperate attempt to get out of jail, an unfortunate retcon spurred by irresponsible legal counsel?)* the activists focus on the unfairness of the case, the worn jackboot of the state, and the salient information to get people awake.

Ironically, like fellow used-to-be-young-turk Jesse Jackson and few others from the 20TH century who met and embraced old age in the 21ST, Abu-Jamal is almost beyond words now, very near to being beyond critique. The imprisoned writer has survived to see his own history on both horizons, his past and future—ones he helped write one radical newspaper, pamphlet, broadcast, column, and book at a time. He may die with his case being forever labeled "controversial," but his significance to the 20TH and 21ST century Left, to worldwide prison writing, to radical radio broadcasting, to American jailhouse lawyering, and now to worldwide radical literature, is beyond dispute.

Here is a "collective biography," written and spoken into being by many activists, scholars and writers. The book's two sections, "Now" and "Then," not only break time in half but divides up collective versus intellectual work.

"Now" contains the March 2021 collective spoken-word and organizing work of Piette of the *Worker's World* online news source, Gabriel Bryant, Wright, Santiago Alvarez, Kaepernick, *The Jamal Journal* online and print news source, the renowned scholar and activist Angela Y. Davis, Fernandez, Gabe Bryant, Yahné Ndgo, Linn Washington, Jr., Pam Africa and Hanrahan, among others.

"Then" starts with Washington and Fernandez setting the tone of the past with an exchange about the MOVE Organization. Then Reginald Schell, Abu-Jamal's former Defense Captain for the Philadelphia branch of the Black Panther Party, and Dick Cluster. Then, a very small sample of Abu-Jamal's FBI files and a chapter on Abu-Jamal's BPP years give a portrait of a turbulent time connecting to a young man who became a radical. Washington then outlines his 1970s reflections of the MOVE Organization and his young, dreadlocked radio journalist friend and colleague. Michael Schiffmann, Abu-Jamal's political biographer, writes about the crime scene and the crimes behind it. Joe Davidson, a founder of the National Association of Black Journalists, writes about Abu-Jamal in a 1995 cover story of *Emerge* magazine, Abu-Jamal's only mainstream media magazine cover. (Abu-Jamal's first-person sidebar exclusively for *Emerge*, "Walkin' in the Shadow of Death," has been reprinted many times, but this is the first time *Davidson's* article has been reprinted.) Legal scholar Daniel F. Blank gives some needed context in an excerpt of a seminal law journal article about Abu-Jamal and Pennsylvania's death penalty. Investigative journalist and author David Lindoff discuss in detail the radical shift Abu-Jamal made with a new legal team at the turn of the century, one apparently more focused on conspiracies that salient, provable facts. Lindoff follows up with the chronicling of a gun test that causes real questions to be asked about justice and that night at 13TH and Locust. The brother-sister Schiffmann team, Michael and Annette, give a visual history of the history of Abu-Jamal protests in Germany, while Wright and Jacque Lederer's fiction speaks for radical France. Kelly Harris, who, like Fernandez, represents the Africana tradition formally as a professor, asks the question if Mumia Abu-Jamal, who is studying for his doctorate at the University of California at Santa Cruz, is recognized within

Africana Studies as one of its own. Kevin L. Clark of *Essence* magazine discusses with Abu-Jamal health care and COVID in prison, a topic that became more timely as 2020 turned into 2021. And Noelle's touching tribute to Abu-Jamal's agent, Frances Goldin, brings the section closer to denouement. But the book is closed out by Miranda Hanrahan Beach and Jennifer Black, with their discussion of Abu-Jamal's completion of his magnum opus—a trilogy, co-written with his filmmaker biographer Stephen Vittoria, about the American empire.

Together, the contributors are representative of a) who chooses to write for Mumia and b) how they choose to do so. Many of these writers have become internationally known for their unambiguous stances on this life and case.

Editor's Note No. 1: There are two names listed here that you won't find in the Table of Contents. Gabe Byrant and Santiago Alvarez are listed here as a tribute to their activism and organizing, particularly during those maniac March days. Although not in the pages *per se*, they are behind many words and images of "Free Mumia" 2020 and 2021 and what is said here.

Editor's Note No. 2: I don't necessarily agree with every description, argument, characterization, or point of view presented here. But I thought it was important to be representative of Abu-Jamal's life arc and his advocates' worldview; four is still four whether its two plus two or eight minus four. I have strived for the narrative arc, one that allows subject and writer/speaker to merge into the same ideas, the same vantage point, containing the same friends and enemies.

They write *for* Abu-Jamal because, in their/our view, he writes for us—the *real* us, not the public *I-like-Joe-Biden-and-Kamala-Harris, no-I'm-not-kidding-I-really-do* us. The *why-you-so-angry-all-the-time* us. The *skeptical-of-the-system/state* us. The us that only comes out of its techcages and plays its angry war drums in the streets when a Republican is in national or state office.

Like his musical contemporary Gil Scott-Heron, Abu-Jamal has never simultaneously stopped creating for, playing to and building his audience. He's the physical manifestation of the underground news service with a full archive. He's the *Black Panther* (newspaper) proletariat type-writer who eventually became the first blogger, long ago dubbed cyberspace's first political prisoner, but who in 2021 is one of the last of that imprisoned radical realm still alive and fully functioning. Ed Bradley's Black radical alter ego doesn't have another 67 years with us, but since he took to the Philadelphia airwaves in 1975, Abu-Jamal has carried himself with distinction. We are left to explain, then, to the present and future why his body of work, his long life and his ideas remain important, and why they never fail to cut the glass of the status quo but, sadly, never leave any permanent cracks on it—with the notably evil exception of draconian "Mumia Exceptions" (a term contributor Linn Washington, Jr. has made famous) created by sore winners and spread throughout Pennsylvania prisons and halls of justice run by legions of doom. Abu-Jamal has taken the underground press and, thanks to the Internet, the World Wide Web, digital printing and a group of devout believers, morphed it into his own *overground-underground*: intellectually decaffeinated audio for those who choose to hear, web*sights* for those who choose to see and click, binded words for those who choose to read paper.

Forty years removed from the streets of Philadelphia, Mumia Abu-Jamal is his own subject, syllabus and lecturer at YouTube University—an intangible edifice that is part of a digital world he largely has never seen, much less participate. But 26 years after he was live from Death Row, the 2021 COVID-diagnosis-rapid-response of his team proves he will not be forgotten like Harrison, another great writer and speaker of the past. The scattered and linked digital breadcrumbs—the hip-hop name-drops, the feature film documentaries, the archived Prison Radio audio, and now even the doctoral dissertations firmly locked in databases will also help. While he lives, he will continue to force himself into relevancy because, 40 years under lock and key, he continues to write about and for the present and the future, not the/his past. He has not MOVE-d; we have. Whether we write about or for, we have the same choice we have always had: his life is ours to carry to 2022 and beyond or just be collectively resigned to look at Abu-Jamal as a now slowly-crumbling museum piece, a Black radical version of a Confederate statue that hegemony will invisibly make every attempt to take down. But you can't dismantle something that lives in both the activist heart and in the ever-retrievable digital air.

MUMIA ABU-JAMAL FAQ: THE VOICE OF THE VOICELESS[4]

THE CAMPAIGN TO BRING MUMIA HOME

WHO IS MUMIA?

Mumia is a revolutionary journalist. He has been writing since age 15, first as Minister of Information for the Philadelphia chapter of the Black Panther Party (1969-1971), then for numerous Philadelphia radio and print venues, including National Public Radio.

His journalism was featured in mainstream venues, but he refused to forget those whom corporate media routinely neglect. He was especially noted for covering police harassment of the MOVE Organization, while other journalists ignored it.

His writings, today, after 39 years in prison, now fill twelve books and thousands of radio and print columns in publications ranging from homeless "street news" papers to *Forbes* magazine and *The Yale Law Review*.

MUMIA SERVED NEARLY 30 YRS. ON DEATH ROW

Mumia was confined for three decades on Pennsylvania's death row before federal courts ruled "unconstitutional" the death sentence he received at age 27 for the shooting death of Philadelphia police officer, Daniel Faulkner. He now is serving a "Life Without Parole" sentence in Pennsylvania's general prison population.

MUMIA IS THE UNITED STATES' MOST INTERNATIONALLY RENOWNED POLITICAL PRISONER

Mumia is known worldwide as a political prisoner, because of the political context of his arrest, sentencing and imprisonment.

He was arrested, tried, convicted and sentenced in the era of rampant police brutality, and also of activists' resistance, under former Philadelphia Mayor Frank Rizzo.

In that period, Mumia uncompromisingly reported on police brutality and racism, exposing officials' brutal assaults on the MOVE family & organization, and on other national and international revolutionary movements.

When he was found already shot at the scene of Officer Faulkner's shooting, police brutally beat Mumia beyond recognition, then charged him with the officer's shooting. He has been imprisoned ever since, on the basis of a trial that systematically denied him due process, involving prosecutors' withholding of evidence, racial bias in juror selection, and a judge's rampant bias.

Further, higher courts have routinely rejected Mumia's numerous appeals on the basis of exceptional rulings that denied him the courtesy of court precedents that often were extended to others who lodged the same appeals on the same grounds.

MUMIA IS A FRAMED MAN

A charge of killing a police officer is the hardest rap to beat, even when innocent, especially for a revolutionary activist of color. Nevertheless, the arguments for Mumia's innocence are some of the strongest that can be made. He has maintained his innocence from the very beginning and to this day. Independent journalists researching his case have set forth cogent grounds that Abu-Jamal was framed (e.g. *Patrick O'Connor, The Framing of Mumia Abu-Jamal,* 2008).

Amnesty International, in its extensive analysis of the case in 2000, called for "a new trial," holding that the original trial "was irredeemably tainted by politics and race and failed to meet international fair trial standards."

Even a lawyer writing for the mainstream *American Lawyer* magazine, who was prone to call Mumia "guilty," nevertheless still summarized at length the evidence for a police frame-up, announcing, "I'm joining the 'Save Mumia' movement, here and now" (Stuart Taylor, Jr., *American Lawyer*, December 1, 1995).

MUMIA'S CASE IS A PRIMER FOR WHAT MANY OTHERS SUFFER

Mumia's case is a veritable primer on the kinds of abuse suffered by the Black, brown and poor in the U.S. today. What happened to Mumia foregrounds starkly what many suffer in police encounters, in dealings with prosecutors, in trial and appellate courts, and in U.S. jails, prisons and detention centers. Consider these links, below, between Mumia's own experience and what is suffered by others in the U.S. today:

(1) Like so many others' bodies, Mumia's body was subjected to a brutal beating by police, on the street and in his ambulance on way to the hospital, before any determination of guilt was even attempted. He was Black, brown, poor – therefore, vulnerable and beaten. Before that, he was subject to numerous cases of "stop and frisk" harassment.

(2) As seen by all too many of the poor, today, who stand before judges, the prosecutors suppress evidence that might work in favor of defendants.

In Mumia's case, the fact of a fourth person being at the crime scene, who was the likely perpetrator (Kenneth Freeman) was never considered by Mumia's jury. The prosecutor in Mumia's case acknowledged during another trial that this fourth person was present at the crime scene where Mumia was arrested and beaten.

Both police and prosecutors also suppressed an independent journalist's photographs of the crime scene. Taken by Pedro Polakoff, these were the first photos taken at the scene. They disprove key points in the state's case and raise numerous other questions undermining the coherence of prosecutors' case. These were never made available to the defense or jurors despite the photographer's offering them to both police and prosecutors.

(3) As experienced by many defendants of color, in Mumia's trial the D.A. used 10-11 of its 15 "peremptory challenges" to target Black jurors for removal from potential service on Mumia's jury. This left Mumia, from

a community that was overwhelmingly Black, with a "jury of his peers" that was over 2/3 white.

Five years after Mumia's trial, a video training tape came to light detailing D.A. strategies to intentionally keep Black jurors off juries when there are Black defendants.

(4) Along with many others, Mumia has suffered harsh constraints of the Anti-Terrorism and Effective Death Penalty Act of 1996 that regulates the appeals process above the state level. This 1996 act, passed when some of Mumia's strongest challenges to Pennsylvania's courts were in process, limited federal powers of review over state court decisions. This effectively blocked Mumia's chances, and those of others, in their attempts to gain relief for even their strong claims. Many of the 198 currently on Pennsylvania's death row, and among the more than 3,000 on U.S. death rows, have been at the mercy of state courts ever since this 1996 Act.

But Mumia has suffered this limitation acutely in his state, having his appeals denied repeatedly while others' appeals have been granted for the same claims! A federal judge on the U.S. Third Circuit Court of Appeals himself noted this fact. The repeated practice of this denial to Mumia came to be called "the Mumia exception."

(5) Along with numerous others throughout Pennsylvania, Mumia faced a biased judge who had an unusually high number of his capital trial decisions reversed. That judge, Albert Sabo, also had been a member of a police union (the Fraternal Order of Police) and was heard in a court anteroom by a court stenographer to say of his work at Mumia's trial, "Yeah, and I'm gonna help 'em fry the n———-."

(6) Like all too many who go to trial without good defense counsel, Mumia was convicted in the absence of basic forensic evidence. The bullet that killed Officer Faulkner could not conclusively be matched to Abu-Jamal's gun. The police also failed to perform routine tests on Abu-Jamal's hands, which would have determined whether he had even shot a gun that night.

(7) Finally, and again like the experiences of many others in Philadelphia, Mumia's arrest and trial conviction were secured in an era when city police corruption was rampant. Less than two years before Mumia's trial, the Department of Justice, in an unprecedented move filed a lawsuit against the Mayor and 21 city and police officials for abuse that "shocks the conscience" (the lawsuit's words).

The officers who arrested and later brutalized Mumia came from the 6ᵀᴴ District, which was under yet another federal investigation for police corruption, approved by the U.S. Attorney General under Ronald Reagan.

As a result, fully a third of the 35 officers involved in Mumia's case, including the top officer at the crime scene, Inspector Alfonzo Giordano, were subsequently convicted of corruption, extortion and tampering with evidence to obtain convictions.

NOW

YAHNÉ NDGO, SPEAKING AT MARCH 6, 2021 MUMIA ABU-JAMAL ZOOM EVENT

We all know that Mumia is an important voice of The People, and that that is one of the primary reasons he has been incarcerated for so long. And so to begin, what I would like to do is just read a few words from his book *Murder, Incorporated* about the white republic. We're speaking here about laws because right now we see that Mumia is subject to these extremely unjust laws, these fake laws. And he is being held based on the idea of the validity of these laws and the credibility of these laws.

And here Mumia and Stephen Vittoria write:

> *The Supreme Court saw itself as the nation's elites saw itself, as primarily white first. It should therefore not surprise us that one of the first congressional acts of the nation, the Naturalization Act of 1790, plainly limited nationalization to all free white persons.*
>
> *And while this proved a law to millions of the Europeans, it proved a snare for the multitudes of color, both within and without the white republic. Within the borders of the U.S., the Aboriginal peoples, the so-called Indians, saw what that U.S. law meant firsthand.*
>
> *In essence, the law meant precisely what the dominant whites wanted law to mean. Whatever they wanted it to mean. As we can see, it could mean one thing one day and a completely different thing on another. For the law was an instrument by which they could achieve their own objectives, which usually meant the taking of Indian lands and territories.*
>
> *Why is this important in the study of the Supreme Court's*

imperial rulings? The answer is quite simple. Imperialism didn't just spring into existence like Athena from the skull of Zeus, for imperialism is an economic reality, no matter the myths mouthed by media or academia.

And so when we talk about the economic reality of imperialism, what we're talking about is capitalism. And capitalism is the economic foundation of the nation's elites. And I personally don't like the term elite because there's nothing at all elite about those motherfuckers, those dregs in the ruling class.

But those individuals use as two of their primary tools racism and classism. And we see how that works through the January 6ᵀᴴ event that had the nation in uproar. Where you had all of these right-winged white people going in and storming the U.S. Capitol, and then surviving that with only one death of those who were insurging. And, and the way those people were treated by those in power as opposed to how those in power treat others. And the truth is that it was a reflection not simply of racism but the reality that this particular group was not actually doing anything to attack or confront the status quo. The actual endangerment of the status quo is the trigger. So yes, the pigs did go ahead and they did sacrifice some of those people by going and putting them in jail; they will do that especially to their lower class whites at times like these, because they are considered easily sacrificial in the shadow of a primary goal like the shoring up of the status quo. So, they were sacrificed. And the agents of the ruling class began to initiate and instill new legislation that they would actually be able to—and going forward would most frequently use against OUR movement, all the while claiming that neither these laws nor their implementation could be racist. Why not? Because of their pretend origins - a response to WHITE so-called insurgency. It would be correct to recognize the classist elements of this situation since the rioters were for the most part only sacrificed—as in jailed—because they were the poorer, lower, utility class of whites, useful only in their purpose of protecting the status quo. Yet we cannot forget that, though the material and the class interests of those rioters are most aligned with our community, individuals like those capital clowns never stand with us because of how capitalism has used racism to pit them against us. Which is why any legislation introduced because of their behavior is also racist. It's racist not only because it will be wielded primarily against us and was truly created to be wielded primarily against us, and not only because the reason the capital clowns didn't die is because they were white. It's racist because in spite of our class alignment our community will support the development of these laws to be used against the movement for the sake of witnessing white people finally being held accountable. It's racist because white people will celebrate as the laws are imposed against us as it will help them to feel closer to "elite." This system will not work without the misalignment of the working class and poor. And working class and poor whites must feel their whiteness makes them special so that they will play their role of protecting the capitalist, imperialist systems that oppress all of us.

Racism is a primary operating stance or a primary operating space from which the enemies of our community engage, and certainly, therefore, the enemies of Mumia.

So these laws that Mumia's talking about, that are being used right now to justify withholding his freedom, these laws are able to be used in whatever way the ruling class decides they want to use them. And they're used against some people and not used against some other people. Not only does their application change from one day to the next, but it also changes depending on who it is on which the ruling class is actually focused.

So now we turn and look at someone like Mumia, who actually does challenge the status quo. He is so well-informed about the nature of the system. He is powerful not only because he articulates the reality of the nature of the system, but because he does it in a way that is so easily consumable.

Mumia's voice is one that can create massive, massive cracks in a system of imperialism and capitalism that is depended upon for the maintenance of the hegemony of the ruling class.

And that is why the ruling class intends to keep Mumia behind bars. But of course, this is not something that we will abide; we must fight for our brother. He must be released and returned to The People.

His voice is so important; as is all of his writings. What I just read is but one example, an amazing read, a segment combining with all kinds of histories going all the way back to the founding of this nation, showing all of its contradictions.

And Mumia has been able to produce this work, this and so many others, while being subject to the unjust, cruel and harsh treatments of incarceration for not years but decades. Imagine what he will give us when he's free.

We have to fight for Mumia and for all of our political prisoners. And Mumia teaches us that all prisoners are political prisoners.

We must continue to build the courage to fight, both within ourselves and within our communities. That is the only way Mumia—and we—will get free.

MUMIA ABU-JAMAL EXPLAINED IN (ROUGHLY) FOUR DATES, 2020-2021: A ZOOM/YOUTUBE ORAL HISTORY

MARCH 3, 2021, IN DOWNTOWN PHILADELPHIA

RALLY ATTENDEE: *Damn!*

JOHANNA FERNANDEZ: I just got a call from Bob Boyle, one of Mumia's attorneys.... uh, oh my God... Mumia has COVID. Um, he's in the infirmary. Their attorneys called our attorneys, he had gotten a rapid test and now they did conducted another test, and it came out positive. So Mumia Abu-Jamal has COVID-19.[5]

Bob Boyle is the health attorney of Mumia Abu-Jamal. He won the lawsuit, along with Bret Grote, that got Mumia the hep C treatment he needed. There is smoke, and I think we need to start a fire, and we need to really bring Mumia home where he can get the care he needs, and Mumia has preexisting conditions. He's got liver damage that was imposed by the Pennsylvania Department of Corrections because it failed to treat his Hepatitis C in a timely fashion.

Mumia has high blood pressure, and, like so many other prisoners, he has been sedentary, in a prison, 23 hours a day, for a year. The kind of deconditioning and lung problems that that kind of isolation produces is epic. We have a state with blood on its hands. At least four people that we know of have died in the prison that houses Mumia. At least four prisoners have died of COVID-19. Those are the numbers that have been released, and we know there are more. Over a hundred prisoners have been killed by the Pennsylvania DOC as a result of COVID in the last year. The numbers that they've released are not the real numbers.

So this is really a moment for the movement to bring Mumia home, domestically, internationally, to fight for Mumia to be immediately released. He's spent 28 and a half years on death row, unconstitutionally. The answer to that wrong is immediate release. He should have been released. He should never have been incarcerated. And now they're attempting execution by other means. We are not going to stand by.

RALLY ATTENDEE: *No!*

JOHANNA: We're going to say, "Release Mumia, release Russell 'Maroon' Shoatz, another Black Panther imprisoned in Pennsylvania, release all aging people in prison...

RALLY ATTENDEE: *Whoo!*

JOHANNA: "... and let our people go."

RALLY ATTENDEE: *Yeah!*

JOHANNA: The white supremacy of the state and of this office of the Philadelphia District Attorney is responsible for incarcerating more Black and brown people in this county, than in any other county in the country. That is white supremacy, nothing more, nothing less. In this age of Black Lives Matter that means, "Let people go that you've put in to a white supremacy system, to white supremacy's policies." People are vulnerable to death, and this is a homicidal system of imprisonment that we are seeing.

So it's time to mobilize and to raise hell, light up the fire, so that we bring Mumia home!

NOVEMBER 16, 2020, VIA ZOOM/YOUTUBE

JOHANNA FERNANDEZ: I'm an associate professor of history at Baruch College of the City University of New York. I'm one of the hundreds of people who have been leading a movement to free Mumia Abu-Jamal, the imprisoned radio journalist and former Black Panther, one of many people around the world struggling to free him, but also other political prisoners.

Imprisonment and the prison apparatus, the carceral apparatus, is the third largest employer in the United States. Third only to Walmart and Manpower Inc. That is a catastrophe of epic proportion. The people who have been disproportionately imprisoned in this period are Black Americans and increasingly Latinos.

Now why do I start with this? Because there was a generation of Black radicals who in the 1960s called attention to the fact that incarceration would be the new face of white supremacy and racism in the United States, after the embers of the urban rebellions of the '60s cooled off. Those radicals include members of the Black Panther Party. There are over a dozen Black Panthers who are today imprisoned.

Those activists in the Black Freedom Movement and the Black Power Movement who fought racism from segregation and lynchings in the South to our current mass imprisonment, many of them have been targeted by the state and imprisoned. Today as a new generation of Black freedom fighters emerge, they too are being targeted by the state for political reasons.

One of the people who was targeted by the state is the award-winning radio journalist, Mumia Abu-Jamal, who spent 28 and a half years in the harrowing torture of Death Row because he was convicted of killing Daniel Faulkner, a white police officer. He was imprisoned in 1981 convicted in 1982 and sent to death row in 1983, but in 2011, after 28 and a half years on death row, a federal court ruled that the D.A.'s office in Philadelphia had obtained a death penalty in his case, unconstitutionally, through trickery. That year his sentence was commuted to life in prison without parole and this year marks the 39TH winter of Mumia's imprisonment.

For over two decades, the Pennsylvania Supreme Court has refused to hear even one of the over 21 constitutional violations in Mumia's case. Why? Because Chief Judge Ronald Castille was irreparably biased—he man who appointed himself to hear Mumia's appeals, to discuss the violations in his case. This man, Ronald Castille, was unduly influenced by the Fraternal Order of Police, the institution most emphatically committed to Mumia's imprisonment and execution.

How was Judge Ron Castille's judgeship a problem? Why should he have recused himself from hearing Mumia's appeals? Because he was funded by the Fraternal Order of Police, and he was named "Man of the Year" by the Fraternal Order of Police, the same institution that has attempted to get Mumia first executed, and who wants Mumia to continue to be imprisoned.

If this weren't bad enough, Ronald Castille was both prosecutor and judge in Mumia's case. This is why we're here today, because a landmark Supreme Court ruling in 2016, *Williams v. Pennsylvania*, finally established the parameters of judicial bias. It essentially said that you cannot be both prosecutor and judge in the same case.

Judge Leon Tucker of the Philadelphia Court of Common Pleas essentially established that that's exactly what happened in Mumia's case, and he ordered all of Mumia's issues that he presented on appeal to the Pennsylvania Supreme Court, reopened.

What has happened since? The widow of Daniel Faulkner, the fallen officer that Mumia Abu-Jamal is wrongfully accused of killing, has filed a rare petition to stop all of the decisions of the lower courts and intervene in Mumia's case.

We are going to talk about why that is happening and what is the new evidence that has emerged in Mumia's case that has the Fraternal Order of Police, the entire establishment of Pennsylvania, and Philadelphia, and the Fraternal Order of Police, running? They know that if the new evidence that has just emerged in this case sees the light of day, Mumia will walk, and the entire apparatus of mass incarceration in the United States and Pennsylvania will be exposed. The framing of Mumia will be exposed once and for all.

JOHANNA: Our first speaker is someone I've known for more than two decades now. She is the person who has singularly kept the case of Mumia Abu-Jamal alive in the public sphere, through thick and thin, through highs and lows, and that is Pam Africa. She is the Minister of Confrontation of the MOVE Organization. She is chairwoman of the uncompromising International Concerned Family and Friends of Mumia Abu-Jamal.

PAM AFRICA: On a move, thank you, Johanna, and thanks to everyone who's participating today. We have here a clearly factually a case of judicial prosecutorial and police misconduct. I like to add terrorism to that.

The Philadelphia District Attorney, Larry Krasner, has released 15 people dealing with judicial and prosecutorial misconduct. Mumia, who has been on the foregrounds, and Krasner know about his case, has not released Mumia. We must demand that Krasner do for Mumia what he did for the other 15 exonerees, 13 Black, one white, and one Latino. We're asking people to help us stop the plot, stop the plan. It's clear that they're trying to kill this innocent man. 15 cases, and just before the King's Bench Act—which someone else would talk about later—just before then, he could have released Mumia.

I can't express enough, Mumia is very ill in that prison. He's not like he was two years ago.

The thing is, he should be on the street based on evidence. We need to immediately put pressure and demand that Krasner release Mumia based on judicial and prosecutorial misconduct. A move that you don't have to come back to court because Krasner released two of the prisoners from prison.

I can't express this enough. The failed plots for 39 years where they tried to kill Mumia, if it wasn't for a judge in Scranton and the movement, Mumia would be dead today. The prison officials were in a plot that got exposed inside the courtroom before a lot of people that they were manipulating papers to kill him.

We're not talking about judicial prosecutorial misconduct. We're talking about a continuous plot to try to kill Mumia. Everyone else is going to speak on details of what it is that I'm talking about. I'm saying, "On a move, long live revolution and free Mumia Abu-Jamal, a Black political prisoner on death row, who is a world-renowned journalist, as well." Thank you, on a move.

JOHANNA: Thank you so very much, Pam. She is having to leave us for health reasons and her family. I want to remind everyone that she was referring to bribery on the part of the prosecutor's office in the case of Mumia Abu-Jamal, the bribery of witnesses to obtain a conviction.

She was also referring to what we discovered in court when Mumia fell ill with Hepatitis C, we sued in court and we learned as the case was developing in court, that the Department of Corrections had attempted to manipulate their own doctor to say that Mumia's critical case of Hepatitis C was not serious.

In court, that doctor said, "Oh no, no, no, no. You tried to get me to say that Mumia was not seriously ill, but the science and the record suggests that he is."

At that point the judge intervened and said, "You all have to figure this out because someone is about to perjure themselves and there are going to be serious problems in the case."

Eventually we won and we got Mumia the health services and care he needed, and as a result of this health lawsuit, other prisoners across the country are now using Mumia's case to sue for treatment of Hepatitis C. We will win again.

MARCH 6, 2021, VIA ZOOM/YOUTUBE

BETSEY PIETTE, JOURNALIST, *WORKER'S WORLD*: Let's talk about now where Abu-Jamal's case stands legally. Linn Washington Jr. Is a Professor of Journalism at Temple University in Philadelphia. He also works as a journalist specializing in analytical commentary and investigative news coverage of issues involving race-based inequities in the criminal justice system. Dr. Johanna Fernandez is a professor in the Department of Black and Latino Studies at Baruch College in New York City. She has written and produced the film *Justice on Trial: The Case of Mumia Abu-Jamal*. Noelle Hanrahan is the director of Prison Radio, a multimedia production studio that brings to the public the voices of incarcerated women, men, and children. She has produced over 3,500 multimedia recordings from over 100 prison radio correspondents, including the critically acclaimed work of Abu-Jamal.

Would one of you like to briefly explain the basis for Mumia's current appeal, and where it's at in the so-called criminal justice system at this time?

JOHANNA: I can start. So what we know and what folks should know is that in December of 2018, the Philadelphia Court of Common Pleas Judge Leon Tucker ordered that Mumia's four post-conviction relief appeals which had been denied from 1998 to 2012, be reheard. Mumia had gone through a series of appeals in the '90s and in the 2000s. They were heard by the Pennsylvania Supreme Court. But because of judicial bias on the part of one of the judges, Ron Castille, who had previously been a prosecutor. And had been involved in Mumia's case and later became judge when Mumia began to appeal his case there was bias. You can't be both prosecutor and judge in the same case. So it was determined that all of these appeals had been denied because of judicial bias. Leon Tucker opened them and said that we need to open all of those appellate processes that Mumia submitted to that court and were denied because of judicial bias.

And what were those issues? So those are the issues that are now before the Superior Court of Pennsylvania. And those issues involve ineffective counsel—that Mumia wasn't effectively represented by his counsel during the original trial. That there was prosecutorial misconduct—that the prosecutor at the time, Joe McGill, withheld evidence that he had agreed to look into, reinstating his key witnesses' driver's license. That suggests that there was quid pro quo, that if you testify and finger Mumia we're going to do something for you. That evidence wasn't presented at trial. There's also evidence that the prosecutor Joe McGill manipulated witnesses, Veronica Jones, into fingering Mumia as the shooter and that the council that Mumia had didn't retain experts on the issue of ballistics. There are a bunch of other issues including that at face value there was bias in the jury selection process. That is a very important issue because if there's judicial bias, if there is racial bias in selecting a juror, then you get a new trial.

There are other issues. This is what I am going to end up by saying, which is very important. A lot of these issues that are being looked at right now by the Pennsylvania Superior Court involve a very important witness of the prosecution. And that is Robert Chobert. At the very end of the process that started with Leon Tucker in the local court over this issue of judicial bias, the judge asked the prosecutor's office to release all of the files involved in Mumia's case. All of them so that we could prove that there was judicial bias. Six boxes emerged over the course of, of that proceeding. And in that box, what emerged was a letter from Robert Chobert to McGill. I have it with me here. It's a startling letter because it proves something we've all known for 40 years. That there was corruption, manipulation of key witnesses. That people were bribed and intimidated.

The letter reads: "Mr. McGill, I have been calling you to find out about the money owed to me. Do you need me to sign anything? How long will it take to get it? How was your week off? Good, I hope. Let me know soon, write me back, Robert Chobert."

BETSEY: We're gonna come back to everybody being able to add to this. It was over a year ago in September 9, 2019, that Mumia's attorneys filed their post-conviction relief act petitions. Later that year, the Fraternal Order Of Police, using the widow Maureen Faulkner, asked to intervene in the case. And subsequent to that in February of 2020, the Pennsylvania Supreme Court accepted King's Bench petition on their behalf, which has delayed Mumia's case now for over a year. And, I'm wondering, Linn, if you could comment on that?

LINN WASHINGTON, JR.: King's Bench, in shorthand, is a very extraordinary power that the Pennsylvania Supreme Court has. It is only supposed to be utilized in matters of grave public importance. In this particular case, the Pennsylvania Supreme Court, which is an issue in Mumia's current appeals, injected itself in this case. Revenge is never supposed to be a reason for this extraordinary King's Bench authority. And that's what happened in Mumia's case. Now, let's understand: this is the same court that years ago would not, would not give King's Bench, designation for the kids-for-cash scandal, where children were being illegally sent to a juvenile jail to enrich their juvenile jail and money was given to the judges who would send them there. Corruption.

NOELLE HANRAHAN: And they all know it. Every single part of the judiciary, the prosecution, from Ed Rendell, Lynne Abraham, Joe McGill, all of them, and Larry Krasner know that the last 30 years has been a sons-of-Rizzo corruption scheme. That the Juanito Kidd injustice center [The Justice Juanita Kidd Stout Center for Criminal Justice] has been a conveyor belt for Black and brown bodies through that system for the benefit of the police—the majority white, 6,500-person police force, who get overtime for arresting poor Black and brown people.

LINN: What happened with the King's Bench, which delayed Mumia's appeal, was that Maureen Faulkner and the Fraternal Order of Police, avowed enemies of Abu-Jamal for decades, contended that Larry Krasner was favoring Mumia.

They just made a naked allegation almost like Donald Trump's "somebody stole the election off me." The allegation was that Krasner's office could not be objective. The facts did not prove that, but the court appointed a judge to do a review. The judge did a very detailed and very thorough review, found out that not only was very crass and are not favoring Mumia, but he would aggressively oppose Mumia's appeals in a judge issued his report.

In an unusual kind of configuration, only three of the seven members of the Pennsylvania Supreme Court actually participated in this. They agreed to accept the judge's ruling, essentially keeping Larry Krasner on the case. However, two members, one dissented straight up saying, "I don't care what our courts investigator, a judge found, I would grant relief and take this case away from Larry Krasner." Another judge, a Philadelphia judge, who just happens to be the brother of a local union leader who is now under his second federal indictment that's pending, said that while he would accept the finding because it was the finding of the court, he would favor giving the relief that Maureen Faulkner asked for. And not only do that, he laid out some reasons about how she could succeed in doing this if she did it again. So once again, with this King's Bench, you see the institutional bias from the Pennsylvania Supreme Court and you see the willingness of members of the court to bend and break the law when it comes to Mumia.

A number of years ago, I came up with a phrase called "The Mumia Exception." It means that the Pennsylvania law means the law except when it comes to Mumia, because there is a clear pattern actually from the beginning of his trial in 1992, where you could see the courts not following their, their own rules. I have to add that with that King's Bench, when the judges rendered their opinions, one of them said that the other two who wrote opinions saying that they would grant relief to, um, Maureen Faulkner, he took them to task. This was the first time in the history of this case that there has been a dissent at the Pennsylvania Supreme Court level. Quite extraordinary, but it just shows you the bias in the court system against Abu-Jamal. Thank you.

BETSEY: Thank you, Linn. And you mentioned the questioner, you know, said that he's fully capable of prosecuting Mumia on this case in February of this year, Krasner did file his response to the petitions filed by Mumia's attorneys in September of 2019.

And I'm wondering if, Noelle, if you can comment on what this new brief by Krasner means and what comes next in the legal challenge.

NOELLE: I think we all have been disappointed in that Larry Krasner's office and some of the people in his office are doing the same types of challenges to cases that they have done for the past 30 years. Frankly, Larry Krasner did not fire enough people because they're using procedural challenges, one of the first, the first seven or eight pages of this new brief opposing relief for Mumia Abu-Jamal, is merely procedural, that there is a missed deadline of 60 days. They are not arguing the merits for quite some time in this brief. And then they go to the merits. Now, the merits of the case, as Larry Krasner and his office see it, are only the rulings of Albert Sabo.

When someone takes their case and they argue the appeals, it's based on the evidence that was developed in the lower courts in the Leon Tucker court in the Philadelphia, the Common Pleas Court. With Mumia Abu-Jamal, 38 years after his original trial, his only evidentiary hearings were before Judge Albert Sabo, the man who said to a court clerk in front of a judge before the trial, "I'm going to help them fry the N-word." That's the only justice Mumia Abu-Jamal has had. Larry Krasner's office is defending the lack of evidence.

All of us have seen a lot of evidence come out over the last 38 years. You can name different evidence, the Polakoff photos [showing items moved at the crime scene], the Robert Chobert piece. That material is not before the court. That material is not in the court. And it has to be. Mumia Abu-Jamal needs a new evidentiary hearing. He needs a new trial.

What game is Larry playing? He said he doesn't want to violate the constitution. So he brought forward new evidence that was suppressed. New evidence found in the prosecutor's office after he took, after he came into office. That's one relief.

But Mumia Abu-Jamal needs relief *now*. He's ill, dangerously ill. He, and we know that this system can turn the key any moment they feel that the people have demanded enough pressure that to let our people go. They can go in there and make up another excuse to let him out.

They can, and we will demand that they will. And it's gonna take the people, more than the legal community, but we do need both. But it will take the people doing it to free Mumia Abu-Jamal.

BETSEY: Thank you, Noelle, you kind of lead me into my final question, which I'll kind of throw open to anyone who wants to comment. You know, before we learned that Mumia had COVID and other serious health issues, there was a debate over whether our demands should be a new trial for Mumia or to release Mumia now. It raises the question, I think, because of the medical emergency really making the focus to release Mumia now: does Larry Krasner have the legal authority to release Mumia? Linn, then, Johanna?

LINN: Well, Krasner has the authority to withdraw the prosecution, which would start the process for letting him out. And him taking that kind of a position on the basis of justice, given all the facts, he could do this. He couldn't individually do it, but he could be a part of the process that gets things going. Actually, the governor of Pennsylvania will be the one that would and should release Mumia immediately based on a compassionate release.

JOHANNA: Essentially, prosecutors across the country have had an enormous amount of power to, to actually release people. Krasner was foundational in the release of the MOVE 9, a group that also was allegedly involved in the killing of a police officer. He was critical there and he can do the same thing today using his wrongful convictions unit. This is one of the most important cases in the history of Philadelphia. On the basis of this case, we cranked up the apparatus of imprisonment. Philadelphia imprisons more Black and Latin ex-defendants than any other county in the country. And they accomplished that by fear-mongering and racism through the case of Mumia Abu-Jamal.

And now we have new evidence that suggests that the prosecution was so corrupt, was so hostile, was so lying, and was so embed with the cops who were corrupt, who tampered with evidence that this case is not defensible.

And in fact, he said that to Amy Goodman of *Democracy Now!* in July of this year. Larry Krasner said that Mumia's case is a microcosm of everything that is wrong with the criminal justice system and with the role of the police in railroading defendants. But now he's playing politics with the life of Mumia and the life of others because if there is a turning point in Mumia's case, as Noelle suggested, and as Linn has said, heads are going to roll. The whole apparatus of imprisonment will come tumbling down because Mumia's case is known domestically, nationally, internationally and it will be a scandal of epic proportions. So we are asking the D.A., not to hold on to the corruption in the nastiness and the hostility to defendants and the white supremacy of his predecessors. He was hired by the working-class Black people of Philadelphia to do the right thing.

MARCH 16, 2021, VIA ZOOM/YOUTUBE

SHAUN KING, JOURNALIST AND ACTIVIST: What is your role as district attorney with Mumia's case? For those of us who hope that USDA could do something about it, what are the barriers there? Now, I say that knowing that anything you say will be used against you politically, but too many people ask, Larry, for me to ignore it. I'm curious as well as one of your biggest supporters, as somebody who not only do I have questions about Mumia's guilt, but even if we just assumed that he was guilty for a moment, is he to spend the rest of his life in jail even if he was guilty for that moment? How do we work that out?

LARRY KRASNER: It's a great question. I can answer a good amount of it. I can't answer all of it, because this is a pending case. The killing we're speaking of occurred on December 9TH, 1981 that we are coming up on 40 years, I was in college in Chicago. I think I was a sophomore when that killing actually occurred even though I am from Philadelphia.

It has been litigated for many, many years before I ever got to the D.A.'s office. The thing that fascinating to me is I have protesters who are in favor of Mumia Abu-Jamal come to the front office, and they protest. Some of them, frankly, take a very strong position that we must be terribly unfair.

Then about 10 minutes after they leave, I see a bus pulling up. It's full of retired police officers and friends of Mrs. Faulkner, who is the widow or the officer who was killed, and they all pile out and they hold up signs. "Krasner is a liar. Krasner is in the bag for Mumia. He's going to do everything to let them out."

They even went so far as something almost unprecedented, which is trying to get me removed from the case, because the Faulkner family insisted I'm so unfair, and I am so biased in favor of Mumia I couldn't possibly handle the case. That litigation went on for months. I had to sift through depositions and then answer questions on it.

Ultimately, the Supreme Court, depending on which justice, cursed me out but also said, "OK, well, I guess we can't really prove he's so terribly unfair." There are people on both sides of this issue who feel just as strongly that I'm completely unfair in opposite directions. I don't know if that means I'm bringing people together or not.

I don't want to make light of their concern, because I know it comes from a sincere place. as long as we're being direct and as long as we're being provocative, let me try to answer your question a little further.

Apparently, some people believe that I actually am the jailer for Mumia Abu-Jamal. I am not. I do not have the capacity to turn the key to let him out. I do not have the legal power to turn the key to let him out, and I do not have the legal power to control his medical care.

It is essential that all inmates receive proper medical care. It is essential that consistent with the law that all defendants have the opportunity to challenge a conviction.

The notion that we're somehow at the beginning, we're back in 1981, and we can just ignore the decisions that made now for decades including the decision that he not be executed because he originally had death sentence is just inaccurate. We do not have the power. What comes to my office is one decision at a time on a particular issue. Sometimes the law is crystal clear, and sometimes it is not.

We are always going to bend in favor of trying to get to the bottom of these issues. That's actually why we got attacked by the Faulkner family and FOP and their crew, because our bottom line was we thought we should get to the bottom of the issues before more witnesses who were involved way back in 1981 pass away.

This has already happened that a significant number of witnesses involved back in 1981 have passed away. That's how I got in trouble with them. When I get 2,000 texts suggesting that somehow I can take out my key and let him out of jail, it just shows a deep misunderstanding of how this works.

SHAUN: Sorry to interrupt you, Larry. Help us understand what power you do have on the case. Where is the case now? As much as you can say it because it is an active case.

LARRY: Let me address the medical issue. There is absolutely no motion that anyone has filed in which I have any say whatsoever in relation to the medical treatment of Mumia Abu-Jamal. There's been no phone call from his lawyers, whatsoever. What there have been are literally hundreds of emails and texts from people who apparently think I can somehow control this.

If a motion in which I had standing to respond was provided, I would respond appropriately given what the actual facts are. Sometimes, the facts are not clear. We have some people who are very adamant that there's been a diagnosis of a certain type, and then other people in the same camp say there has been no such diagnosis. There's simply a symptom, that sort of thing.

Whatever the facts are, we would respond and take an appropriate position. The Eighth Amendment to the U.S. Constitution requires constitutionally adequate medical care. I think it should require more than that. Frankly, I've litigated this myself as a defense attorney in federal court for a woman who had thyroid cancer.

I think people in custody are entitled to good medical care. If there was a motion presented, if I had standing on anything, we would respond. I would like to think we would try to be as fair as we could with reference to the rest of the case.

There has been a lot of going around and around in which we essentially took the position that we were OK with getting to the bottom of certain issues and doing hearings. The whole system went nuts, and the family went against us. It all got tied up in the Pennsylvania Supreme Court for a long time.

As I mentioned earlier, they grudgingly said, "OK, I guess we don't have to take it away from you and give it to Josh Shapiro, our attorney general," who, by the way, has been sending people into court to advocate for the death penalty in cases where we are opposed to the death penalty, has repeatedly opposed pardons in cases where we have supported them, and has opposed commutations in cases where we have supported them.

It is a very, very complicated process that will require us on a motion-by-motion basis to respond, and we will do so. I can tell you this. You may like what we do or you may not, but we are going to try to be fair with the facts and the law just as we have been fair when we exonerated 18 people on 19 cases—18 people, not as well known, not as famous as Mumia Abu-Jamal but 18 people nonetheless.

I heard none of this energy, *none* around those individuals. That's worth reflecting because, frankly, a prosecutor ought to treat famous and unpaid famous people the same; rich people, poor people, the same; smart intellectual people, the same as people who have low IQs. We should treat them all the same.

SHAUN: I appreciate your thoughtful answer there. Part of my hope was that people who have decided that fighting for Mumia's freedom and care to hear from you on that. Thank you for allowing me to ask that question. For those of you who are here for Mumia, I hope you do see that Philadelphia as a district attorney who will engage us on hard questions.

MARCH 17, 2021, VIA JAMALJOURNAL.COM

JAMAL JOURNAL: What is your reaction to Krasner's comments to Shaun King about Mumia Abu-Jamal's case and the power of his office to release him?

LINN: D.A. Krasner danced around the core issue of justice for Abu-Jamal during the interview. The misconduct that led Krasner to end the wrongful convictions of 19 persons is even more pronounced in Mumia's case. Krasner defends being unfair to Abu-Jamal as acting fairly.

NOVEMBER 16, 2020, VIA ZOOM/YOUTUBE

COLIN KAEPERNICK, ACTIVIST AND FORMER NFL QUARTERBACK: When I was invited to speak on behalf of Mumia, one of the first things that came to mind was how long he's been in prison, how many years of his life had been stolen away from him, his community, and his loved ones.

He has been incarcerated for 38 years. Mumia has been in prison longer than I've been alive. When I first spoke with Mumia on the phone, I did very little talking. I just listened. Hearing him speak was a reminder of why we must continue to fight.

Earlier this year, the United Nations Human Rights Office of the High Commissioner issued a statement noting that "Prolonged solitary confinement, the precise type often used in the United States, amounts to psychological torture." Mumia Abu-Jamal has spent roughly 30 out of his 38 years in solitary confinement.

In his book, *Live from Death Row,* Mumia wrote that "prison is a second-by-second assault on the soul, a day-to-day degradation of the self, an oppressive steel and brick umbrella that transforms seconds into hours and hours into days." He has had to endure this second-by-second assault on his soul for 38 years.

He had no record before he was arrested and framed for the death of a Philadelphia police officer. Since 1981, Mumia has maintained his innocence. His story has not changed.

Mumia was shot, brutalized, arrested, and chained to a hospital bed. The first police officer assigned to him wrote in a report that "The Negro male made no comment," as cited in "Philly Mag."

Yet, 64 days into the investigation, another officer testified that Mumia had confessed to the killing. Mumia's story has not changed.

But we're talking about the same Philadelphia Police Department whose behavior shocks the conscious, according to a 1979 DOJ report—behaviors like shooting non-violent suspects, abusing handcuffed prisoners, and tampering with evidence.

It should, therefore, come as little surprise that, according to Dr. Johanna Fernandez, over one-third of the 35 officers involved in Mumia's case were subsequently convicted of rank corruption, extortion and tampering with evidence to obtain convictions in unrelated cases.

This is the same Philadelphia Police Department where officers ran racial profiling sweeps, like "Operation Cold Turkey" in March 1985, targeting Black and brown folks, and bombed the MOVE house in May of that year, killing 11 people, including five children and destroying 61 homes.

The same Philadelphia Police Department whose officers eight days before the 2020 presidential election shot Walter Wallace Jr. dead in the streets in front of his crying mother. The Philadelphia Fraternal Order of Police has unrelentingly campaigned for Mumia's execution. During their August 1999 national meeting, a spokesperson for the organization stated that they will not rest until Abu-Jamal burns in hell.

The former Philadelphia president of the Fraternal Order of Police, Richard Costello, went as far as to say that if you disagree with their views of Mumia, "You can join him in the electric chair," and that they will make it an "electric couch."

Today, we're living through a moment where it's acceptable to paint "End Racism Now" in front of the Philadelphia Police Department's 26TH District Headquarters. Yet, a political prisoner, who has since the age of 14 dedicated his life to fighting against racism, continues to be caged and lives his life on a slow death row.

We're in the midst of a movement that says Black Lives Matter. If that's truly the case, then it means that Mumia's life and legacy must matter. The causes that he sacrificed his life and freedom for must matter as well.

Through all of the torture Mumia has suffered over the past 38 years, his principles have never wavered. These principles have manifested themselves in his writing countless books while incarcerated, in his successful radio show, and the time and energy he has poured into his mentorship of younger incarcerated folks, and the continued concern with the people suffering outside of the walls.

Even while living in the house of the prison system, Mumia still fights for our human rights. We must continue to fight for him and his human rights.

Mumia is a grandfather. He is an elder with ailments. He is a human being that deserves to be free. Free Mumia.

JOHANNA: In 1973, there were approximately 250,000 to 300,000 people in prisons today. There are 2.4 million people in prison. We know that the United States incarcerate more people than any other country in the world.

In the early 1970s, the person we're about to hear from began to ring the alarm on a mass incarceration and proposed that we don't need prisons and that the future worth fighting for is a future without prisons. We know who that person is. She has been celebrated off late across the country and across the world.

Finally, an idea that seemed impossible in the 1970s and in a previous period has now been popularized and mainstream because of her work, but also because movements change history. They shift the terms of debate and open up a new vision and possibility for organizing our society. We know that the movement for Black Lives has transformed the way we talk about the police and prisons.

It was Angela Davis who opened up this conversation in the United

States. Angela Davis has many things. Among them, she is professor emerita at the University of California at Santa Cruz.

ANGELA DAVIS, ACTIVIST, AUTHOR AND FORMER PRISONER: I'd like to thank all of the phenomenal speakers who preceded me. I am so grateful for this opportunity to once again register my unwavering support for Mumia Abu-Jamal. He has played such a pivotal role in the processes of popular education that have led us to this critical juncture.

What one might call the century-and-a-half-year-old effort to acknowledge the structural and systemic character of racism and to take seriously demands for abolition of the death penalty of prisons of police. It is right and just that we should accelerate our efforts on this new terrain to finally free our brother comrade.

Much attention has been focused on Philadelphia recently from the elections to the police killing of Walter Wallace because he was experiencing a mental health crisis, to the arrest by federal agents of the teacher and community activists, Anthony Smith.

We know that barely a week before his arrest *Philadelphia* magazine had applauded Anthony Smith's community service and his exceptional leadership. All around the world, we've followed the work of Anthony Smith's organization, the Black Philadelphia Radical Collective. Many of us passionately support the 13 demands they have submitted.

We know also that the city council and Philadelphia recently offered an official apology for the 1955 bombing which killed 11 MOVE members, including 5 children, and completely destroyed 61 homes.

I've been asked to briefly discuss Mumia's case in the context of the long history of political repression in this country. In the context of the utilization of the critical of the criminal legal system to produce pretext for incarcerating people who have chosen to develop radical resistance strategies in relation to racist state violence.

Mumia is a relatively younger member of a generation of Black radical activists and intellectuals who have challenged the structural and systemic character of racism long before this recognition helped to accelerate efforts to reimagine some of our society's fundamental institutions. Because of our radical stances, we were targeted by the state.

In many instances, the state demonized and railroaded countless numbers of Black radicals. Some of us who were freed, but many of whom have been imprisoned for as many as five or six decades. Mumia was targeted by the Philadelphia Police and COINTELPRO, beginning with his membership in the Black Panther Party.

His declassified 500-page FBI files show that the Philadelphia Police in consultation with COINTELPRO, for many years had tried to peg a crime on Mumia. We also know that at least one-third of the police involved in his case were jailed after it was discovered that they had systematically tampered with evidence in large numbers of cases across the city of Philadelphia.

I think that few people know that the investigation of the killing of Daniel Faulkner, the policeman whom Mumia is accused of killing, that this investigation was conducted not by the homicide unit of the Philadelphia Police Department, but by its Civil Defense unit which was the local police arm of J. Edgar Hoover's COINTELPRO.

Mumia was sentenced to death. From death row produced brilliant critiques of the prison industrial complex, mass incarceration, capital punishment, and other institutional consequences of racial capitalism. Many of us are aware of the fact that his widely circulated writings have helped to humanize people in prison and people on death row.

Like many others of my age, I've been an active supporter of Mumia for many decades. I've had the honor of speaking on his behalf at United Nations conferences and in other international venues where Mumia, for example, was declared an honorary citizen of Paris. The last person before him to receive that distinction was Pablo Picasso. I participated in that ceremony in Paris as his surrogate.

Leonard Peltier, Mutulu Shakur, Russell "Maroon" Shoatz, Ed Poindexter, Romaine "Chip" Fitzgerald, David Gilbert, and my former co-defendant Ruchell Magee are a few of the U.S. political prisoners who have spent the vast majority of their lives behind bars, and as we know are currently the most vulnerable with respect to COVID-19.

Thanks to international organizing efforts, Mumia is perhaps the most well-known political prisoner in the world, and these international efforts saved his life when he came dangerously close to execution in 1995.

Mumia's case exemplifies the lengths to which the state will go to silence, those who speak truth to power and this is why the fraternal order of police has been unrelenting in its attempt to silence him and his supporters.

Now, that structures of policing have finally been exposed for their systemic racism, and as we call for justice in the names of Breonna Taylor, George Floyd, and Walter Wallace and so many others, and now that the city of Philadelphia has issued an official apology to MOVE, now is the time to accelerate our campaign to bring Mumia home.

Let's not forget that Mumia's identification with MOVE and his empathetic reporting on the city's repression of MOVE rendered him a major target of the Rizzo administration. As you've heard from Johanna and others, Linn Washington, Jr. for example, that Mumia's case is riddled with violations, especially the concealing of exculpatory evidence. The concealing of the presence of Kenneth Freeman at the scene of the killing of Daniel Faulkner.

The same night of the MOVE bombings, Kenneth Freeman was found dead in a parking lot, gagged and handcuffed. We know that there were clear violations in relation to the selection of the jury. A 11 out of the prosecutions, 14 peremptory challenges were used to eliminate Black jurors.

This in itself as this already pointed out supports the call for a new trial. The Supreme Court has ruled that the elimination of jurors on the basis of race is a major violation and as Johanna and others have pointed out, newly discovered filed boxes in the D.A.'s office, which were there for 37 years or so contain a list of potential jurors highlighting their race.

Perhaps even more egregious are the instructional tapes that were produced by Philadelphia Assistant District Attorney Jack McMahon, who pointed out that educated Black people should not be selected to serve the jury. He said that Blacks from the low-income area are less likely to convict and as a result I'm quoting "I don't want these people on your jury." As he said, and it may appear that you're being racist or whatnot, but again you're just being realistic—you're trying to win the case.

Finally, the framing of Mumia and his incarceration are part of a larger story of structural racism and repression linked to global capitalism, linked to racial capitalism. Racism drives incarceration and infects policing all over the world, from Rio de Janeiro, to Johannesburg, to London, to Paris. Here in the U.S., mass incarceration especially affects indigenous people and Black and Latinx communities.

We need to emphasize the fact that the very same forces that have driven the creation of the prison industrial complex are responsible for the fact that many people in other countries and countries of the Global

South have seen their home economies destroyed by capitalist incursions. They have no other choice than to flee.

Thus the borders, and the walls, and immigrant detention facilities are integrally linked to racist policing and the prison industrial complex. I should point out that abolitionist strategies emphasize the connections of all of these institutions.

Finally, at a time when critiques of structural racism are gaining traction and specifically its centrality to policing, we gather here to demand the release of Mumia Abu-Jamal and other political prisoners whose trials and sentences were irreparably influenced by their political beliefs and by their challenges to this very system.

URGENT CALL TO ACTION
MUMIA HAS COVID-19
IMMEDIATE IN PERSON ACTION:
SATURDAY FEBRUARY 27TH 12 PM

MEET AT DA LARRY KRASNER'S OFFICE AT 3 PENN SQUARE PHILADELPHIA, PA AT 12 PM

MUMIA ABU-JAMAL IS MEDICALLY VULNERABLE AND IS EXPERIENCING SHORTNESS OF BREATH AND CHEST PAINS

FREE MUMIA!!!
FREE ALL ELDERS OVER 50!!
FREE ALL POLITICAL PRISONERS!!!

FACEBOOK LIVE STREAM @PAMAFRICA

SCRIPT

MY NAME IS _____ AND I DEMAND:

1. THE IMMEDIATE & UNCONDITIONAL RELEASE OF MUMIA ABU-JAMAL, WHO HAS COVID-19 AND IS VULNERABLE.
2. THE IMMEDIATE RELEASE OF ALL POLITICAL PRISONERS.
3. THE IMMEDIATE RELEASE OF ALL ELDERS, AGING PRISONERS OVER THE AGE OF 50, PEOPLE WHO HAVE CONTRACTED COVID, AND ALL OTHERS WHO ARE ESPECIALLY VULNERABLE TO DEATH THOUGH COVID-19.

WE DEMAND THAT MUMIA BE MEDICALY TREATED IN A HOSPITAL AND RELEASED IMMIDEATELY!!!

@MUMIAABUJAMAL   @BRINGMUMIAHOME

After these public protests and meetings, Mumia Abu-Jamal had been treated for COVID but still has a host of medical conditions as 2022 approached. He underwent open-heart surgery on April 19, 2021. On April 24, 2021, Abu-Jamal's 67th birthday, Pam Africa announced at "Free Mumia" birthday rally that doctors had misdiagnosed Abu-Jamal's heart problems—he had clogged arteries—as congestive heart failure.

Mobilization4Mumia

Mobilization4Mumia.com, mobilization4mumia@gmail.com

PRESS RELEASE April 14, 2021, 6:01PM

FOR IMMEDIATE RELEASE
PRESS CONTACTS: JOHANNA FERNANDEZ, 917.930.0804; SOPHIA WILLIAMS, 917.806.0521

MUMIA ABU JAMAL UNDERGOING EMERGENCY HEART SURGERY THURSDAY! CALLS FOR HIS RELEASE INTENSIFY! EMERGENCY PRESS CONFERENCE 4/15

After days of not being heard from by his loved ones, we just learned that imperiled, world-renowned Black Panther journalist and political prisoner Mumia Abu-Jamal had been moved to an unknown hospital, complaining of chest pain. We have since learned that tomorrow, April 15th, Mumia will be undergoing emergency heart surgery at a hospital as yet unknown to his immediate family and supporters.

An emergency press conference will be held Thursday, April 15, 2021, 4pm EDT. Register at linktr.ee/mumia. Speakers will include Angela Davis, Marc Lamont Hill, Pam Africa, Johanna Fenandez, and grandson Jamal Hart, Jr.

This dramatic and dangerous new development comes on the heels of Mumia surviving the onslaught of Congestive Heart Failure (CHF) and Covid19 several weeks ago, exacerbated further by an acute skin rash condition, a residual health challenge that emerged from Mumia's bout with Hepatitis C several years earlier. That skin rash, which includes open lesions, has made him susceptible to infections. As he was finally being treated for the CHF and Covid19, his condition was further adversely affected by the insistence of state authorities to shackle Mumia.

The International protest campaign in support of Jamal was key in getting him that urgent medical care. Supporters and organizers are insisting on and demanding several key items:
I) That Mumia be allowed immediate contact with his wife Wadiya Jamal, his principal spokesman Pam Africa, his personal physician Dr. Ricardo Alvarez, and his spiritual advisor Dr. Mark Taylor;
2) That Mumia 'not be shackled' over the course of this treatment so as not aggravate his skin condition;
3) That Mumia - an innocent man - be freed on the basis of a compassionate medical release because "release is his only real treatment option," according to his personal physician Dr. Ricardo Alvarez.

He will be the subject of a weekend of support and protest activity on the weekend of April 24th, which will be his 67th birthday. Those activities are detailed at letmumiaout.com.

ALL OUT FOR MUMIA!
We Free Him Or He Dies
Mobilize to Shut Down Philly April 23-25

The People for Mumia
Friday 4/23 @6PM EDT (3PM PST)

Virtual Fundraiser & Speak Out:
Activists, Youth, Writers, Musicians, and Former Political Prisoners express what Mumia means to the Movement today.

GUEST SPEAKERS AND PERFORMERS:
TOM MORELLO, ALBERT WOODFOX, SUSIE ABULHAWA, ROBIN DG KELLY, MIKE AFRICA JR., MARC LAMONT HILL + MORE

Register, Donate & Live Stream:
LetMumiaOut.com

THEN

INTRODUCTION BY JOHANNA FERNANDEZ AND LINN WASHINGTON, JR.

NOVEMBER 16, 2020 ZOOM/YOUTUBE PRESS CONFERENCE

JOHANNA: We have another question coming in about the recent statement on the part of the City Council in Philadelphia. The Philadelphia City Council has formally voted to apologize for the aerial bombing of the MOVE house in 1985.

The question is what is the relationship between this bombing of the MOVE Organization and Mumia's case? There's a request to comment on the meaning of the statement of apology on the part of city hall about the MOVE bombing of 1985 and what it means from Mumia's case. Does anyone want to speak to this?

LINN: I could address that if you would like.

JOHANNA: Sure.

LINN: In May of 1985, May 13TH 1985, the Philadelphia police department dropped a bomb on the MOVE house in trying to get some members of MOVE to surrender. That bomb started a fire. The commissioner of police at the time, a guy named Gregore Sambor, gave a direct order to allow the fire to burn.

That fire turned into an inferno. That inferno killed 11 people inside the MOVE house, including five children, burned down 61 homes, left 250 people homeless. Here, we have a connection but not a direct connection but is parallel. The then district attorney Ed Rendell, who had prosecuted Mumia under his administration, went to federal court in fact, to block a grand jury investigation. He won.

His successor, a guy named Ron Castille, the one that we're talking about in a Mumia case, convened a grand jury, then came out with a multi-hundred-page report where he said that there was no crimes committed by the police anywhere, including the police who perjured themselves before the grand jury.

We have Ron Castille whitewashing the MOVE bombing, and then he later, or at the same time, is fighting against Mumia's appeals. Then later, when he gets elected to the Supreme Court of Pennsylvania, through support by the FOP, financial and campaign support, then he rules against Mumia having some appeals a couple of times.

Again, we just see the gross nature of injustice embedded deeply in the justice system of Philadelphia. That apology, I want to add while it was approved by city council, the initiative in the effort to effectuate an apology was done by a Philadelphia community activist named Ulysses "Butch" Slaughter, who had been working for over two years to get all of the parties together.

The city council, through new councilperson Jamie Gauthier, did push the resolution through. That was commendable.

I think it's of importance that the members of MOVE, and particularly those who have been released after serving more than 40 years in prison for their wrongful conviction for killing a police officer during an incident on August 8, 1978, their position is: "We don't want your apology. You killed our family. You killed some of our children. That apology will never bring them back. If your apology is real and sincere and it means something, release Mumia Abu-Jamal."

This is their consistent position. MOVE doesn't want an apology. They want to release Abu-Jamal.

1969-1970

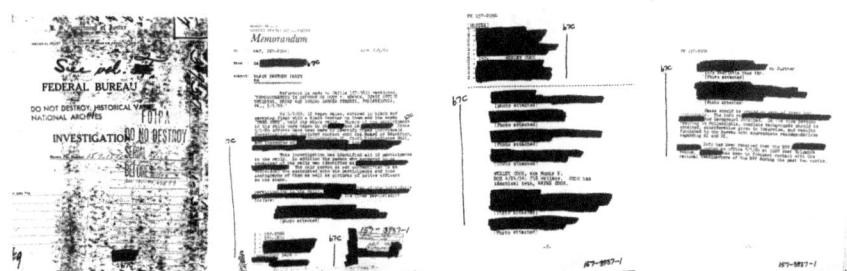

A WAY TO FIGHT BACK: THE BLACK PANTHER PARTY IN PHILADELPHIA[6]

REGGIE SCHELL

(as told to Dick Cluster)

In October of 1966, two young Black men sat in the back room of an anti-poverty office in Oakland, California, and drafted a 10-point platform and program for a new political party. Its name: the Black Panther Party for Self-Defense.

The panther came to California from Lowndes County, Alabama, where it had become the symbol of the Lowndes County Freedom Organization. Earlier that year the Freedom Organization had launched one of the first attempts to put into practice SNCC's new doctrine of Black Power by running independent Black candidates for county offices to unseat the white Democratic Party power structure.

Lowndes County was Ku Klux Klan territory. Not only were Blacks routinely attacked and intimidated by gun-wielding Klansmen, but even a Northern white supporter, Viola Gregg Liuzzo, was killed as she drove through the county during the Selma-to-Montgomery voting rights march. The Freedom Organization decided that to organize freely they would have to abandon the position of one-sided non-violence, and that they would have to do what was necessary to defend themselves if they were attacked.

Alabama law required that all political parties on the ballot have an animal as their symbol. Freedom Organization chairman John Hulett explained his party's choice this way: "This black panther is a vicious animal as you know. He never bothers anything, but when you start pushing him, he moves backwards, backwards, and backwards into his corner, and then he comes out to destroy everything that's before him."

The new Black Panther Party formed in Oakland represented one of the most striking and most popular attempts to transfer the inspiration and the new lessons of the Southern movement to the cities of the North.

Huey P. Newton and Bobby Seale, the party's founders, were born in the

South but grew up in the Oakland ghetto, where they learned that legal equality was a long way from freedom. They met at Merritt College, a two-year school on the edge of the ghetto with a large proportion of Black students. Tired of academic discussions of Black nationalism and revolution, they set out to form a revolutionary organization of "brothers off the block."

Their program, written primarily by Huey Newton, was and still is as follows:

WHAT WE WANT

1. We want freedom. We want power to determine the destiny of our Black Community.
2. We want full employment for our people.
3. We want an end to the robbery by the CAPITALIST of our Black Community.
4. We want decent housing fit for shelter of human beings.
5. We want education for our people that exposes the true nature of this decadent American society. We want education that teaches us our true history and our role in the present-day society.
6. We want all Black men to be exempt from military service.
7. We want an immediate end to POLICE BRUTALITY and MURDER of Black people.
8. We want freedom for all Black men held in federal, state, county and city prisons and jails.
9. We want all Black people when brought to trial to be tried in court by a jury of their peer group or people from their Black communities, as defined by the Constitution of the United States.
10. We want land, bread, housing, education, clothing, justice and peace.

Each point was accompanied by a corresponding point of "What We Believe," explaining the necessity and justification for the demand.

The Party's first activity consisted of patrolling the streets of Oakland with guns and lawbooks to protect Black citizens from illegal abuse by police-and to back up their knowledge of legal rights with weapons equal to those of the police. Stories of Panther patrols facing down the astounded cops began to circulate around the ghetto.

"It was an educational point we wanted to get over," Bobby Seale explained years later in an interview. "We wanted to get the idea over of self-defense, and then educate the people, not only for self-defense against racist police attacks and bullets, but to defend themselves against hunger, famine, rats and roaches, dilapidated housing, unemployment, etc."

The Panther Party burst into the glare of national publicity in May 1967 when they appeared in the California state legislature in Sacramento with their guns-to read a statement opposing a bill, aimed at them, which would outlaw the carrying of loaded weapons on the street. Misdirected by reporters, they actually marched onto the floor of the legislature rather than to the spectators' gallery as they had intended.

Bobby Seale and five other Panthers were sentenced to six months in prison for disturbing the peace of the legislature. For the next four years, one or both of the Party's founders was in prison at all times, charged with a variety of crimes including first-degree murder. The charges on which they were arrested, except for the original Sacramento misdemeanor charge against Bobby Seale, were all eventually dismissed. Yet both men suffered solitary confinement and threats of death penalties in the meantime, and they were freed only after years of massive outside protests against their actual status as political prisoners.

These charges were part of a national campaign by the FBI and local police forces to disrupt the Panther Party's political activities through arrests, shootings, infiltration, and the portrayal of the Party as mindless, bloodthirsty hoodlums. The purpose of this campaign, as the Senate Select Committee on Intelligence learned in 1976 from an FBI memo, was to "prevent the rise of a 'Black messiah' who would unify and electrify the militant Black nationalist movement."

The FBI sought to prevent the Panthers and other militant Black groups from achieving "respectability" and "long-run growth." FBI chief J. Edgar Hoover reported to President Nixon that he was particularly concerned about the Panthers because "a recent poll indicates that approximately 25% of the Black population has great respect for the Black Panther Party, including 43% of Blacks under twenty-one years of age." One memo directed each FBI field office to submit, every two weeks, a report on actions against the Party.

More than twenty Panthers died as a result of this campaign. The most *blatant murder—but not the only one—was that of Illinois Black Panther Party chairman Fred Hampton, who died along with another Panther, Mark Clark, when Chicago police raided an apartment where they were staying on December 4, 1969.*

The supposed purpose of the raid was to search for illegal weapons which an informer had claimed were in the apartment. Yet the police passed up an opportunity to search the office when it was empty the evening before. Instead they staged a surprise attack at 4:45 a.m., guided by a map of the apartment supplied by an FBI infiltrator; they fired more than seventy-five shots to the Panthers' one. Hampton, who had fallen asleep in the middle of a phone conversation the night before, never woke up or moved during the entire raid; yet he was shot four times, twice in the head. A private autopsy performed for his family found that he had been heavily drugged.

Other Panthers were killed by members of rival groups. In December 1968 the FBI informed its field offices of a growing conflict between the Panthers and a Los Angeles-based group called US. It instructed its agents to "fully capitalize upon Black Panther Party and US differences" with "imaginative and hard-hitting measures aimed at crippling the Black Panther Party." While Black leaders attempted to mediate the dispute, the FBI planted phony letters and cartoons to increase hostility and suspicion; it also used undercover agents to inform US of the times and places of planned Panther events. In the course of 1969, four Panthers were killed by US members.

Despite this disruption, Panther chapters sprang up in cities across the country. Modeled on and directed by the Oakland headquarters, they carried out campaigns against police brutality, conducted political education classes, and encouraged Black people to see that "political power grows out of the barrel of a gun." They also provided community services including free breakfasts for school children, free clothing and medical care, and free alternative schools for Black children. The Party acquired several thousand members, about equally composed of women and men. The Black Panther, the Party's newspaper, reached a circulation of 30,000 in Chicago and 35,000 in New York.

The Panthers encouraged Blacks in the U.S. to identify with the socialist countries and revolutionary movements of Asia, Africa, and Latin America. They taught that the enemy is not white people in general but the capitalist system. They insisted on the necessity for a Black-led revolution to overthrow that system, and they pointed to the success of the Vietnamese revolutionaries in resisting the armed might of the U.S. government. "The power of the people," said Huey Newton, "is greater than the Man's technology."

On the Labor Day weekend of 1970, the Party held a "plenary" (open) session of a Revolutionary People's Constitutional Convention in Philadelphia. More than 6000 people participated, about half Black Philadelphians and the rest representatives of other Panther branches, other Black groups, Puerto Rican organizations, anti-war groups, Women's Liberation groups, poor whites, Indians, and other ethnic and political groups from across the country.

In an atmosphere of tremendous determination and emotion, the convention adopted scores of resolutions explaining the principles of the new society for which partici-pants were struggling. The convention did not, however, formulate any common political strategy or tactics for carrying on the struggle. Huey P. Newton, just out of prison after nearly three years (most of it spent in solitary confinement), delivered a keynote speech about the political and economic origins of the existing Constitution and why the necessary changes would not come from working within it.

The intense government repression and internal problems began to take their toll on the Party. In March 1971, a faction led by exiled Minister of Information Eldridge Cleaver left the Panthers because of the Party's refusal to begin an immediate underground armed struggle. In April, Huey Newton issued a criticism of the Party's past actions from the opposite direction, stating that it had "defected from the community" by overemphasizing the gun and the slogans of revolution while isolating itself from potential supporters in the Black com-munity. He called for renewed emphasis on the service programs, programs of "survival pending revolution," to rebuild the Party's base.

Though many branches eventually closed, the Party succeeded in regaining its strength in Oakland. In 1973, Party officers ran in the city's municipal elections on a platform of establishing community-controlled cooperatives to meet basic needs. Minister of Information Elaine Brown received more than 30,000 votes for city council; Bobby Seale placed second in the primary vote for mayor and got 36% of the vote in the runoff election.

Since that time, Seale and Brown have both left the Party, and Panther support has fallen off somewhat amid charges of corruption and violence within the Party leadership. But, longer-lived than most organizations of the 1960's, the Black Panther Party continues to operate its survival programs and do political organizing and education in Oakland.

Reggie Schell was Defense Captain (the highest local post) of the Philadelphia branch of the Black Panther Party in 1969 and 1970. He was interviewed where he still lives in the North Philadelphia Black community, across the street from the first Party office.

Can you tell a little bit about your life before you joined the Black Panther Party?

There isn't nothing to tell. I mean, I could say that in three sentences. I was just an average, what I call, a street nigger. We weren't what you call poor—well, I guess we were poor, because there were days we didn't eat, days we went without coal, times that I went without stuff that I figured I needed. I messed around with street gangs, and then I went out and joined the service. That's when I got my first lesson in racism—in the service. Because you know up until the time I joined, when I was 17, fighting white people was just like fighting with another gang. I was going to South Philly High, which was at that time about 75% white, mostly Italian. We used to have to fight our way in sometimes or fight our way out. But some Italians we found were just as nice to us as we'd be with each other; if something's jumping and they know you, they'd tell you to watch yourself, and try to take some of the weight off you.

That just wasn't the same degree as what I found out by racism when I joined the service: this deep intent to control and to dominate you because you happen to be something else. It was in the service in Germany where I really got exposed to it. Most of the company commanders were from the South, and they were just openly racist. It really, really brought me down.

I remember listening to Malcolm X somewhere in there. Malcolm was on TV a couple of times, and I was really impressed by him. He was on a show called *The Dissenters*. He used to call white people "devils" at that time, and him and this white guy were arguing, almost fighting on the show. And I was impressed because I thought, "Well, shit, at least he's not just gonna sit there and act like he has to apologize for what he belkves."

Then I came home and went to work in a sheetmetal plant. They made porch lights, ventilation screens, everything. And I saw then how the bosses can divide people. Upstairs in the shop it was all white, they ran machines. Downstairs in the foundry, sheetmetal department, punch-presses, it was all Black. The people upstairs got paid more. When I got there we were talking about putting a union in. People were afraid, I guess I was afraid too, but I knew we needed more money, or something, you know. So I worked with the union, helped fight to get it in, and that's when I first started seeing how things go.

I worked on that job about four years. I used to argue with the superintendent because I saw shit being done to Black people, and I know he used to tell me, "One day it's gonna get you in trouble, because you try to take up too many people's fights." Well, one day it did.

How I got in the Movement, I guess, is I began to develop political consciousness around the time of Selma, Alabama.[7] I used to come home from work and just watch how the police beat the women and the children. You know, just about every day I used to think forward to watching that, because it did something to me inside. Like I say, I had started to pick up some kind of militancy on the job. Then I met with some people and started talking about trying to do something or join something that we thought would help change the situation for Black people in this country. After a couple of months of just kicking around, reading, and studying together, we decided that it would be this new group, the Black Panther Party.

I think the first time we heard about them was when the Panthers stormed Sacramento with guns. We heard about it on TV and in the papers. We knew then that after looking at Selma and Birmingham, and continually just watching people being beaten and there was no struggle back—I think that was really the thing that excited me about it: that at least we'd have a chance to fight back now.[8]

Of course, when we first opened we were just ad hoc, really, we weren't Panthers, we weren't anything. But one of the things that impressed me early on in the Party was when we decided we wanted to be Panthers we called out to California and June Hilliard told us, "Look, you don't got to be no goddamn Panther to struggle."[9] So we went out (this was in 1968) and we were just basically doing our thing because we didn't have any idea what Panther work was. But we set up our first office, right down here on Columbia Avenue. We were doing work around police brutality and situations like that. Police were shooting fifteen-year-old kids, mentally retarded children, and we started calling press conferences and trying to organize the people to do something to fight back.

After a period of time we started sending to California for papers; we were selling the Panther Party paper, though we still weren't recognized as a chapter. Then Field Marshal Don Cox came and inspected the branch, put us through a rigid kind of inspection to see if we were qualified to become a branch of the Party. This was early 1969, and it was also when the cadre selected me to become Defense Captain.

How did the Party start out its work?

The politics that we were trying to develop was to inform Black people about things that happened. I mean, we knew they knew, but we also knew that they didn't have any idea what they could do about it and we wanted to try to break them from this stranglehold that bootlicking politicians had on them and the white power structure had on them. Our strategy was to win their confidence first, to gain people's confidence in our desire, at least, to make some fundamental changes.

Besides what had been and still is a continuing problem of police brutality, there was a problem right at that time with sewers backing up. These were the kinds of things that we initially started, to get roots into the community. We had blocked off Columbia Avenue in protest at one point and had people come out with us, and after that we were on our way politically, as far as having some validity in the eyes of the people.

We started our free breakfast for children program somewhere around September of that year. I think the breakfast program really shot us into the community. It was held across the street in that little blue building right there. We'd cook on hot plates 'cause there wasn't any gas or anything in there, It was hard but everybody enjoyed it because it was our first real program and our first attempt at trying to do something fundamental for people in the community.

We got the bulk of the food from merchants in the area. At first we had problems. They said we were Communists, Black radical militants, and they tried to urge people to get us out. Some of the merchants (it was kind of funny because they were white merchants that had spearheaded this) were starting to circulate a petition to try to get us removed off Columbia Avenue. But it really didn't go over anyway, you know. We didn't bother with it, we just felt that if that's what they wanted to do, fine—we had a program we wanted to institute and try to get this community stabilized.

So we kept on doing that and after a while that whole petition thing just fell through.

Right after that, though, we had our first confrontation with the police. They busted me because they said there was an M-14 found at my sister's house. I had some papers there at her house that had my name on them. So along with the M-14 they found these papers and right away, bam, they raided the office. I remember it well. We used to have community classes, community meetings. They were well-attended, we always had thirty or forty people, sometimes more, because I think during that period everybody wanted to be identified with at least fighting back. We used to go into this bar over here afterwards, and I'd be sitting, talking to some people about some of the discussions in the classes. The FBI came in there and came up to me, and they had this police inspector with them, George Fencl, the head of the "civil disobedience squad." They asked, "Are you Reggie Schell?" I turned around and said "No." So Fencl said, "Don't play with me. That's the motherfucker right there." And they read the warrant and I was arrested. They arrested all the other Panthers that were on the street, they broke in the office and ransacked every damn thing, all our files and everything. At that point we weren't organized well enough to have our security intact. We were just really getting the feel of the community when we got hit with this raid. Even though we knew that the system and the police, especially, didn't want us to set up shop, we didn't have any idea about how fast something would come our way. But it didn't stop us from dealing with the police. We did extensive work around police brutality, organizing different communities, getting down with lawyers, helping set up different agencies that we could funnel these problems through.

Probably the most classic example of the way the police acted here was their murder of a young guy, Harold Brown. He was shot and killed in West Philadelphia. He was killed by four highway patrolmen; and the highway patrol in Philadelphia has always had the reputation for being the most vicious and most murderous of all the police. They had stopped this young brother and killed him, shot him. People heard him begging on his knees. Witnesses heard him begging the cops not to kill him, but they just shot him.

We talked to his mother. His father was a postal employee, his mother was a school teacher. He was a good student at Cardinal Daugherty, which was a predominantly white school. By now the Party had gotten itself organized to the point where we could wage a hell of a campaign. We started circulating leaflets, we went up into the area where he was killed and talked with people, with witnesses. We had tape recordings of conversations with witnesses who saw certain things, who had heard the police tell them to "Get the fuck back in the window before we blow your heads off," and stuff like that. We had taped conversations with his mother and his father and we'd done a 16-page booklet on police brutality; and we spearheaded this by putting out wanted posters on the four police.

That set the city administration off. Rizzo was police commissioner and he was calling for something to be done, because we'd put a price on these policemen's heads by putting out a wanted poster on them.[10] You know, what was actually happening, what was transpiring at that point, was that sides were being taken. I think that people who once feared the Black Panther Party because of the shootouts across the country began to see it as a legitimate organization that wanted to try to make some fundamental changes. The campaign that we raised with the police killing of Harold Brown was probably one of the most significant to get us involved with people and to get more people involved in the Black Panther Party. It caused a tremendous amount of anti-police support, because even the major papers had to pick it up. *The Inquirer* did a full expose on the whole thing and finally the cops were sent to a mock trial; you know, they walked in with their guns and their uniforms on, and finally they were exonerated completely. But by that time the political atmosphere in terms of the street, the people on the street, was beginning to change.

Those who had controlled it before had absolutely no control, or very limited control, over what was happening, and I think that's when the Party started really taking off. Around racial problems, you know, people would call the Black Panther Party with almost any problem that had any significance. The people would call the Black Panther Party first before they would call the old established Black leadership, and I think that the campaign itself-the Harold Brown campaign—probably was the catalyst for that.

How much did the Party grow?

I guess, even though I'm no longer in the Black Panther Party, I still have some of the indoctrination about numbers. We never liked to give out specific figures that could be used by the police. We had tremendous numbers up until 1970. After the police raided our office a second time in August 1970, and shot it up, within a week or two weeks hundreds of people had joined the Party. When we had drill we had to use a schoolyard because there were that many people there. I imagine some of them were just fools or curious people, but we used to have to use a schoolyard because there were that many people; we couldn't fit on a city block or a lot anywhere.

What was the role of guns in the Party? Was the idea, as the media often put it across, that picking up the gun meant that right then and there the Panthers would conduct a revolution, or was it more of a symbol?

You know, I think that whole idea was manifested by the police, because I know that the police believed it. The times I was arrested they seemed to put emphasis on the fact that, "We know you all got guns, motherfucker, but we got the firepower, and we'll kill you." Just like the FBI told us, "We got the superior firepower, you can't win." We talked about guns because it was a constitutional right, you know. We also had other ideas about making revolution, but the police and the media had taken this, as you say, symbol and projected it as if we were trying to organize 500 Blacks to get guns and then just commit revolution.

We weren't talking about that, we were talking about people exercising their right to bear arms and to fight in defense of their homes if police come at them, kicking in their door without any valid reason or search warrant. And I think after a period of time Black people understood that.

We did have weapons classes. They were restricted to Panther members, not community workers. If community workers wanted Panthers to come and talk to them about weapon treatment, they would have to set up a meeting at a site of their own choosing and have their own weapons; and then somebody would come in. We did stress that people have a right to own a shotgun or rifle or pistol and that they had best do that; and again, I think that people liked that. Even though they were silent all the years of the peaceful nonviolent demonstrations, they couldn't take it any more than I could take it when I saw what was happening in Selma, Alabama, every day.

It was clear that of course we would take guns and we would defend ourselves and there were times we took guns to situations, like racial confrontations. There was a situation where four Black women had moved into a previously all-white neighborhood through a redevelopment kind of thing and used to get their windows broke out; their children used to be chased home. The women had called us about it. Well, they only called us after somebody fired a shotgun. We went down, we looked at the situation; by that time Fencl and the police were there, but the police offered absolutely no protection. We stayed maybe a week with them, protecting their home.

Can you say more about the Party's idea, the idea of people who came into the Party at this time, about what kinds of changes were needed?

In the early stages of the Party when people first joined, the only fundamental change that they thought had to be made was to at least let the world know, and let the system know, that they would fight. Before the Party came into existence, Black people just were looked on as people who will take a nice little ass-whipping, for a job or something.

I know that we had a lot of men coming in that were leaving their families. They'd come in and work part-time, working on the job and then coming into the Party on the weekend or evenings. They'd go out and sell papers at night; they'd sell 'em through the bars up until the bars closed. And after they'd do that for a while they'd get, you know, that spirit. I don't know what infected them, but we'd find that a lot of them just left their jobs and lived like we lived, from hand to mouth, out on a limb. When we saw them every day, we were seeing that they were fundamentally satisfied with themselves maybe for the first time in their life.

These were people that were frustrated about the entire situation of Black people, and more or less frustrated about themselves, about their own inability to let the system know that "Goddammit, I will fight, and I don't like it but I will get down and you just can't keep on messing over me like that." When I joined the Party I was married and I left my wife for fundamentally the same reason: the question was, as we'd talked about it, either go back to work and get out of this crazy shit, or leave.

I'm talking about a man who's been on the job for eight years. He's not satisfied with the wage scale. He's not satisfied with the relationship that the boss has with him and other people around him. But he just takes it and takes it and takes it, because it is essential that he bring home the bread and butter. Now these men, or these individuals, these human beings, are in a constant state of turmoil with themselves; and the Black Panther Party, when it came out, existed as something that was totally opposed to that—kind of "You won't take advantage of us anymore." And when they marched into Sacramento with guns they were telling America, "This is it, I mean Selma's gone, all that other, you forget that; this is the new human being, this is the new man and the new woman that's emerging."

When people saw that, you know, they'd take that and say, "Well, let me go into the Party and see how Bobby or Eldridge developed this, what they'd think, tremendous courage to stand up before thousands of people and call Richard Nixon a pig, stand up before corporation heads and call them enemies and just deal with them. That was the thing that people came in for-to find out what was this secret formula that the Party had. And they found out later that it wasn't a secret formula; it was just a question of them understanding the forces around them and understanding themselves, knowing what they had to do and what they could and couldn't say.

I don't know if that explains it, but I think that what I'm saying in a nutshell is that people live in a dual world until they find something that they can really believe in. You know, you believe here when you're here and you believe there when you're there. But when something exists that has some principled foundations, something that you can believe in and that you know how to relate to and still be free, you know you won't be like a plastic human being.

I found a lot of people, young people, just breaking with their parents for the same thing, for the same reasons. Some were seventeen, coming in and just wanting to be part of what they figured was a tremendous force that was gonna change American society, which I think that the Party did to some extent. People just seemed to be people who wanted a fundamental change. I don't know if it was so much at that point to change or revolutionize the whole society or just to begin to revolutionize their own self over, to make them free mentally. Based on what I saw as the Defense Captain of the Party, I felt that at first most people wanted to revolutionize themselves. They saw the Party as the vehicle that perhaps was supposed to revolutionize the whole society, but they came in to deal with themselves first, because only through the Party could they gain a better understanding of what the hell we were talking about . Then, as they began to change, they began to see that it gave them more confidence to go out and change others. But they initially needed that themselves.

What were the ways that the Black Panther Party changed the society?

Initially, society looked at Black people as people who, probably legitimately, had some claim for some equality; but at the same time, will these people fight for their equality'? Really, what will they do for it? March and pray and get their legs broken with high-pressure water hoses?

The Party said that was the end of that. We're human beings—we recognize we have certain rights, we have a right to fight for those rights, and we have a right to organize for those rights. We'll do what is necessary; confrontations over the years between the police and the Black Panther Party had let the U.S. know that we will. This is not a fad that you're dealing with now, this is a real emergence of a new human being. And you would find that people would readily identify with Panthers: "They're damn right when they see the police brutalizing somebody." "The Panthers are right, they ought to kill you all." Before that they'd just watch the brutality and go on about their way. So it changed society in that respect.

It also had its effect on the people at the controls of society. I believe that the Black Panther Party—and it's still my belief—was close to flipping this society over. We had established international relationships with other countries; this probably was the first time that it was done on this scale by any Black revolutionary movement since this country existed. In the Party we had made contact with people in Hanoi and we were supposed to begin making deals with the U.S. government to exchange pilots for political prisoners here. We were in Algiers, we were in Cuba, and we had better relations with those people than the head of IBM. So the rulers in this country—not the president, but the rulers, the corporate capitalists—understood that they had to do something.

They understood that the more they attacked the Party, the more Black people came into the Party, and that the more Black people came into the Party, then around the world the more Third World people became conscious of the tremendous surge, the tremendous will that was developing in this Black ethnic group or race here in the U.S.

They knew that they couldn't eliminate us, because by the time they really started escalating the killings of Panthers across the country, the seeds of revolution were already sown in the people. When they raided our office a second time, Rizzo really tried to degrade us by stripping us naked and lining us up against the wall and shooting over our heads. I imagine it was to get the people to believe that this is finally what happens to you. The police took everything out of the office, tinned up the front, and put up a sign: "Unfit for human habitation." What happened the next day was that people on the block stripped the tin off and replaced the furniture. When the police told them they couldn't, they said, "Don't tell us we can't!" The very next day the people just went back up there and ripped it all down, put a refrigerator in, chairs and tables, and began to set the office back up—and the police couldn't do a damn thing about it.

This was happening across the country. It happened in Chicago when they killed Fred Hampton and Mark Clark—this tremendous surge on the part of the people. So the ones at the controls had to do something.

So they took the breakfast program from the Party and coopted it into a national organization. They set up the Urban Coalition, they funded neighborhood health clinics, they had this outshoot of food stamps.[11] They came forth with these different reforms—fundamentally the same programs the Black Panther Party had initiated.

All these things came about not so much because it was the Black Panther Party, but through revolutionary action and consciousness on the part of the people. And the government had to do something to stop Black people from going too far to the left, because if they continued to repress and oppress us—as important as it was that they try to break us—they would have lost millions of Black people and they would have been in big trouble around the world.

People can say Rap Brown inspired the riots, or the Black Panther Party inspired the riots, but it wasn't.[12] You know, I believe it was just the development of a consciousness of revolutionary action, of Black revolutionary action, of Black men, Black women saying, "No more; we took this shit, and whatever we have to do we will do." And this became instilled in the people and what they saw in '64 and '65 were like tea parties compared to what they saw in '67 and '68 throughout the cities in this country.[13] I wouldn't say that it was just the Black revolutionary action and the development of these things that called for the corporate capitalist class to do something. I really think it was the Black revolutionary action going from about '66 up until around '71, when things started to just collapse.

How did the collapse, or the decline in the Party, happen?

Really, from my point of view, it was right after that plenary session of the Revolutionary People's Constitutional Convention that was held here in September 1970. The government tried to stop it, with the raid on us and other things, but they couldn't. There was a tremendous amount of people here then, and if some kind of clear-cut program could have emerged from that, I think that the corporate capitalists would have had a hell of a war on their hands.

There were Indians, Asians, Puerto Ricans, White people, Black people, everybody. Every ethnic group in this country was represented at that plenary session and any kind of clear-cut, basic, fundamental plan to go back into communities—if it was nothing else but to make sure that the government couldn't coopt what was existing at that point—could have helped us funnel more and more people into our struggle.

This rag-tag outfit of Black people, with these other little rag-tag outfits of poor whites and Indians and Chicanos couldn't by themselves pull together nothing of that magnitude; but the support we were getting was tremendous all over the country. Masses of people in this country were beginning to side with the left wing, both white and Black.

But I think the U.S. has got a system that people have got to be very, very conscious of. That is, it projects leaders, and then it breaks leaders. I was out in California that summer when Huey P. Newton got out of jail, and I watched it when people from the community came up and talked with him, congratulated him for coming home and told him how much they missed him and supported him. And I saw that he couldn't talk to them. His conversation was gone, he was a million miles away from them.

At the plenary session what he said just lost people. When he spoke to the people at that session, he spoke to ordinary people in the street way over their head, while they were talking about committing themselves to going back to their areas and making some very fundamental changes in people. I'm not sure if it wasn't a pre-arranged plot to allow Huey to come out at that time.

Because, you know, everyone was talking about turning the Party around. Internally there were certain things happening that left a lot of people across the country dissatisfied. There was drug use, there were problems at the top; and Bobby Seale was in jail in New Haven, Connecticut, and Eldridge Cleaver was outside the country and couldn't return. We were hoping that Huey could turn it around, but when he came home we found out that he wouldn't or couldn't do it. and the Party just started falling, people just started leaving it. The desire was gone.

It's not a question of individuals, really. But the people at the top, the central committee of the Party, they were the ones that we looked up to, the ones that inspired us to do more, and when we couldn't get that inspiration any more, then chapters and branches across the country just started to fall apart.

I know one thing that happened to me when I came out of jail after the raid. Money was needed for bail and to replace the things the police had taken from us, even our clothes. I tripped up when I came out to find out about some central committee members talking about buying some damn expensive jump suits so they could look sharp for the plenary session. It took me down to the lowest, just about the lowest point I'd been since I'd been in the Party.

Another problem I would say, based on what I think I saw, is that the Party tried to exert itself too much. It tried to form coalitions with other groups and then it tried to lead the coalition before it had first established what the coalition was supposed to do within the Party's own boundaries—in the Black community, or in their own areas, if there were six or seven Black groups. It seemed like the Party was more interested later in projecting itself rather than dealing with a program.

It's like I said before, what impressed me early on about the Party was when we called California and June Hilliard said, "You don't have to be no goddamn Panther to struggle." You know, that set. Even though I really, I just wanted to be a Panther because it symbolized this new human being ready to fight, when he made this statement we sat around and talked about it and said, "You know what, he's right; it's nothing but a name."

But after a while the Party started to act different-and it wasn't just on the Party's part. I think that just about every group, every ethnic or national group wanted to ... seeing what they believed was revolution emerging at a very fast pace, they wanted their politics to dominate, you know, and I think that they just forgot about the fundamental reasons for this developing, that is because people across the country were moving our way, the way of the left or the way of revolution.

In what I'm trying to do today I tell everybody in the Movement I won't be so conscious of being a part of the Movement as much as being a part of the community. Because I think the people carried the Panthers, and they carried the Young Lords, and just about all the other organizations. The people carried them and pushed them forward and they gave them protection when they needed protection.

So to get in a damn meeting without the people in there and try to push your politics forward without talking about the common good, that is what I believe was a tremendous mistake-that the Party and other groups wanted to control and dominate everything. And a lot of people rebelled at that and then when they left the coalition, they would do the same thing, set up another coalition and the same thing for themselves.

Another factor was the amount of repression the government brought to bear on the Party. What form did this take in Philadelphia, and did it come from the Philadelphia authorities or the FBI?

Well I think that the repression, it had come down from both, and I base that on that first arrest about that M-14. I don't even know how to describe the FBI people at that time. They were talking like fools as far as I was concerned. They were asking me questions and answering them for me. "What are you? What's your occupation?" and then they'd say "freedom fighter" and write it down. Just little shit like that, and "You're a fucking freedom fighter, you're gonna end up dead."

Then, well, Fencl and his Philadelphia cops used to get a kick out of fucking with everybody; I guess that was the way he got his. You know, you'd just be walking down the street or driving in a car and he'd pull over, stop, search you, take you down to the station for "investigation." That's the way they used to get all the Panthers, everybody they saw continuing to come to our office; one day they'd just get stopped, pulled over, taken down, and they'd ask for what—"investigation."[14]

I know that people in my family, cousins, old friends, told me that the FBI stopped down and asked them what I was like when I was young. I don't know what the purpose of that was. I know my mother called me; she was worried and said that the FBI came to the house and said that I was gonna be killed by some other Panthers or something, and she had best tell them where I was and what I was doing. You know, that kind of shit, that general harassment. There were infiltrators, too. Even a cop told me about one. I don't like to have any relationships with no kind of police because I don't trust them, but I had one that called and told me about this one fellow that was in the Party for a while; he says he's a cop. Sure enough, he was a Black highway patrolman.

But the August 1970 raid was the big climax between the Panthers and the police here. A police park guard was killed, and Rizzo was making all kind of statements, saying he was gonna round up every revolutionary in the city before sun-up, citing us as being fundamentally responsible. We had an idea they'd be coming. About five o'clock that morning I was asleep, and somebody woke me up (we used to pull guard duty in the Panthers anyway) and said, "They're here."

I looked out the window, and they're lined up across the street with submachine guns, shotguns; they're in the alley. I saw the head man clearly, he had a pistol and a gas mask strapped to his leg; he was bending down, and then all hell broke loose. Finally, we had children in there and the gas got to them too much so we had to come out.

Each cop took an individual Panther and placed their pistol up the back of our neck and told us to walk down the street backward. They told us if we stumble or fall they're gonna kill us. Then they lined us up against the wall and a cop with a .45 sub would fire over our heads so the bricks started falling down. Most of us had been in bed, and they just ripped the goddamn clothes off everybody, women and men. They had the gun, they'd just snatch your pants down and they took pictures of us like that. Then they put us in the wagon and took us down to the police station. We were handcuffed and running down this little driveway; when we got to the other end of it, a cop would come by with a stick and he'd punch us, beat us. Some of us were bleeding; I know I was bleeding, but really I thought it was gonna be a whole lot worse.

We had three offices at that time: West Philly where 14 Panthers had barricaded themselves, the North Philly office up here, and a small office in Germantown. They raided them, and they raided everyplace where we stayed. When they took the office, they took everything, they even took the rugs off. And I couldn't understand the reason, but they took all the clothes, the machines; they took everything. I mean I never seen anything as thorough as that—kitchen tables, kitchen chairs, everything we got, refrigerators; they didn't leave us nothing. When we finally got out we had to pay for suits from the prison.

They arrested everyone from the North Philly and West Philly offices, and set the bail at $100,000 apiece. But the support out on the street was really picking up. I think something about them stripping all the clothes off and taking pictures was the shit that backfired. Meanwhile Rizzo was talking all this shit about how he wanted to take us all, one Panther and one cop, and we'd do battle on the street. Finally bail was lowered down to $3,500 apiece, and we got out after a week or ten days and got together for the plenary session.

What happened after you left the Party?

Well, the branch here kept operating until I think 1973 when they took what was left of the cadre and called them out to California to help on Bobby Seale's campaign. But I left a little while after the plenary session, and there were some other people that left then too.

I don't know, if things had been different I might have just said "Fuck revolutionary struggle," and gone back to doing what I was doing before the Party—hustling, working, trying to be slick. But it was really because of the dedication I saw in the Panthers I had known: their loyalty, not to me as an individual, but their loyalty to try to really turn this shit around here in this country. I didn't want to do anything else but to try and do something to carry that forward.

I would say that 98% of the people that joined the Party, of the real cadre of the Panthers, were dedicated, were truly serious. The workload would be so tremendous, like going to sleep at 2:00 and getting back up at 6:00, and people would just do that without crying all the damn time. They never asked for nothing, the women or the men. You know women may like to look sharp from time to time, to dress up from time to time.

But we'd be going out selling papers at night and they'd be wearing combat boots just like the men. They stayed in that kind of garb. Some women would be wearing shoes with holes in them. They wouldn't complain. Somebody else would have to come up and say something to the finance officer, say "You know, so-and-so ain't got no damn shoes." And then we'd send somebody to look at them and jump on the person for not saying something sooner, so we could have got them shoes. Some of the people were on DPA [public assistance], and they would use that money to finance the revolution, to help finance it.

I never saw anything like it before, you know, because people—listen, you're out on the street, you know people are fundamentally selfish because they have to think about themselves as being number one; but when those people came inside the Party, it was something else. They were very good people.

So anyway, in 1970 we set up an organization called the Black United Liberation Front to fundamentally do the same things around police brutality, a free breakfast for children program, a free clothing program, a bus that used to take people to visit relatives and friends in prison. For the first time that I know in my political activity we took a militant stand against drugs and on crime, Black crime, gangs.

We organized all the gangs on this side of Broad Street at one point in 1971-72 and got them, instead of fighting each other, to start turning over abandoned cars, throwing trash and garbage that the city wouldn't collect, and blocking up the street demanding that the city turn over the abandoned houses in the Black community and allot money so that they can hire people to clean them up and to begin to rehabilitate them and make them liveable and sell them to the people at what it cost.[15] That was successful; and we ran a breakfast program and then we became involved in different political activity, like a campaign to stop Rizzo from becoming mayor again. We helped to knock off politically some of the Blacks who supported Rizzo in the past. We'd go into different communities and do extensive work and we'd find that Black people would really get down with that.

Our organization folded about 1975 or maybe early '76; that's when the shit started coming down on us, funds were cut off, we just couldn't get any kind of outside help to do anything so we just had to shut down the office in 1976. In the last two months people have told me a new theory that you're allowed to become a civil rights leader, or a political leader, but you don't do both. And I know when we did the anti-Rizzo campaign we used to get arrested quite frequently. and bail would be high and stuff like that.

Lately I've been trying to fix something up, get something going again, some of the things that we did. And to begin to do some other things. The gang problem doesn't hardly exist here anymore. Most of the young guys now are hustling dope or something, just trying to live and be sharp, so they don't have time just to kill for nothing. They kill you for your money. The city, they're statistical, they like to say there's only one gang death now, or gang-related death. But murders still are being committed because of drugs-for $45 a man get his head blowed off. In the course of a year there might be fifty dope killings and they never include that. So I'd like us to do something around that situation.

Really, you know, I guess I still got too much of that what you call street niggerism in me, because I know people over the last couple of years, they're telling me I don't have no upward mobility, I don't want to change. Probably one of the reasons I've been catching so much hell for the last two years is that some people are afraid of me. It's not so much that I'm a violent person, because I haven't been violent with anybody, but I think this is a question of me not being ready to adapt to reevaluating my entire political perspective. I've made some adjustments, but some things you know I'm gonna stand firm on. What the Party gave me, fundamentally, principally what I joined the Party for was because it did not limit my right to fight for what I believed I should be fighting for. I still believe that.

It would be a relief to me to know that at least people have an idea of what the hell happened then, because the dedication that I saw from people across the country—it shouldn't go unnoticed and like it was just a faddish kind of period that they were entering in and nothing more than that. I know now I see a lot of people that for some reason or another left the Movement, and they see the necessity of something happening again because they see this tremendous economic crisis. And I'm almost confident ... well, one thing that I am sure of is that revolution will come about; you know, I believe what Mao Tse-tung said, that it's inevitable. it's independent of people's will and people can't stop it.

I would like to see more and more people who had some faith in the

Movement become re-involved in it so that the mistakes that were made, we won't allow them to happen again, so we don't keep setting our own self back. Outside of that there's nothing you can say, really, to prove that it wasn't a passing fancy, a fad, some kind of fetish that people were supporting. There's only what you can do.

3 PANTHERS BUSTED FOR CONDUCTING PROPAGANDA WORK AMONG THE MASSES

On Friday, the 4th of July, 3 members of the Black Panther Party, while conducting educational, and political work among the people, were busted and charged with soliciting papers without a permit. They were arrested in Atlantic City, New Jersey.

Arrested were, Milton McGriff, age 30, Elijah Graham, age 18, and Eugene Wells, age 23, with an initial fine of 30 dollars.

Later, after the news hit the hierarchy of the fascist pig setup, the pigs changed their game to $100 a piece.

Back in Philadelphia, the Party found little of nothing could be done in terms of legal help, because of the laws of licenses. In addition to this, the 3 brothers, not being residents of New Jersey, found that they would have to pay in cash. So--we were forced to get the only money available--paper money.

The case is supposed to be floored on Monday morning, July 7th, 9:00, at Atlantic City. These bull--t charges and fines show the inevitable necessity for a UNITED FRONT AGAINST FASCISM---- PEOPLE'S POWER!
ALL POWER TO THE PEOPLE

Mumia X
Lt. of Information
Philadelphia Chapter
Black Panther Party

P.17 "Black Panther"
San Francisco, Cal

Date: 7/19/69
Edition: Vol.III, No.13
Author:
Editor: Eldridge Cleaver

FD-209 (Rev. 9-13-65)

UNITED STATES GOVERNMENT
Memorandum

TO : SAC ▇▇▇ b2,b7D

FROM : SA ▇▇▇ b7C

SUBJECT: ▇▇▇ b2,b7D

DATE: 8/11/69

☐ CI ☐ SI ☒ R (Prob)
☐ PCI ☐ PSI ☐ R
☐

Dates of Contact

Titles and File #s on which contacted

BPP	157-2004
BPP - Publications	157-4012
Hiroshima Day Rally - PH	100-50745

Purpose and results of contact WESLEY COOK — 157-3937

☐ NEGATIVE
☒ POSITIVE — Source ▇▇▇ rally held at
☐ STATISTIC — Rittenhouse Square ▇▇▇ and stayed
until ▇▇▇ The rally ended about 9:30 p.m.

Source said there were several speakers from new left groups and one soldier who supposedly is now in the service. Attendance was over 200. There were no incidents. One of the speakers was the minister of information for the BPP (Philadelphia) who gave an extemporaneous speech and called RIZZO a Pig. Source said the BPP member who spoke was WESLEY (LNU), and he said the usual trash about the oppressor and the roll of the Vanguard interspersing his talk with the usual obscenities.

☒ Informant certified that he has furnished all information obtained by him since last contact.

Rating: Excellent

Coverage: ▇▇▇

157-3937-5

SEARCHED ___ INDEXED ___
SERIALIZED ___ FILED ___
AUG 11 1969
FBI - PHILADELPHIA

1 - ▇▇▇ b2,b7D
1 - Each above listed file
b7C

Red Flag Flutters For A Day

by Alan Oslick

Imagine, if you will, that you're a "junior commander" of a Veterans of Foreign Wars post in Virginia. Or a lean VFWer from oil-baron-ruled Oklahoma. And you've read in your READER'S DIGEST ET AL how the coastal cities are crawling with longhaired creeps, freaks, and comies. So, harboring secret envy of the freedom these people exhibit, when the VFW brings you into Philadelphia, you scurry down to Rittenhouse Park.

Now here's the scene Saturday on the Square, an uncommon sight for even this uncommon park: a high red-lettered banner stretches across a stage, reading "Socialist Workers Campaign '69" or some such message. It's late afternoon, about 3:45, and a group calling itself "The Elizabeth" is belting out strong progressive rock.

Off on the south side of the stage, Paul Boutelle, SWP 1968 vice presidential candidate and 1969 N Y C mayoralty candidate, has eschewed rest after an earlier speech, and is talking softly against the background of The Elizabeth. Some young men are asking him, in effect, why they sould link up with a "socialist" outfit as they are Black, and the SWP fully endorses the Black Panther Party for Blacks. At least that seemed to be the question. I left Boutelle trying to get the SWP off the horns of its own dilemma as I retreated to preserve my ear drums.

Around the edges of the crowd of several hundred rock fans, some VFWers were seeking out sympathetic police ears to find out what the scene was all about. Also Black Panthers were present to peddle their paper and accept contributions, programs.

Edging into a circle of his friends, I talked to West Mumia Cook, Communications Secretary of the Philadelphia Black Panthers. An intense and fairly articulate spokesman, Cook is a young man who has no tolerance for anyone not adhering to the revolutionary line pushed by the Panthers.

This isn't our thing," he said of the "Red Revolution in Rittenhouse Square" affair. As for the minority S D S that emerged with Panther support from Chicago, Cook repeated the latest Panther turnabout (by Dave Hilliard), and denounced the S D S and virtually every other left group as "objectively fascist." "S D S criticized the Panther United Front Against Fascism as 'Stalinist," complained Cook, "What they called 'Stalinist' is the revolutionary Panther discipline."

Later I noticed in the Black Panther newspaper (8/16/69) an item headed "Philadelphia B.P.P. Purge, Let This Be Known and Acknowledged By All Extremities of the Black Panther Party." In an article expelling one Willie McIntyre, summing - up paragraphs read:

"One must never lose sight of the revolutionary truth. 'The individual is subordinate to the organization' - and that no one person may ever move to endanger the people's revolution or the political work of the Party.... Fight fail, fight fail, fight again, fail again, fight until ultimate victory. Smash the State."

No specifics were listed as to what special considerations McIntyre demanded that labeled him "ultra-democratic."

The music subsided, the Panthers moved out. On stage, Jim Quinn, formerly of what was the TEMPLE FREE PRESS, was introduced onto the stage. Brushing his mane away from his eyes, Quinn struggled awhile with his mike before piercing the technical truth of maintaining adequate distance between mouth and mike.

Quinn saluted comrades in the S.W.P. for keeping up the fight outside of the Democratic-Republican framework, "The life-styles we want to live can maybe lived after the Revolution." Listing the three "M's" of the revolution as "Malcom, Marx, and Marijuana," Quinn lashed out at Tate, Rizzo, Berger, and Specter as being "the enemy." He had a few kind words to say of "good pigs," and other words for the others. If they were listening, the police around the greatly diminished crowd didn't visibly react to the "pig" bit.

Quinn then called on the audience to attend to what SWP district attorney candidate John Benson had to say.

Benson enthusiastically saw a great upsurge in the desire for change: "The willingness to struggle in the streets, has transformed the anti-war movement against the most barbaric and criminal warin mankind(?), in the process of struggle, into a struggle for power, not just anti-war but into a movement from capitalist America to a socialist America." He called for participation in the Nov. 15 anti-war demonstration in Washington that will be "half a million to a million marching on the White House demanding that the war end now." Benson reiterated the SWP slogan of "black control of the black community."

p. 4 - "The Distant Drummer"
Philadelphia, Pa.

Date: 8/22-29/69
Edition No. 47, Vol. 34
Author: Alan Oslick
Editor: Don DeMaio

Anyone wanting to read the SWP Philadelphia campaign material can write to the SWP-YSA at 686 N. Broad, Phila., points in the crowd, who admitted to being present when Boutelle spoke, what he said. They didn't recall.

Posters of Malcolm, Che, and "Bring the Troops Home, Vote Socialist" hung from the stand. One striking poster that hung from each side of the stand bore the declaration "Revolution Until Victory, Defend Arab Revolution." It portrayed a girl guerilla in various positions as she swung a semi-automatic gun around. I walked up closer to see the name of the issuing Arab terrorist group, and read off the Young Socialist Alliance's name and a New York City address. (YSA is the youth arm of the SWP).

To me the SWP preaches opportunism. They cool talking about what socialism means to the point that they never seem to publicly talk about it. "Black control of the Black community" within the context of capitalist America doesn't seem revolutionary nor necessarily forward. Nonetheless, whatever you think about peace demonstrations, the SWP has given of its efforts to the point of exhaustion to build up a nonsectarian peace movement.

While within its own ranks it practices a rigid discipline typical of Trotskyite groups following Leninist models, within the broader left movement the SWP has always defended the right of others with whom it disagrees to speak, others with whom it disagrees to speak-- an attitude other left parties and SDS of all varieties could learn from, fears of "ultra-democracy" notwithstanding.

After waiting another forty minutes for a tardy dance group to appear, I left the SWP, park people, guards, and VFWers at the Square. "We're all tired now from organizing this, and we've got our national convention (closed to the public) coming up Labor Day weekend, but, yesh, we'll be back with more this fall," asserted one weary but happy SWP worker.

62-2036 (SWP)
57-2004 (BPP)
?-4652 (SDS)
-JSMS (YSA) b7C
+ 157-3937 (COCK)

FBI

Date 9/25/69

Transmit the following in _____
                                  (Type in plaintext or code)
Via AIRTEL   AIR MAIL (REGISTERED)
                            (Priority)

TO: DIRECTOR, FBI (105-165706 Sub 3, 37)

FROM: SAC, SAN FRANCISCO (157-2255)

SUBJECT: BLACK PANTHER PARTY - PHILADELPHIA DIVISION
         RM - BPP

Reference is made to San Francisco airtel dated 9/25/69, concerning the first reports of arrests of members of the BPP in Philadelphia.

███████████████ a highly confidential source, gave further information on this situation on the date of 9/24/69. His information was as follows:

A person named ███████████ of the BPP in Philadelphia, was contacted by BPP ███████████ reported that six from Berkeley, Calif., on 9/24/69.

2 - Bureau
2 - Baltimore (157-3241)
    (1 -
⑧ - Philadelphia
    (1 - 157-2004)
    (1 -
    (1 -
    (1 -
    (1 -
    (1 -
    (1 - 157-   WES COOK)
3 - Los Angeles (157-1618)
    (1 -   (1
2 - New York (100-161993)
3 - San Francisco
    (1 - 157-3063) (ARRESTS)   (1 - 157-1810) (BALTIMORE)
    (20)

Approved: _____ Sent _____ M Per _____
          Special Agent in Charge

1.

157-3737-27

SF 157-2255
b7C

Panthers had been "busted." Those arrested included RENE JOHNSON, with the title of Assistant Officer of the Day; PEGGIE SCHELL; ROLANDO or ORLANDO HEARN, with the nickname of MONTE; CRAIG WILLIAMS, Officer of the Day; CLARENCE PETERSON, Financial Secretary; and WES COOK, Branch Secretary.

As of 10:00 a.m. on 9/24/69, REGGIE and MONTE were still in custody. REGGIE was to be arraigned at the Federal Building at 2:30 p.m., being charged with possession of a stolen M-16 rifle. This rifle had been recovered at the home of ▓▓▓ and had been listed as stolen from Camp Lejeune.

b7C

▓▓▓ further reported that MONTE had been arrested on a bench warrant for contempt of court and failure to appear. The arrest had been made allegedly by the FBI and the Civil Disobedience Squad of the Philadelphia PD. MONTE was to be arraigned at Philadelphia City Hall at 2:30 p.m. and the other four persons named above had been released at 7:00 a.m. with no charges against them.

Later in the afternoon an unidentified man from Philadelphia advised ▓▓▓ that REGGIE had been released on $2,500 bond but ORLANDO was still in custody with bail set at $3,000.

The source had no further information concerning this particular item which was brought up by ▓▓▓.

2

157-3937-27

SF 157-2255
▓▓▓▓ b7C

The same source advised that ▓▓▓▓▓▓ of Baltimore had been arrested in Baltimore allegedly on an outstanding Calif. fugitive warrant. ▓▓▓▓▓▓ talked to ▓▓▓▓▓▓ in Los Angeles, seeking information on ▓▓▓▓▓▓ was informed that ▓▓▓▓ had been arrested on some sort of a traffic citation and when the police were checking him out they discovered he was wanted on a fugitive warrant. ▓▓▓▓ wanted to know when ▓▓▓▓ was due in court.

▓▓▓▓ said she believed it was on 10/4/69. ▓▓▓▓ said he was interested in trying to find out what kind of a fugitive warrant was outstanding against ▓▓▓▓

The same source advised that at 12:20 a.m. ▓▓▓▓ was successful in reaching a woman he called ▓▓▓▓ (PH) ▓▓▓▓ in the past, has been the nickname for ▓▓▓▓ wife of ▓▓▓▓ known as ▓▓▓▓

▓▓▓▓ then talked to the husband of ▓▓▓▓ and informed him that all things were messed up in Philadelphia where the whole leadership of the Party had been arrested. ▓▓▓▓ said that Headquarters had no information of any kind about what had gone on back there. ▓▓▓▓ also said he had learned that the police had 'busted' ▓▓▓▓ in Baltimore on some outstanding fugitive warrants from Calif. ▓▓▓▓ wondered if ▓▓▓▓ had any information concerning this matter.

▓▓▓▓ thought that ▓▓▓▓ was on probation or parole, but he was not certain as to that. ▓▓▓▓ said that Headquarters had attempted to get ▓▓▓▓ working on this matter inasmuch as she had many contacts in Philadelphia, but ▓▓▓▓ did not know what she had been able to find out. ▓▓▓▓ said a person named ▓▓▓▓ (PH), not further described, should have information about ▓▓▓▓ ▓▓▓▓ still thought it was nothing more than a probation case, but possibly he was not permitted to leave the State. Neither ▓▓▓▓ nor ▓▓▓▓ knew if ▓▓▓▓ had

3

SF 157-2255
b7C

any restrictions as to travel. ▓▓▓ then made
the comment 'the pigs had gone crazy.' ▓▓▓ promised
to work on this matter and inform Headquarters.

As of later on 9/24/69, Los Angeles had not given
San Francisco any further information concerning the
Philadelphia arrests.

Also on 9/24/69, brother ▓▓▓ from New York
talked to ▓▓▓ about the arrest of ▓▓▓ in
Baltimore. After ▓▓▓ was arrested on a traffic warrant
the 'feds' moved in on him saying they had a fugitive
warrant for him from Calif. and there was "$10,000
reward' on him. This was not further explained.

The above material is furnished to Baltimore
for its information to show the interest of the
National Headquarters in the arrest of ▓▓▓ Copy is
sent to Los Angeles with the request that the status of
▓▓▓ in Los Angeles insofar as probation or other
violations is concerned be ascertained.

Copy is sent for the information of New York
to show the interest of ▓▓▓ in this matter.

Any further developments will be called to the
attention of offices concerned.

b7C

MUMIA ABU-JAMAL'S BLACK PANTHER PARTY DAYS: "DO SOMETHING, NIGGER, EVEN IF YOU ONLY SPIT!"[16]

TODD STEVEN BURROUGHS

Like many urban Black members of the Baby Boom generation, the young Wes Cook came of age with and, to a certain extent, within the Civil Rights and Black Power movements. Aspects of his life are familiar to those Black Boomers who grew up yelling for power, wearing Afros, and openly and romantically discussing how they would disrupt, destroy or subvert The Man. He was 10 years old when Philadelphia became one of the first American cities to go up in flames kindled by racial and economic injustice. He was 12 in 1966—a year after a young Muslim minister was killed in the Audubon Ballroom.

In Oakland, California, two community college students acted on the minister's suggestion that Blacks form rifle clubs to defend themselves. They wanted to see if revolution could come to the United States the same way it had come in Cuba and several African nations—through a guns' barrel. The duo, Bobby Seale and Huey P. Newton, formed a Third World Marxist political organization. The new group emphasized community service, political education, and self-defense against Oakland's racist white police force attacks. Stokely Carmichael, a Student Nonviolent Coordinating Committee leader, was organizing an independent political party in Lowndes County, Ala., to test Blacks' newly-won voting power. Seale and Newton asked to adopt the party's name and symbol, a black panther, as their own. Carmichael and the other SNCC organizers had no complaint.

Something a little closer to home helped place Wes Cook on the Panther's path: Rizzo's violent response to the Black student protest in 1967.

Rizzo did his best impersonation of Birmingham's Eugene "Bull" Connor. Nightsticks. Broken bones. Blood. No officers punished.

The following year, a young Christian minister from Alabama was killed for attempting to force the United States government to re-commit to the War on Poverty. Many young Blacks wanted to avenge his death. Some did by looting and busting windows in scores of cities. In the aftermath, thousands of young Blacks had another idea: they wanted to join that group of radical cats they had heard about in Oakland. So they set up or flooded existing local chapters and branches. They purchased rifles, Black jackets and Black berets. *Since Brother Martin's way didn't work*, they thought, *let's try Brother Malcolm's.*

Ungawa. Black Power. A 1968 George Wallace for President rally in Philadelphia. Cook and his friends booed and hissed Wallace and his supporters. Some Wallace supporters decided to respond as a gang. A frantic Cook happily spied a policeman. What happened next Abu-Jamal recalls in *Live from Death Row*: "The cop saw me on the ground being beaten to a pulp, marched over briskly—and kicked me in the face." [17] (Cook's FBI file, in contrast, stated that Cook struck the officer.[18]) Another not-so-insignificant event happened in Cook's life that year. One of his high school teachers gave him a new name, a Kenyan named Timone Ombina. His new name was a royal one to Kenyans, one historically identified with leadership and struggle. Cook took to his nominal rebirth immediately. It coincided with the new identity created by puberty. [19]

During all of these changes, he discovered something that galvanized him in all his parts: a weekly tabloid newspaper. Its volatile mixture of newsprint, words, drawings and pictures stirred the Scout and the United Nations within him. The newspaper was *The Black Panther*. Cook's entire life—including his courtroom struggle to not be put to death—would be defined by the ideas expressed in its contents. His attraction and commitment to the Party were complete. He joined up with some other Black men who could trace their outlines within the Panther's shadow. The remaining challenge: customizing a West Coast idea for Philly.

Cook was turning 15. In transition from boy to man, his embrace of the Black Panther Party symbolized the beginning of his quest to find three primary things that gave his world definition—revolution, writing and family. He was well suited for his task. Cook thrived on intellectual challenge and had always fed on the adrenalin rush of the journey. He was a teenager in search of his manhood and identity during a time when his people openly sought their destiny. Like many Black teens of the time, Cook wanted outlets—for camaraderie, expression, resistance, and *nia* ("purpose" in Kiswahili). There were many choices for young Blacks who were also looking for those things. They included the Nation of Islam, the NAACP, and various Black cultural nationalist organizations in colleges and/or on the streets. For Cook (or Wes Mumia Cook, as he would call himself as a Panther), the Black Panther Party's Philadelphia branch satisfied those four needs.

From a Death Row cell, Abu-Jamal publicly ruminated on the tenuous state of young Black manhood. As the third decade of the 21ST century continues, very young African-American males still have the choice he faced decades ago: to be consumed by anger or constructively channel it; to embrace self-pity or seek higher ground. "One can emerge with the poison of aloneness, or the shared sense of commonality," he postulated in an anthology published by *Essence* magazine. [20] The teenage Cook chose to be pro-active, to emerge with the latter. He was also fortunate to have a Black Power Movement that easily absorbed his energy. By embracing his adventure into young manhood through the prism of a Black Panther, Cook gained a new family that was helping to fuel a revolutionary spirit of Black unity. He enjoyed both while they lasted.

The Philadelphia branch was formed in the spring of 1969.[21] Abu-Jamal recalled that it was difficult to give an exact date because several groups formed at the same time—one in South Philadelphia, one in North Philadelphia and one in the city's Germantown section. The Germantown group sold only *The Black Panther*, Abu-Jamal recalled, and died out, while the remaining groups combined. Wes Cook was there at the very beginning—at both the bookstore meeting and in a subsequent confab in a South Philadelphia apartment, watching Bill Crawford and Terry McCarter lobby to lead the group. The fledging rank-and-file chose McCarter as Defense Captain—the highest rank a branch offered. McCarter, however, did not mesh with his followers and had problems with alcohol. So the group chose again from among their ranks, settling on Reginald Schell, an Army veteran from North Philadelphia. [22]

The branch's members made their debut at a small May Day gathering, a "Free Huey" rally, at the State Office Building. The FBI's informants took pictures of the "12 Negro males," tracked down names, and opened files on 10 of them.[23] The Black Panther Party quickly became a priority to the FBI because the Party combined the two things the bureau feared most: Leftist political activity and Black insurrection.[24]

Acting on Williams' instruction to get a site on West Columbia Avenue, a Black community thoroughfare, Schell chose a site, a storefront with a big glass window on 1928, and after military-style inspections from Deputy Field Marshals Henry Mitchell and Sister Love, the branch's headquarters was established.[25] The branch members lived and worked on the ground floor and the basement, with the building's top floors housing apartments. One of the Bureau's informants listed the date of the branch's opening as June 7, 1969.[26] By the next month, its breakfast program was up and running.[27]

Bonding quickly developed between Cook and his fellow Panthers, most of whom were at least five years older than him.[28] Cook's "father hunger," as he would label it later, was particularly satiated by his relationship with Schell.[29] The recent death of "Mr. Bill," Cook's father, had, like the Black Power Movement, moved adulthood a little closer. Acting more like a big brother at home to try to fill the absence of "Mr. Bill," Cook would happily embrace the role of Schell's little brother while they worked for the people.[30] Their friendship and the working relationship would be birthed by, and would survive, the Party. Years later, Schell described the young Cook as "highly intelligent" and "highly motivated."[31] Wes, explained Schell, projected himself as an adult by his personality. "He didn't look old, but his mind was way beyond his years—the way he carried himself, you wouldn't believe he was 14 or 15. He looked young, but the way he carried himself, his demeanor, was that of a full-grown man.... .I think that at 15, 14, Mumia was making decisions that some grown men couldn't make... I had full confidence in him from Day One." Schell thought he "was born to be a Panther."[32]

His adolescent path set, Cook became a full-time revolutionary. The energy of youth was lit under the fire of zealotry.[33] He slowly phased out of Benjamin Franklin High School and took up residence in the branch's headquarters. Cook's family trusted him to find his own way, so they put up no resistance. As spring became summer and summer became fall, Cook's days and nights in 1969 quickly became centered around three things: Party work, his family, and a young woman named Francine Hart. Even though he was younger than her, she was attracted to the tall, Afro-ed Panther with the deep voice. Cook gave her a new name fitting a revolutionary—Habibah. Soon he and Biba, as she was nicknamed, seemed attached to the hip, becoming regulars at rallies, streetcorners (selling the newspaper) and Robbens bookstore downtown.[34] The Party, meanwhile, would continue to grow during Cook's tenure.[35]

The Party not only gave Wes Mumia Cook (as he now called himself) a second family, but also a single outlet for his creativity, his intellect and his sense of rebellion: revolutionary journalism, in the form of his post as the branch's Lieutenant of Information. Being a propagandist suited him; Schell noticed Cook could put words together well, both verbally and in print. (Schell learned about Cook's talents during the branch's study sessions of Chinese Communist Party Chairman Mao Tse-Tung's *The Red Book* and the BPP 10 Point Platform and Program. "We would have classes, and you could see in Mumia that Mumia was the kind of person that could take information and turn in back into something that's understandable and intelligible for the community to digest it and to get their interest. You didn't have to be a rocket scientist to see that Mumia was destined to be the Lt. of Information." [36]) In addition to his Black Panther dispatches, Cook wrote leaflets, press releases and pamphlets for the branch. [37] As a Philadelphia BPP Party representative, Cook visited Party offices in Harrisburg, Pittsburgh and other Pennsylvania cities. [38] He spoke at Panther events, such as the Philadelphia commemoration ceremony for Fred Hampton and Mark Clark, Chicago Panthers assassinated by that city's police officers in late 1969. [39] The young Philadelphia Panther, who saw for himself the bullet holes in the Chicago chapter office on a quick post-shooting tour, gave interviews to local Philadelphia media. One such interview, published one month to the day after Hampton and Clark's death, landed Cook on the front page of *The Philadelphia Inquirer* on Sunday, January 4, 1970. His image—young, Afro-ed, on the phone in the Panther office, hard at work for Black liberation—would be remembered. [40] So would his quoting of Tse-Tung—the one about how political power gushes out of a gun's barrel.[41] He also did all the other typical Panther tasks—assisting with the breakfast program, standing guard over the headquarters, working with the other comrades on the various community service programs. In between, there was time for food and sleep, all with his fellow Panthers.

In the community of Party chapters and branches, Philadelphia, a branch, made its name through community service and providing information, not gun brandishing. The city's Panthers did not patrol the neighborhood watching the police. Instead, the Philadelphia BPP spent most of its time protesting or lobbying for people who either did not know how to, or could not, make local government agencies respond to them.[42] For instance, if city officials wouldn't take action to fix the constantly backed-up sewers on Columbia Avenue, then the Panthers would block the street until the bureaucracy moved in their direction. Some Panthers might run for seats when a City Council election was upcoming, as Milton McGriff and Craig Williams did.[43] If Philadelphia had a gang problem, the Panthers would hold a weekend conference of political education for them, telling the gangsters that they needed to save those weapons "for your own defense and the defense of your people" and that they should instead for "A People's Army." [44] And if four Black women were being harassed after moving into an all-white housing development, then the Panthers would stand by those sisters for as many days it took until the mob gave up. And if a young Black man named Harold Brown was fatally shot by white highway patrolmen when he and witnesses begged them not to shoot, then Cook would write a 16-page pamphlet about it, and he and the other Panthers would circulate it, along with "Wanted" posters of the four officers, around the city. [45] All of this did not escape the attention of the police. Harassment became a fact of life for members of the Philadelphia branch.

Cook, absorbing the way of the Panther, learned all of his duties with military-like precision. But his writing had begun to stand out. By the 19TH of July, "Mumia X" had begun writing articles for *The Black Panther*.[46] His Black Panther bylines varied with his nicknames: Wes Mumia, West Mumia, Mumia X and Bro. Mumia. Sometimes he signed his birth name and used one title or the other; sometimes it was just "Communications Secretary, Philadelphia Branch." The only other Philadelphia Panthers who signed their names to articles were Lynn Smith and Rolando Montae, but their names only appear occasionally. All Panther branches and chapters were encouraged to submit articles to the paper's office at National Headquarters. The paper's editors would pick the best of the lot, giving its organ national scope.[47]

Cook's articles, which, typically, documented recent police brutality incidents of the day and attempted to rally young Black people to the

Revolution, read like those of a recent convert ("Throughout our history, some niggers have refused to bow down and be beaten into the dust"), reflecting the defiant anger—and, some Panthers and others would say years later, the political immaturity—of the time. [48] Like his castigation of a "pig pastor" who wouldn't support the group's breakfast program. "He has yet to fulfill them by his religious ranting about fire and brimstone. Not having a good, hot nourishing diet takes you all too close to that hot place anyway.....You have defined your position. We have defined ours. We have constructed a clear line of demarcation, not too far different from the one your Christ defined. And we are the DO-ERS." [49] The commentaries, like most in the Party newspaper, would end with some sort of proletarian call to action: "Do Something, Nigger, [Even] If You Only Spit!"[50]

The young Panther had a lot to write about. One incident was very close to home: the police raid on the Panther headquarters on September 23, 1969. The way Schell remembers the story, Lt. George Fencl, head of the city police's Civil Disobedience Squad, along with some FBI agents, walked up to Schell and the other Panthers, including Cook, while they were in Webb's Bar, a frequent Panther hangout across the street from the group's West Columbia headquarters, around 11 p.m. "They asked, 'Are you Reggie Schell?' I turned around and said, 'No.' So Fencl said, 'Don't play with me. That's the motherfucker right there.' And they read the warrant, and I was arrested." [51] Led by Fencl, the authorities then raided the headquarters, seizing security reports, files, a mimeograph machine and an M-14 rifle that they claimed had been stolen from a military training base.[52] The Panthers were led by gunpoint to the police station. Cook said to *The Temple* (University) *News* that police gave no warning and had no warrant and that the Panthers didn't resist.[53] A Panther duo stayed in custody—Schell for possession of stolen government property, Rolondo (Monte) Hearn for armed robbery and contempt of court—while the other Panthers—including Cook, Rene Johnson, Craig Williams (the "Officer Of The Day") and Clarence Peterson—were set free the next day.[54] Cook was quoted as saying that a police lieutenant told him the following during his release: "We don't want any more inflammatory statements coming out of your office. We know you. We've got more firepower than you. That's not a threat, you know." [55] The Philadelphia branch, of course, covered its own raid for *The Black Panther*. In an unsigned article complete with pictures, Party members wrote in the Panther style about their own raid, led by "Lt. Georgey-boy Faggot Fencl." One paragraph seems to carry Cook's touch: "Historically, all reactionary forces on the verge of extinction invariably conduct a last desperate attempt to eliminate the revolutionary forces, and some revolutionaries are apt to be deluded for a time by this phenomenon of outward strength but inner weakness, failing to grasp the essential fact *that the enemy is nearing extinction while they themselves are approaching victory.*" [56]

Cook had found a career that he would use to define himself as his life took many turns. School just couldn't compete with the intellectual immersion that journalism required and the excitement it and the other Party work generated. It wouldn't be the last time Cook would bounce back and forth between formal education and its more gregarious, dynamic, lower-class, creative, free-spirited and attention-seeking cousin, Black community activity.

By 1969, the year Wes Mumia Cook began writing for *The Black Panther*, Black newspapers had enjoyed 142 years of often-militant fighting for the rights of Black people. With the increased emphasis on Black radio news and the development of Black public affairs radio and television shows as a result of the scores of urban insurrections between 1964 and 1968, the Black press was becoming the Black media. From the beginning, Black activists over the decades used Black newspapers and magazines, and now Black media, to seize control over their own personal destinies, allowing them, in turn, to use their vehicles to push for other Blacks to control their collective destiny.

The Black Panther was created in 1967 by BPP founders Bobby Seale and Huey P. Newton, along with BPP leader Eldridge Cleaver. The newspaper was put together in the Black Panther Party's headquarters in Oakland, California. It relied on members of its chapters and branches to be correspondents. The weekly newspaper was unapologetically Black and Marxist. It named friends and enemies in unforgettable, and perhaps even reckless, ways. Emory Douglas, the newspaper's official artist, created agitprop images that allowed illiterate people to see who the Panthers were (heroes) and who the police were (pigs). It publicly named and printed the pictures of those the Party considered "The Enemy of the People." In *The Black Panther*, the people were the vanguard, the police pigs, and capitalists and other members of the establishment were bloodsuckers.

The new big, Black radical newspaper cat was a harsh, brash, radical, outspoken great-grandchild of sorts of *Freedom's Journal*—the first Black newspaper, published in 1827 by some of the "founders" of Black America—and the newspapers that followed. The historian Lerone Bennett Jr. has postulated that Black America was founded from 1787 to 1837 by free Blacks. Bennett divides the era of the founding of Black America into two time periods. The first period, 1787 to 1816, was when free Northern Blacks began to found schools, lodges, churches and other institutions after the Revolutionary War. [57] The second period, 1817 to 1837, was when Blacks had completed building their main institutions and begun their agitation for full civil and human rights. [58] One institution that developed during this second period was the Black press. In the beginning, the Black press served as offense and defense. It began both as a response to white media supremacy and the vehicle for free African-Americans to see their own words. The heart of African communication—the drum and the word *(nommo)*, the voices of the village–met the technology of the European-created printing press with empowering results. Bennett writes that the creation of periodicals allowed for different colonies of "Black America" [to] co-exist in the same time zone" and "brought the Black community together and focused its thinking." [59] *Freedom's Journal* was a signal to the predominately white abolitionist movement that free Blacks were ready to define themselves.[60] So they did. However, they also used the vehicle to record births, deaths, marriages, and other parts of free Black American life that the white press chose to ignore.[61] This duality of purpose—to explain and defend Black life while documenting its everyday happenings—would become Black media's permanent raison d'etre. The idea of Blacks achieving self-determination through self-definition of objectives, friends and opponents had been established. Technology would change the medium and transform the audience, and the society of the day would determine the tone, but the necessity of the message would remain a constant. Black media created the space for Black people to talk to themselves, see themselves, and hear themselves. It allowed questions to be asked and answered. Black media helped define and sustain a Black public sphere—the cultural, political, social, economic and spiritual center of Black America. Black media created and recreated Black America, following and leading it.

But if *Freedom's Journal* set the stage for *The Black Panther* to appear

140 years later, it was David Walker's *Appeal* that set the tone. Walker was a Boston abolitionist, a used clothing dealer, and the city's agent for (and occasional contributor to) *Freedom's Journal*. He was born free in Wilmington, North Carolina, in 1785 and left the South while in his thirties. On his birthday, September 28, 1829, two years after *Freedom's Journal* was born, he published a 76-page pamphlet called *Walker's Appeal, in Four Articles: Together with a Preamble, to the Coloured Citizens of the World, but in particular, and very expressly, to those of the United States of America, written in Boston, State of Massachusetts, September 28, 1829*. It was a document that called for a holy crusade against slaveholders (*"Fear not the number and education of our enemies, against whom we shall have to contend for our lawful right; guaranteed to us by our Makers...."*). [62] It led to his arrest and subsequent disappearance. Walker's *Appeal* resonated—among Blacks who were not afraid to fight for freedom and among whites who were afraid that such a fight would indeed occur. Like *Freedom's Journal*, his words inspired those in the fight to abolish slavery. His essay frightened those who wanted to maintain the status quo of racial oppression. "Like a cry of fire in a crowded theater, like the sound of screeching tires on a crowded thoroughfare, these words constricted hearts and made sweat run down backs," Bennett wrote. [63] Walker's call would inspire other manifestos to be written. Other documents of protest would be produced, with Blacks, in the tradition of Thomas Jefferson and Thomas Payne, turning their voices into sirens, their pens into swords and ink into blood. [64] These publicly distributed documents would continue to inspire resistance against white supremacy. Like Walker, Frederick Douglass, Mary Ann Shadd Cary, Ida B. Wells-Barnett and other Black publishers discovered over the decades as the 19th century turned into the 20th that to be truly free was to be free in everything—in word, in voice, in flesh and in spirit.

The Black Panther had another thing in common with the Black periodicals of old; it was an organ for a national organization. Here it joined historic company: *The Crisis*, *Negro World* and *The Messenger*—the organs of W.E.B. Du Bois and the NAACP, Marcus Garvey's Universal Negro Improvement Association and A Philip Randolph's The Brotherhood of Sleeping Car Porters, respectively—served tens of thousands in the 1920s. *The Black Panther* and *The Messenger* were radically Socialist in perspective, with the goal being to rally Black workers.

It had an older, contemporary journalistic sibling of sorts as a radical 1960s organ: *Muhammad Speaks*, the weekly newspaper of the Nation of Islam. Both were sold on Black America's streetcorners by the faithful, and both had circulations in the hundreds of thousands. *The Black Panther* also had another similarity with *Muhammad Speaks*; it listed in every issue its "10-Point Program and Platform" in much the same way the NOI listed "What We Want" and "What We Believe." Both were substantial national vehicles to promote and raise funds for their respective organizations, and both used poetry, art, and angry prose to make their positions known. The papers were "overground" vehicles to communicate directly to working-class, everyday people who worked and lived on urban streets. The papers defended themselves from white mainstream media attacks and distortions of themselves and their respective missions. Used as fundraising vehicles for their organizations, the newspapers also educated the public on their respective organizational missions and detailed how they were under attack by police and each other. Abu-Jamal would recall an encounter he had with his NOI counterpart on a Bronx street corner as they sold their respective newspapers. The political bantering between the rivals displayed many of the ideological differences of those in the Black Revolution. [65]

Cook's association with *The Black Panther* were just part of the latest chapter of the story of how ex-slaves metaphorically took hold of words and transformed themselves and others—how they used *nommo* (generative word power) on their own terms, for their own purposes. Their words became powerful because of their ability to inspire others to act. The generation coming of age in the Black Power Movement of the late 1960s to mid-1970s—particularly those who went into professional broadcasting, like Mumia Abu-Jamal would just a few years later—paid attention to the successes the publications had in educating and organizing Black America.

With so much activity around him, Cook had decided to go with the revolutionary flow, embracing whatever it had to offer. He would spend the winter of 1969 in New York and the spring of 1970 in Oakland, living and working with comrades in those cities. "One could be transferred in the blink of an eye, for reasons that were beyond one's ken," recalled Abu-Jamal. "A Panther accepted this with equanimity or even looked forward to it with anticipation." [66] As a Panther, Cook had become a visible, committed revolutionary, so he was "excited" to be shipped to the Bronx branch of the New York City chapter, to the BPP's East Coast Ministry of Information there.[67]

"Although a ghetto then," remembered the writer, "it still had the buoyant spirit of hope within it. Blacks and Afro-Ricans worked to affirm the people's inherent dignity in their human right to self-defense. BPP's free breakfast and other such programs enhanced feelings of community solidarity while serving some basic needs." [68] He told an interviewer about day-to-day Panther communal living there: "I worked out of the Bronx. And there was some rough stuff in the Bronx.... We lived in a Panther pad in the Bronx, not far from the office. The Information Ministry was on Boston Road in the Bronx. And we got used to gettin' in that shower, and the water just [snaps fingers] just comes on, and you had to jump out of that thing real fast. Turn it off, right?—because that water would change temperature [snaps fingers] like that... Without warning... You know, you'd hear a little thump. That was, you ain't, you couldn't fake it—you had to jump out of that shower.... I remember getting to the Bronx in the spring, and walking down the street, sellin' papers, and, you know, somebody's saying something in Spanish. And you lookin' up, movin' out of the way, and a bag of garbage is coming at you. They weren't throwing it at me, 'Yo, we gonna get you, Black Panther.' That's just how people got rid of their garbage. They opened their window and threw it out there." [69]

Wes Mumia Cook sold newspapers and did the usual duties that winter. During the spring of 1970, he was transferred to Oakland to, among other things, write for *The Black Panther* from its home office—the Party's national headquarters. He was excited by the opportunity to travel. Just like in New York, he quickly got used to the scene, earning the respect of his boss, *Black Panther* editor Judi Douglas, as he wrote and edited dispatches.[70] He learned that what Oakland residents called a ghetto looked to his Northern-project-raised eyes like a suburb. He learned the hard way to never fall asleep while on guard duty, and to never jaywalk in California, experiences he gives first-person and self-deprecating treatment in *We Want Freedom*, his Panther historical study and memoir.[71] By the time Cook began his second year in the Black Panther Party, however, he would see the hopes of a people hoisted and dropped by, respectively, the promise and failure of revolution. He had returned home from his Oakland stint braver and more confident about the future he and his comrades were created. However, that vision was blurred by the struggle tearing his revolutionary family asunder from without and within.

The tension began to rise when the National BPP decided it was going to hold a national convention—a Revolutionary People's Constitutional Convention—at Temple University in Philadelphia in September of 1970. The cradle of Revolutionary War-era liberty would be the site of new American revolutionaries. Representing many different groups, these radical activists of all colors would also demand liberty or death. The idea that revolutionaries of all stripes would descend on Philadelphia frightened the city's law-and-order police commissioner, Frank Rizzo, to no end. His town was *not* going to be overrun by Black Power advocates and white, Leftist hippies. With revolution discussed openly throughout the country and the BPP-sponsored meeting on its way into the city, Rizzo put the Philadelphia police in ready mode. His worst fears—or hopes, depending on the perspective—were realized when, during a weekend of reported violence against police officers, one of his men, Frank VonColln, was fatally shot. Although Party members were not involved, it was the excuse he needed to clamp down on Black militancy, once and for all.

Claiming the men involved in the fatal officer shooting were members of a local militant group called the Black Unity Movement, Rizzo announced the department would round up *every* Black revolutionary by sunup. The man who ordered his men to beat up Black protesting schoolchildren three years previously ("Get their Black asses!") had now, in 1970, given himself the authority to attack *any* and *all* Black militant organizations.[72] Schell said branch members were used to police harassment, so the Defense Captain thought he had an idea what was coming next. Rizzo was as good as his promise. By the morning, the Panthers had been stripped down to their underwear in front of their headquarters (and in front of a police department-friendly news photographer) and packed away in jail, with bail set for $100,000.[73]

The Panthers—especially the Philadelphia ones—were not going to be deterred. The convention went ahead as scheduled. "Finally, bail was lowered down to $3,500 apiece," recalled Schell, "and we got out after a week or ten days and got together for the [convention's] plenary session."[74] Huey Newton was not unaware of Rizzo's terror tactics. "I understand Bozo's off his leash," the BPP Minister of Defense was quoted as saying to supporters and reporters at the airport when he arrived in Philadelphia for the convention. "That's Rizzo's name: 'Bozo, The Mad Dog.'"[75]

Cook was not arrested the night of the raid because he wasn't in any of the Panther offices at the time. But he played a role of minor importance at the convention. Cook—"always a small fry in the Panther organization," as he would describe himself years later—was assigned to bodyguard Newton.[76] "I doubted he knew my name, but I loved him," Abu-Jamal remembered.[77] But Cook would share the disappointment of many when Newton, fresh from prison, delivered his plenary address. The masses had expected to hear the charismatic, dynamic symbol of the "Free Huey" movement rally the troops in a dramatic call-to-arms. Instead, they got a dry political science lecture about "democratic capitalism" versus "bureaucratic capitalism."[78] Schell recalled Huey had just "lost" the crowd.[79]

Schell was convinced the many problems he saw with the Party were not going away. He was disappointed in hearing about Central Committee members buying expensive jump suits for the Convention while his branch, attempting to recover from the raid, had to scrounge for such basic necessities as clothes.[80] The Party had tried too many coalitions with too many other groups too soon ("It seemed like the Party was more interested later in projecting itself rather than dealing with a program"[81]). And now it was slicing itself into two. He also balked at a transfer to New Haven, Connecticut.[82] So he left the Party after the convention. Cook was one of those who followed Schell out. He had been in the Party for less than two years. Schell, Cook and other activists set up the Black United Liberation Front, another militant organization, but Cook's very brief tenure as a fulltime revolutionary had come to a close.[83]

In the coda of *Live from Death Row*, Abu-Jamal remembered his sickening rage over watching his beloved Party destroying itself, thanks to a feud between his "hero," Newton, and his "idol," Cleaver.[84] Strongly encouraged by behind-the-scenes FBI machinations, the two Party leaders had divided the Party into two factions: East Coast (Cleaver) and West Coast (Newton). The organization that FBI Director J. Edgar Hoover had once called the greatest internal threat to America's security was degenerating into a kind of political gang rivalry. Although Cook's FBI files show him listed as a correspondent for *Babylon*, a Cleaver-factioned publication, Abu-Jamal has said he did not choose a side between

Cleaver and Newton because he wanted no part of a family feud. "I didn't join the BPP to get in a goddamn gang war!" he recalled his thoughts at the time. "Shit! I could've stayed in North Philly for this dumb shit!.... Frustrated, angry, I drifted away from a Party that had drifted away from its moorings in the people." [85] As an older man speaking from Death Row, it seemed Abu-Jamal's only regret about his Party involvement was how its destruction impeded the advancement of a new civilization, one perhaps glimpsed, only for a moment, at the Revolutionary Convention. "I felt that it was proper to fight the system, but when the system can manipulate you into fighting your own, then the system wins and the people lose," he explained to an interviewer for a book. [86]

The post-convention exit of Schell and his cadre from the Party made *The Philadelphia Sunday Inquirer*'s front page.[87] Cook had returned to Benjamin Franklin when he made his way back to Philadelphia. He was suspended for passing out "revolutionary" literature. *The Inquirer* quoted him as saying that he left the Party to organize his fellow students. [88] The FBI fretted about him wanting to start a citywide, radical Black student newspaper and followed him as he joined Schell's BULF and eventually transferred to Roxborough High School later that November.[89] He wrote only a few articles for *Babylon* (he failed in print, for instance, to see any satirical humor in a new, controversial television sitcom, CBS' *All in The Family*) because he understood it was time to move forward. [90] The movement took him outside of the physical and psychological confines of the Philadelphia projects; as 1970 closed, his Panther adventures had taken him to major cities on both American coasts and in the mid-West, along the way creating lifelong friends and enemies while planting the seeds of a lifelong vocation. But now, the new decade created new priorities, which, in turn, created new responsibilities. He drew closer to his girlfriend Biba, the connection between his past with the Panthers and his future. By doing so, Cook's new life would, in turn, help create a new life, and the forthcoming child would name the parent.

Cook morphed from Panther to father as quickly as he resumed using his Kenyan name permanently. In a book, Abu-Jamal recalled how his definition of manhood changed—how he had changed—as a result of both leaving the Panthers and creating a new family with Biba. Instead of man meaning "militant defense, service, and sacrifice for one's people, one's community and one's Party," it now meant "becoming a committed lover, companion, and father. And it meant the tortured mix of love and dread that marked the birth of a brown-skinned boy in this land—a feeling as perverse as it is terrible, a feeling as true as that two plus two equals four."[91]

The Black Panther Party for Self-Defense may have been a flash in the pan. But that flash provided illumination. It became a defining point in the lives of many young Blacks who were drawn to it. The Party not only showed thousands of young people the positives of grassroots organizing, but it exposed them to the world and their responsibility to it from a radical, de-colonized perspective. One of those thousands of young Black people, a teenager named Wes Cook, found friends and an outlet for his energy in the electricity created by the Party. He also found his life's purpose as a communicator. In short, he found himself as a young man. Although he would obtain outward signs of mainstream American so-called "success" during the desegregated era of the 1970s—some private college education here, a middle-class, high-profile career in the public sphere there—at the core, he would still think and act like the young, working-class, mentally liberated Black Panther for the rest of his life, consequences be damned.

1971-1979

In 1972 and 1973, amid new, energizing activity in Black America, the Federal Bureau of Investigation was looking for Abu-Jamal.[92] There was that time that the FBI searched Abu-Jamal's luggage after he flew to San Francisco. Jesse Jackson Sr. wrote decades later of the incident in a book attacking the death penalty: "The most threatening item they found after ripping his baggage apart was an X-Acto knife, the kind artists use for cutting paper. He was charged with the possession of a dangerous weapon, although the absurd charges were soon dropped."[93] The Bureau would continue its tactics, or at least try to:

> *On February 23, 1972, [BLOTTED OUT] Vermont State Police, Montpelier, Vermont, advised that Wesley Cook was attending Goddard College, Plainfield, Vermont, and is residing on campus.*[94]

The FBI was not allowed on Goddard's campus, so the Bureau was reduced to looking for a Molotov cocktail in a haystack.[95] In early 1973, Richard Sharples, the governor of Bermuda, was assassinated by Black men who were associated with a group called The Black Beret Cadre. The FBI wanted to know if Abu-Jamal, on a campus filled with counterculture hippies, knew anything or anyone involved:

> *.... COOK'S TELEPHONE NUMBER WAS LOCATED IN AN APARTMENT LOCATED IN NEW YORK CITY OCCUPIED BY [BLOTTED OUT] AND OTHER BLACK PANTHER PARTY-CLEAVER FACTION AND BLACK LIBERATION ARMY ASSOCIATES. BECAUSE OF COOK'S BLACK EXTREMIST BACKGROUND, HIS POSSIBLE INVOLVEMENT IN THE URBAN GUERRILLA ACTIVITIES OF THE BLACK*

LIBERATION ARMY, AND HIS ATTENDANCE AT GODDARD COLLEGE [,] WHICH ATTRACTS BLACK EXTREMISTS FROM BERMUDA, THE INVESTIGATION TO LOCATE HIM SHOULD BE INTENSIFIED AND EFFORTS SHOULD BE MADE TO DETERMINE IF HE HAD BEEN OUT OF THE COUNTRY OVER THE WEEKEND OF MARCH 9-11, 1973.[96]

The FBI interviewed Edith in March, who told them Abu-Jamal had gotten a job at Bell Telephone and resided with her at Wallace Street.[97]

But he wouldn't stay at Bell Telephone long, since the Zeitgeist was coming for him like the lighting found by the kite of the man whose high school Abu-Jamal first scoffed and later abandoned in order to fight in his own American Revolution. He would locally and nationally provide the news during an extraordinary decade's playlist explosion of Black music unrestricted of format and ideas, the decade begun in music by Soul Train, Marvin Gaye and Aretha Franklin, and followed up by Issac Hayes, Stevie Wonder, Earth, Wind, and Fire, Parliament-Funkadelic, Bob Marley, and in film via Blaxploitation flicks such as *Sweet Sweetback's Baadasssss Song*, *Shaft*, *Superfly*, *Cleopatra Jones* and *Foxy Brown*. Black was now political, social and cultural—a flowering, then sputtering, of radical Black consciousness attempting to answer all questions. Black people were getting their African spiritual needs met through the now-open world of Black music, and receiving their civic information and political socialization, on Black American socio-politico terms, through the Black radio newscasts and its (and television's) public-affairs shows. The FBI didn't have to call Edith Cook after 1975. Soon, everyone in the Philadelphia metropolitan area and in the newly connected Black radio nation would know where to find Abu-Jamal, always at the top and bottom of the hour. He would merge his radical past with his inquisitive nature, and blend both with Nommo, the news-talk part of an electric-generated and Black-created groove.

MUMIA, MOVE & ME: REFLECTIONS OF A 1970S PHILLY JOURNALIST

LINN WASHINGTON JR.

Philadelphia police killed a Black man late on the evening of Monday, July 10, 1978. That incident registered a new low even for Philly's police, with their notorious history of brutality and racism. Police had viciously pummeled Winston Hood with their fists during a malicious attack. After police cuffed the hands of the dazed and bleeding Hood behind his back, one cop rushed up, gun drawn and shot Hood in his stomach at point blank range.

The next morning when I went to report from the site where police killed Hood, I saw a fellow journalist, Mumia Abu-Jamal. Bumping into my friend Mumia while reporting on police brutality was an all-too-regular occurrence during 1978. Police lawlessness from beatings to fatal shootings had seemingly accelerated in the months before Hood's death.

Philly's then-mayor, Frank Rizzo, proudly approved that abusive policing. Rizzo, the city's former police commissioner, had an infamous reputation for racism. Philadelphia police fatally shot 23 persons in 1978. Those fatal shootings exceeded the number in 1977 (19) and 1976 (13). Eleven of those fatal shootings in 1978 involved unarmed persons like Hood. Bracketing those fatal shootings, where many more non-fatal shootings and even more brutal beatings.

The killing of Hood came less than two months after the end of a 56-day starvation blockade Rizzo mounted against a counter-culture group, MOVE. It was a local radical organization whose ideology and lifestyle triggered brutal clashes with police during much of the 1970s. That shocking, headline-grabbing blockade arose from contentious disputes between MOVE and Rizzo rooted in police brutality. Rizzo initiated that blockade to force MOVE members barricaded inside their commune to surrender for arrest. The commune also contained children.

The blockade sealed off all access to the commune, located in twin Victorian-era three-story houses. Rizzo shut off utilities (water-gas-electric) and denied MOVE access to food.

When I saw Mumia that day, he stood a few feet from where that cop killed Hood. A radio reporter, Mumia had his broadcast microphone thrust skyward at the end of his outstretched arm. *What was Mumia doing?* I wondered as I walked up. When Mumia lowered the mic and shut off his tape recorder, I asked.

"Getting ambient sound," Mumia replied.

Mumia referenced an audio production procedure I hadn't heard since taking broadcast classes at Temple University, located a few miles from the site of Hood's fatal shooting. I nodded in awe at Mumia's professionalism. *He's getting "sound" from the scene to augment his reportage,* I noted mentally. *He's covering all 5Ws of journalism: the Who, What, When, Where and Why.* That ambient sound helped with the Where and we both knew the Why: More racist brutality from racist Philadelphia police.

Mumia's skilled reports on news the mainstream media generally overlooked had garnered him respect citywide and beyond. His precise, passionate reportage on issues that impacted the poor and ignored had earned him the title "The Voice of the Voiceless." Interestingly, the notion that news media had a responsibility to report on the marginalized was not formally embraced by the Society of Professional Journalists until 1993. That's when SPJ included a new provision in its Code of Ethics that urged journalists to "Give voice to the voiceless."

Less than one month after Hood's death, an incident of peculiar brutality by Philadelphia police would have a profound impact on Mumia's professional career and his personal life. That August 8, 1978 incident was the gunfire-filled Philadelphia police raid on MOVE.

During that August 8TH raid, Philadelphia police fired over one hundred bullets and dozens of smoke bombs into the basement of MOVE's commune, where 12 adults, including women holding small children, were holed up. Police finally used a high-powered, truck-mounted Fire Department deluge gun to blast over 100,000-gallons of water into that basement, flushing out those in that basement then facing death by drowning.

MOVE members arrested during that August raid had endured that

March-to-May starvation blockade that ended in a settlement intended to preclude future confrontations. MOVE and Rizzo each blamed the other for failure to fully comply with the terms of that settlement. Each side shared blame, although Rizzo, as usual, bore the bulk of non-compliance with settlement terms.

During that August raid, where a policeman was fatally shot, four officers savagely beat surrendering MOVE member Delbert Africa. That atrocious assault–captured by TV and newspaper cameras–received headline coverage worldwide. During a press conference hours after that raid, Mayor Rizzo castigated the news media. He blamed the media for that policeman's death. Rizzo leveled that blame even though police had filed murder charges against MOVE members for that officer's death. A question from Mumia that challenged police accounts of that raid ignited Rizzo's outburst. Rizzo's rant included a veiled threat against reporters.

Less than two years after that August 8TH raid, I had a serious *talk* with Mumia about MOVE. The contentious disputes between MOVE and Rizzo was a big story in Philadelphia, one Mumia covered prior to that raid.

Distinctively, Mumia was one of few Philly journalists whose reportage included MOVE's side. News coverage of MOVE in the 1970s routinely distorted or suppressed their voice. That anti-MOVE/pro-City Hall slanted coverage violated the existing SPJ Ethics Code provision that "News reports should be free of bias and represent all sides of an issue."

That *talk* we had centered on Mumia's growing alignment with MOVE. After that 1978 raid, Mumia had moved from insightful, balanced reportage on MOVE to open advocacy for MOVE.

Mumia's attachment to MOVE was having a deleterious impact on his journalistic career. His pro-MOVE reportorial posture, coupled with his occasional direct participation in MOVE activities, prompted pushback from supervisors at the Philadelphia radio stations where he worked. Supervisors – white and Black, friend and foe – saw his advocacy as a breach of the arms-length objectivity that journalists were supposed to maintain in their reportage.

I told Mumia that I thought his desire to elevate the exposure of MOVE and counter media-fanned misconceptions about MOVE could be accomplished effectively through his maintaining an appearance of journalistic objectivity. I felt that with the high esteem Mumia enjoyed in communities citywide, plus the respect he had among most journalists in Philadelphia, he could adroitly present the MOVE perspective from his platform as a journalist in ways that a street activist could not. I argued that his loss of access to a broadcast microphone due to advocacy would eliminate his ability to do what he wanted to do for MOVE.

My suggestions to Mumia were not predicated in some rote adherence to recognized journalistic standards. We both knew that the standard journalistic practice of "objectivity" too often compromised accurate coverage of non-whites and radicals like MOVE. In most newsrooms at the time, objectivity was defined within the context of the prevailing status quo that included embedded institutional racism ignored by reporters and editors.

Mumia and I had a good *talk*. Needless to say, Mumia had a different point of view. Mumia, like MOVE, saw an overarching imperative to confront injustice, speaking Truth-to-Power, irrespective of personal consequences like limitations on his career in journalism. Countering my arguments, Mumia's position was conventional practices of journalism that constrained "the work" of confronting systemic oppression could be/should be shed like heavy winter clothes in summer's heat.

There were natural points of affiliation for Mumia with MOVE. Mumia was a vegetarian like MOVE members. Mumia, like MOVE members, wore his hair in dreadlocks – a non-conventional hairstyle at that time. Mumia had adopted an African name, legally changing his birth name of Wesley Cook to Mumia Abu-Jamal. MOVE members adopted Africa as their last name. MOVE member Delbert Africa was once a member of the Black Panther Party, like Mumia. (Delbert became the leading face of MOVE in the late 1970s after John Africa went underground to avoid arrest.) And Mumia, like MOVE, firmly believed America's political system and its materialistic culture were inherently corrupt and corrupting, immune to mere reform. Mumia and MOVE believed The System needed transformative change, achievable through revolution.

I thought I understood what Mumia was going through with his internal conflicts arising from MOVE coverage because I'd gone through similar professional and personal turmoil related to MOVE. The injustice-filled tribulations MOVE experienced from The System that incensed Mumia were incidents that vexed me. It was emotionally jarring for me to witness the assaults and insults slammed on MOVE. Seeing that naked repression week-in-&-week-out for years impacted me in ways that caused me to question the responsibilities of journalism and my role as a journalist.

Those incidents of official misconduct against MOVE included hundreds of bogus arrests of MOVE members instituted to break the group, brutal beatings from curbsides to inside courtrooms when MOVE members challenged official oppression and defiant refusals of authorities to even investigate any of those injustices. Egregiously, authorities ignored the miscarriages of pregnant MOVE women resulting from being deliberately kicked in their vaginas during assaults. Prior to that August 1978 clash, I had written articles on the police-involved deaths of two MOVE babies, heart-wrenching incidents for me as a father of young children at the time. Those fatalities included a March 1976 clash where a policeman [allegedly] stomped a MOVE baby to death. I knew that Mumia, also a father of young children, felt pain from the deaths of those MOVE babies.

MOVE was a story I'd covered constantly since my first weeks as a full-time reporter in the fall of 1975. I worked for *The Philadelphia Tribune*, the oldest African American-owned newspaper in the country. As the new reporter on staff, *Tribune* editors assigned me to MOVE. That assignment happened because MOVE members had grossed out other staff reporters with their dogmatic attitudes and their practice of consuming large amounts of garlic that left them reeking with odor. MOVE said it used garlic for its medicinal benefits. I often wondered if MOVE saw an ancillary benefit in weaponizing the smell of garlic as part of its armament employed in its in-your-face campaigning against The System it considered putrid.

Through reporting on MOVE, I met all the MOVE members and most of the group's core supporters. As an entity, the technology eschewing/environmental consciousness extolling organization was then and remains today an enigma for me. During those turbulent 1970s, MOVE ingratiated and annoyed simultaneously. MOVE members, for example, generously assisted the elderly and others in need. Yet MOVE fiercely assailed critics like some of the liberals living near its commune. The neighbors objected to the profanity-laced tirades MOVE blasted from loudspeakers mounted outside its commune. The outsides of that commune often smelled like a barnyard, odors incompatible with inner-city spaces. Odors emanated from MOVE's then ahead-of-the-times composting practices, and the feces from the many stray dogs MOVE cared for. However, the two times I was inside MOVE's sparsely furnished cloistered commune, it was spotless, eat-off-the-floor clean.

I knew about MOVE before I began reporting on MOVE. When I moved to Philadelphia, the first apartment I rented was at 33RD and Powelton – across 33RD Street from what would become the MOVE commune. I remember MOVE founder Vincent Leaphart from the neighborhood before he assumed the persona of the elusive John Africa. When I first moved into Powelton Village, Leaphart was then known as Vince The Dog Man due to his love of canines. At that time, I dismissed Vince as half-crazy, not knowing the streaks of brilliance in that self-educated brother. I followed the growth of MOVE's activities in Powelton and around Philadelphia. I read the weekly column MOVE once had in the *Tribune*, frequently trying to make sense of their often-rambling, always inventive-filled commentaries.

Yes, I had respect for MOVE, not for its mysterious ideology or its *different* lifestyle but for the fact that they fought back against brutal police. With the refusal of officials from the mayor to the District Attorney to City Council to act against abusive policing, MOVE's resistance to that scourge seemed like vigilante justice. While police always subdued MOVE during clashes through overwhelming with sheer numbers, some officers left those clashes with physical and emotional wounds. I also liked the fact that MOVE castigated duplicitous authorities—elected, civic and religious—publicly and impolitely, citing their failures to address systemic inequities like abusive policing, double standards of justice and institutional racism that systemically impoverished the poor of all races.

Somehow, the misconduct I saw directed at MOVE caused me to overlook contradictions in the organization that proudly-&-loudly proclaimed its dedication to exposing contradictions in The System. For example, the self-professed "revolutionary" MOVE did not participate directly with another revolutionary/radical groups in Philadelphia, fighting police brutality and other important issues. With MOVE during the 1970s, it was either their way or get out of the way. MOVE declared it had all the answers... solutions provided by their prophet John Africa. MOVE's self-righteousness sidelined natural allies who found that stance off-putting. Those who did work with MOVE against Rizzo did so not from an affinity with MOVE's ideology, but from their realization that if Rizzo's moves against MOVE succeeded that meant increased dangers for all.

While MOVE was definitely victimized, I began to recognize that MOVE was also victimizer. And, in some circumstances, MOVE victimized Black people. Increasingly MOVE's vaunted non-compromising our-way-or-the-highway stance annoyed me. To me, these self-declared revolutionaries frequently injected defeat into victory. I felt the psyche of Philly's Black community desperately needed winners, not martyrs. (I must note that the MOVE of today does *not* exhibit an our-way-only stance while still maintaining fidelity to the principles of founder John Africa. And, I must note that irrespective of MOVE's provocations, the reactive responses of authorities were wildly disproportionate.)

So when I had that *talk* with Mumia, what I really didn't know was that I really didn't know Mumia. I didn't realize that I failed in the fulfillment of those 5 Ws of journalism: I hadn't fully reported on the Who – as in who Mumia really was before I met him.

I first met Mumia sometime during the 1973-1974 time frame when we both worked at WRTI-FM. We were volunteers at WRTI, Temple University's radio station. It then operated with a strong community-service orientation. Mumia did a community affairs program, and I was a jazz music DJ. A few years later, we became much closer when we both worked as reporters in Black media, he in radio, me in print. Reporting is often hurry-up-&-wait for things to get started. That dynamic afforded us plenty of time to talk before the real reporting began. In July 1977, Mumia and I were among seven media practitioners to receive recognition for providing "truth and information" to Philadelphia's Black community. A coalition of progressive Black community groups organized that ceremony. That was the first award for reporting that Mumia and I received.

At the time of our *talk* we both worked for white mainstream media in Philadelphia, again Mumia in radio and me in print. It was one of many conservations Mumia and I had on and off the job. Topics of those discussions ranged from the struggle against apartheid to astrology, illegal governmental surveillance to Philly's failing public schools, reparations to reefer. We talked about political empowerment, economic uplift, Black

Power and the Black Panthers. Those conversations were more analytical than autobiographical. Mumia, for example, never mentioned his student activism, like trying to change the name of his high school from Benjamin Franklin to Malcolm X High. The school's student body and its principal supported the name change, but Philadelphia's school board, including Black members of that body, opposed that effort. Mumia was expelled from Franklin.

I did know Mumia helped others more than boosting himself. In retrospect, now knowing Mumia's humility, it was not surprising that Mumia never mentioned his Black Panther Party membership during our many conversations, much less brag about it as many former BPP members did at that time. I didn't know that as a teen, Mumia was the information officer for Philly's BPP branch. I didn't know that he worked for the BPP's newspaper – a nationally distributed publication that I read. Through his work with the BPP newspaper, Mumia's orientation to journalism was a vehicle to facilitate advocacy.

Not knowing Mumia's full background prevented my ability to fully contextualize Mumia's move toward MOVE at the time of that *talk*. The Mumia who saw televised images of MOVE member Delbert Africa violently assaulted by Philly cops during that August 1978 raid was the same Mumia who a decade earlier endured a merciless assault from a Philly cop. That November 1968 attack occurred after that cop refused to arrest the racists who beat Mumia when he participated in a protest at a Philadelphia rally for segregationist presidential candidate George Wallace. The 14-year-old Mumia thought the cop would protect him from the racist, but instead that cop pummeled Mumia then falsely arrested him. The cop that beat Mumia falsely claimed Mumia attacked him.

The same Mumia who experienced that bullet-filled August 1978 assault on MOVE was the same Mumia who in December 1969 – as a teenaged BPP member – visited the bullet-riddled bedroom in Chicago where police had recently murdered charismatic Black Panther Party leader Fred Hampton.

By the time we had that *talk*, Mumia had witnessed the failure of Philadelphia police officials to discipline the officers who beat Delbert Africa on August 8, 1978. Mumia had witnessed a federal judge cavalierly dismiss the U.S. Justice Department's unprecedented 1979 lawsuit charging Rizzo and 22 top city officials with aiding-&-abetting abusive policing – the first such lawsuit ever filed against city officials in America.

And before that *talk*, Mumia had witnessed the cop who killed Winston Hood receive a disability pension. Philadelphia officials approved that cop's pension request based on his repugnant rationale that the hatred people held against him for his proclaimed "accidental" shooting of Hood impaired his ability to perform as a policeman.

At the time of that *talk*, ample evidence existed to dispel any illusions about the efficacy of journalism to effectuate substantive change despite its ability to influence public perception.

In the months after that *talk* Mumia's career soared and cratered. He won national awards for his reportage and garnered prestigious recognitions. He was elected president of the Association of Black Journalists of Philadelphia, now known as the Philadelphia Association of Black Journalists, a proud and active affiliate of the National Association of Black Journalists. And, in January 1981, *Philadelphia Magazine* placed him on its list of the "81 People to Watch." That listing of noteworthy people in the Philadelphia area praised Mumia for bringing "a unique dimension to radio reporting."

During that post-*talk* time frame, nine MOVE members were convicted of third-degree murder for the death of that policeman on August 8, 1978. Police had no forensic or eyewitness evidence that the gunshot that killed Officer James Ramp came from a gun fired by a MOVE member. Compelling but ignored evidence indicated 'friendly fire' from a fellow officer felled Ramp. The MOVE 9 each received 30-to-100-year sentences, including four females who police testified were holding children not firing guns.

Also, the three cops eventually arrested for that televised beating of Delbert Africa were acquitted by a Philadelphia judge. That jurist issued a directed verdict of acquittal – an action rarely initiated by a judge. That judge, deceptively, declared those cops acted in self-defense because they feared a possible attack from unarmed Africa known for his strength. That specious acquittal was particularly outrageous because court officials had specially imported a jury from out-of-town to ensure the accused brutalizers received a fair trial. The judge's acquittal stopped the trial before the jury even began deliberation and even before the defense presented its case. That unusual acquittal was not unusual given the anti-MOVE/pro-police attitudes then held by many Philadelphia judges.

Mumia's escalating pro-MOVE reportage turned his career potholes into roadblocks, eventually leaving him without a full-time reporting job. Since freelance reporting didn't provide enough income to support his children, Mumia began driving a cab a few nights a week to generate additional income. It was while driving a cab during the early morning hours of Wednesday, December 9, 1981, Mumia happened upon an encounter where he saw a policeman strike his younger brother, Billy. Minutes later, Mumia was shot, beaten by cops, and arrested for killing the officer who struck his brother. Before sunrise that day, Mumia's life had changed forever. Weeks after his December 9TH arrest, another life-impacting event happened: Mumia announced his full support of MOVE.

That announcement came during a press conference in the early evening of Monday, January 4, 1982. Mumia's wife, Wadiya, came into the Press Room inside City Hall to read a statement prepared by Mumia's family and read a letter Mumia wrote from jail. Wadiya told assembled news media that police had harassed her and threatened Mumia's family.

Mumia, in his letter read by Wadiya, declared his innocence. He denied killing Officer Daniel Faulkner. His account: police beat him at the shooting scene, beat him in the hospital emergency room as he awaited surgery for the serious wound from Faulkner's gunshot and beat him during his recuperation days later. Mumia said he had filed a formal complaint with police officials about those beatings that left him with broken ribs, a punctured kidney and serious head injuries.

Perversely, the official investigation into Mumia's complaint about police brutality produced dubious evidence that helped secure Mumia's murder conviction months later. During that investigation, the prosecutor handling Mumia's murder case asked police officers involved in the December 9TH incident if anyone heard Mumia confess to the murder of Officer Daniel Faulkner. During meetings with that prosecutor two months after Faulkner's murder, two policemen suddenly claimed they remembered that Mumia admitted he killed Faulkner while in the emergency room, critically wounded, awaiting surgery. Incredibly, one of those two officers making that belated claim of hearing a confession had guarded Mumia in the emergency room on December 9, 1981. That officer filed an official report on December 9TH that stated Mumia made "no comments."

Before the emergence of that claimed emergency room confession in February 1982, the prosecutor had relied on a claim from a ranking police inspector that Mumia confessed to him on December 9TH while Mumia laid wounded inside a police van at the crime scene. But in early 1982, that Inspector faced arrest by the FBI for multiple instances of corruption that included falsifying evidence. The prosecutor knew his case against Mumia could suffer if he used the corruption-stained inspector at trial. During Mumia's June 1982 trial, the prosecutor used the February 1982 confession claim and acted like that December 9TH confession claim never existed. Incidentally, that inspector was one of the cops Mumia cited in his brutality complaint about beating him at the crime scene on December 9TH. Police Department officials dismissed Mumia's brutality complaint. They ignored civilian eyewitnesses that confirmed those beatings, and they ignored Mumia's documented injuries from those beatings.

An interesting point is that in 1968 when Mumia was hospitalized from the beating by racist George Wallace supporters and a Philly cop, police officials ignored that cop's brutality and his false arrest of Mumia. A judge dismissed that cop's falsely filed assault charge during a court hearing where Mumia appeared, his face "a mass of bruises" according to a November 1968 newspaper account.

Wadiya's January 4, 1982 press conference announcement of Mumia's full allegiance with MOVE created short-term strain for Mumia but a long-term gain for him. Organized community support for Mumia slipped after that press conference while his support from MOVE surged.

The "Defense Committee For Mumia Abu-Jamal" formed hours after Mumia's December 9TH arrest splintered due to reticence by groups within that coalition to associate with MOVE. A Committee meeting scheduled for the evening of January 4TH was abruptly cancelled. That committee, which met almost daily between Mumia's December 9TH arrest and that January 4TH press conference, consisted of "over 35 multiracial community organizations," according to a press release issued on the afternoon of December 10TH, 1982. Committee members sought fairness from the legal system and fairness from the news media. "People are angry over why so much media attention is being directed into portraying Mr. Jamal as a radical fanatic, when literally hundreds of people knew him only through his service work in the community," the Committee's spokeswoman stated on December 10th.

The Philly media drubbing of Mumia drew criticism from some within the profession. One columnist, a moderate, assailed colleagues for shirking objectivity. That columnist criticized the "prejudicial passion" in coverage that reduced in the public's mind "any possibility of innocence...." That columnist called for the assignment of a special prosecutor to handle the trial of Mumia as a "way of convincing the community that justice in the case will be done."

Philly authorities had no intentions of taking steps to ensure fairness for Mumia, such as appointing a special prosecutor or importing an impartial jury as was done in the trial of the cops charged with that August 1978 assault on Delbert Africa. That stance against justice for Mumia conflicted with repeated Pennsylvania Supreme Court rulings on fair trial rights. One 1959 ruling declared criminal defendants are "entitled to all the safeguards of a fair trial" irrespective of whether the judge and/or prosecutor "believes the defendant to be guilty."

MOVE members and MOVE supporters served as liaisons providing the jailed Mumia with assistance in preparing for trial. Mumia, in the tradition of MOVE, opted to represent himself. His right to self-representation was snatched by the trial judge – a former police union member – at the request of the trial prosecutor during the jury selection phase. The prosecutor claimed Mumia scared potential jurors, an allegation that conflicted with news accounts that Mumia's self-representation was non-threatening.

Mumia asked for John Africa to represent him, a request denied by the trail judge. John Africa never appeared at Mumia's trial, even as a spectator. MOVE members said John Africa did advise Mumia through those liaisons. Mumia's trial ended with a conviction and a sentence to death by execution.

Mumia rejected claims that his announced allegiance to John Africa and MOVE caused his conviction. Mumia refuted those claims in a commentary published in the *Philadelphia Tribune* weeks after his July 1982 conviction. "Did any black-robed MOVE member deny me the most basic so-called rights of this country's constitution?" Mumia wrote. "Did Judge Africa deny me the right to counsel of my choice, John Africa?"

Mumia blamed the bias of the prosecutor and the judge for his conviction plus the failings of his defense lawyer, not MOVE.

After Mumia's trial, MOVE member Pam Africa founded the International Concerned Family & Friends of Mumia Abu-Jamal, one of those liaisons. Indefatigable, she became integral in what emerged as the international movement to free Mumia. Pam Africa repeatedly crisscrossed America to win Mumia's release. Initiatives by activists like Pam Africa coupled with work of lawyers defeated the death penalty Mumia languished under for nearly 30 years.

Mumia has produced more journalism than most full-time journalists ever generate during a comparable time span during his decades in prison. He's produced articles, broadcast commentaries and books from prison, inclusive of Death Row isolation. Mumia's journalism is done without access to resources that most journalists take for granted, such as writing on a laptop computer and using the Internet for research.

A recurring reference in Mumia's prison journalism has been the injustices endured by MOVE, particularly the incarceration of the MOVE 9 and the horrific 1985 bombing of a MOVE compound that killed 11 people, six adult MOVE members and five children. The parents of three of those dead children were incarcerated MOVE 9 members. John Africa died during that raid where gunfire from police snipers prevented MOVE members from escaping a fire ignited by the bomb. That inferno was allowed to burn on orders of Philadelphia's then Police Commissioner, Gregor Sambor. That fire also destroyed 61 homes, leaving 250 Black people homeless.

Beginning in the summer of 2018 and completed in January 2020, all seven surviving members of the MOVE 9 were paroled from four decades behind bars. Two of those MOVE 9 members died in prison. In May 2020, during the 35TH recognition of that 1985 bombing/burning, released MOVE 9 member Janine Africa said if the City of Philadelphia really wanted to atone for that worse incident of police brutality in American history, instead of offering MOVE an apology "release our brother, Mumia!" Mumia and I have talked many times before and after his incarceration, but a conversation with him as a "free" man again is *the talk* I most want.

1981-1983

Declaration of Linn Washington on the Events of December 9, 1981

Mumia Abu-Jamal's new legal team held a press conference on May 4 and released the following affidavit.

DECLARATION OF LINN WASHINGTON

I, LINN WASHINGTON, declare:

1. This is an account of events that transpired on the morning of December 9, 1981. This account is my true and accurate recollection of these events.

2. I submit the following account understanding the federal and state laws pertaining to perjury and submission of false information.

3. This account principally examines two areas: (1) the unusual of police presence at the 13th and Locust Sts. crime scene site of the shooting of Officer Daniel Faulkner and (2) events at Thomas Jefferson Hospital, where Officer Faulkner and Mr. Abu-Jamal were taken for treatment.

4. My name is Linn Washington. I am currently a columnist for The Philadelphia Tribune newspaper. Further, I am a freelance journalist for publications nationwide. I write extensively on matters involving the criminal justice system and racism. Additionally, I am an Assistant Professor in the Journalism Department at Temple University in Philadelphia. I hold a Master Degree from the Yale Law School and a B.S. in Communications from Temple University.

5. At the time of the events detailed below, I was working as a reporter for the Philadelphia Daily News. My assignment for the Daily News then was a municipal beat reporter assigned to cover the 17-member City Council in Philadelphia. I was assigned to the City Hall Bureau of the Daily News. I had worked as a full time newspaper reporter in the city of Philadelphia since October 1975. As a reporter, I covered a variety of assignments including police beat/crime reporting and investigative reporting. By

December of 1981, I had received awards for some of my journalistic coverage.

6. On December 9, 1981, I knew Mr. Abu-Jamal professionally and personally. I knew Mr. Abu-Jamal as a fellow journalist whom I had worked closely covering a variety of assignments including news events involving allegations of abusive misconduct by members of the Philadelphia Police Department. Additionally, I knew Mr. Abu-Jamal as a friend, having first met him nearly seven years earlier at WRTI-FM, the radio station for Temple University, the college where I completed my undergraduate studies.

7. On the morning of December 9, 1981, when I awoke, I turned on Philadelphia s all-news KYW radio station. Tuning into KYW when I awoke was my reportorial practice at the time. I did this to become acquainted with the major news of the respective day.

8. The lead story on December 9 when I turned on KYW sometime after 6AM was the shooting of Officer Faulkner.

9. This news item immediately caught my attention for two reasons beyond the tragic shooting of a police officer.

10. First, the KYW report declared that police had apprehended journalist Mumia Abu-Jamal at the scene. I knew Abu-Jamal, as stated above.

11. Second, the KYW report declared that when the first officers responded to reports of a shooting at 13th and Locust, they found one man spread eagle on a building wall and another man slumped on the curb.

12. The man on the wall, KYW reported, was William Billy Cook, the brother of Abu-Jamal. I thought it was unusual that Cook was spread eagle on the wall before being ordered to do so by arriving police.

13. I knew William Cook as Abu-Jamal's brother. I also knew that Cook was a street vendor in downtown Philadelphia. During the late 1970s and early 1980s, Philadelphia Police frequently harassed Black Street vendors, incidents that I had reported on as a journalist. I first met [illegible] close

friend of Cook's, Kenneth Freeman. Cook and Freeman were constantly together, leading me to initially think that they were relatives.

14. I met Kenneth Freeman in the mid-I970s when he came to the offices of The Philadelphia Tribune after receiving an alleged beating at the hands of Philadelphia police. I then worked as a reporter for the Tribune.

15. Throughout the 1 970s, Philadelphia police frequently beat Black men in general and Black street vendors in particular, as amply documented in numerous official reports during that era conducted by federal authorities and local monitoring agencies.

16. After hearing that KYW report when I awoke on December 9, 1981, I called the City Desk at the Daily News to see if the editors had a specific assignment for me regarding this story. I was given a typical generic assignment of getting whatever information you can and report that information to editors on a periodic basis.

17. When I left home sometime around 7:30 AM, in route to downtown Philadelphia, I decided to visit the [illegible] Jefferson Hospital. Jefferson, as stated above, was the medical facility where Officer Faulkner and Mr. Abu-Jamal were taken.

18. When I arrived at the 13th and Locust crime scene, the first thing that struck me was the absolute absence of any police. When I arrived at the [illegible] scene around 8:30 AM, there were no police officers in sight. There were no uniformed officers, no detectives, no special detail officers (like crime scene investigators) at the location of the shooting.

19. I found this total lack of police presence at a crime scene to be highly unusual.

20. As a veteran of much police beat reporting then, I knew it was generally standard practice to at least assign a uniformed officer to guard the crime scene. I found it highly unusual that no police were maintaining the integrity of this crime scene, particularly since this incident involved the shooting of a police officer. I had covered previous shootings, including some non-fatal

shootings of police officers, where police kept the crime scene cordoned off from the public for days.

21. However, while the lack of police presence was unusual, it was not unprecedented. I had observed Philadelphia police do unusual things with crime scenes in a few prior instances. Most notable was the police destruction of a crime scene on August 8, 1978 a few short hours after the shoot-out between members of the MOVE organization and Philadelphia police that resulted in the death of Officer James Ramp.

22. Police razed the compound that MOVE members occupied during the shoot-out within three hours after the last MOVE member surrendered. During the surrender, MOVE members climbed out of the compound's basement that had been flooded with water and tear gas by police to force their surrender.

23. It is my belief that police destroyed this MOVE crime scene before the passage of sufficient time to conduct a reasonably thorough investigation. Police personnel were in the darkened (no electricity) ramshackle MOVE compound for less than two hours before a demolition crane leveled the property.

24. Questions about the sufficiency of the police investigation of the August 1978 crime scene arose repeatedly during the contentious trial involving the MOVE members charged with Officer Ramp's death. During this era, questions frequently arose about the adequacy of police investigations into incidents of alleged abuse by police. I feared that the lack of police presence at the December 1981 13th and Locust Sts. crime scene would have an adverse effect on the sufficiency of the police investigation involving the charges against Mr. Abu-Jamal.

25. At 13th and Locust Sts. on the morning of December 9, 1981, I visually inspected the crime scene. I wanted to familiarize myself with the scene, gathering as much visual data as I could. Yet I wasn t looking for anything in particular because details of events regarding the shooting were sketchy at best then.

26. Billy Cook's VW was still at the crime scene. The car was unlocked. I opened the passenger side door and looked inside the parked VW. It is my

recollection that I saw a few drops of blood on the floor in the back behind the driver s seat.

27. My inspection of the VW was brief. However, during the time that I remained at the crime scene, no police arrived.

28. From the unguarded 13th and Locust Sts. crime scene, I traveled to Jefferson Hospital. I think this was shortly before 9:00 AM.

29. I proceeded to the Emergency Room at Jefferson. Philadelphia police and hospital security blocked access to the Emergency Room from inside the hospital. Other reporters were milling around the hallways outside the Emergency Room. My recollection is that police/security were denying access to the Emergency Room even to some hospital personnel, presumably those not specifically assigned ER tasks at that particular time.

30. I then tried to gain access to the Emergency Room from the outside entrance but that too was blocked, by a bevy of Philadelphia police. This police cordon prevented even walking up to the ER s outside door to look inside.

31. Sometime after arriving at Jefferson, I have a recollection of seeing a hospital worker who knew me as a reporter and this person said that police were beating Mr. Abu-Jamal in the ER. I had no way of confirming this allegation, being denied access to the ER and the unavailability of police or hospital spokespersons. However, that allegation of assault did not surprise me given the pattern and practice of abusive acts by Philadelphia police repeatedly documented by federal government and local media investigators at that time.

32. While at Jefferson, I eventually made my way to an atrium type area, where food was served. While getting food, I saw two other reporters that I knew.

33. It is my recollection that during a conversation with them one stated that he had talked with a person he knew in the hospital who told him of having seen police assault Mr. Abu-Jamal in the ER. This account was

consistent with the account I had received from the hospital worker who approached me with information about a beating.

34. I remember staying in Jefferson for another hour, awaiting reports from hospital press information spokespersons. I don't remember receiving any reports from hospital spokespersons.

35. While in contact with my editors at the Daily News from the Hospital, they told me to return to my office in the City hall press room. I left Jefferson Hospital sometime after noon on December 9, 1981.

I declare under penalty of perjury under the laws of the United States of America that the above is true and correct and was executed by me on May 3, 2001, at Pittsburgh, Pennsylvania.

(signed) LINN WASHINGTON

THE GOOD OLD FRAME-UP: HOW POLICE, PROSECUTION AND THE COURTS TURNED MUMIA ABU-JAMAL INTO A "MURDERER"[98]

MICHAEL SCHIFFMANN

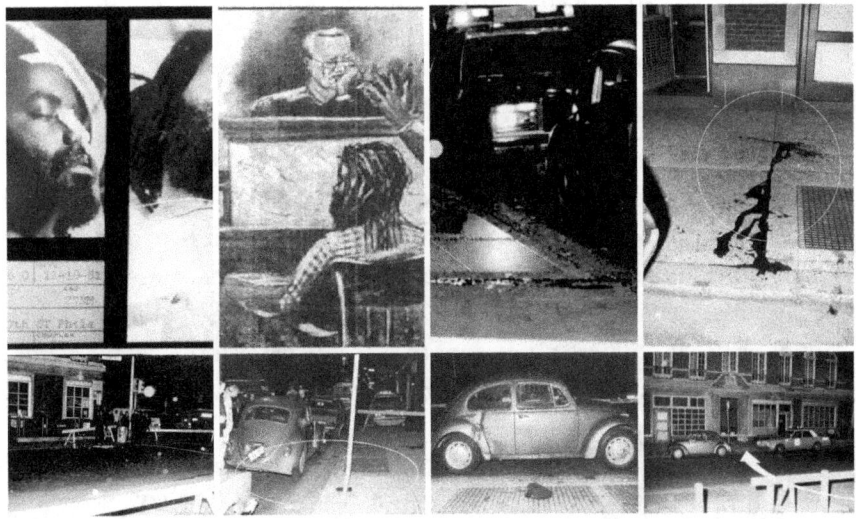

The case of Mumia Abu-Jamal begins on December 9, 1981, with an event that, despite its perception by many U.S. citizens as occurring very often, is in actual fact quite rare: the killing of a police officer.[99] The very fact that its rarity also extends to Philadelphia[100] contributed to the sensational character of the murder trial against Abu-Jamal in the summer of 1982, which ended July 2 with a guilty verdict from the jury and a death sentence the day after.[101]

But other, more general factors also played a role. Like the overwhelming majority of cops in 38 % Black Philadelphia, the officer who was killed was white,[102] while the alleged perpetrator Mumia Abu-Jamal was African American. In addition, like most persons in the U.S. who are accused of a capital crime and an even larger percentage of those who are then sentenced to the maximal punishment, death,[103] as an underpaid freelance journalist and part-time taxi driver Abu-Jamal belonged neither to the upper- nor to the middle classes, but to the underclass.

From that angle, the profile of the accused corresponded exactly to the cliché of the violent Black underclass criminal as the main threat for the happy lives of free white U.S. citizens, a notion that has a painfully long history of suffering for the victims of this stereotype. While the civil rights movement of the 1950s and 1960s had succeeded in at least questioning this picture, the 1970s already saw the start of a massive countermovement that has swept enormous numbers of Black and other underprivileged Americans into prison, and which continues up to this day.[104]

THE OFFICIAL VERSION

"Policeman Shot to Death; Radio Newsman Charged"—this phrase and similar ones provided the headline for Philadelphia's newspapers the day after.[105] The description of the events by the prosecution, which was closely reflected in the media, certainly underwent an evolution, which cannot be discussed here for reasons of space. Whatever the details, before Mumia Abu-Jamal's murder trial even started, the following official version[106] had already crystallized:

Just before four o'clock in the morning on December 9, 1981, Abu-Jamal's brother Billy Cook, who is driving his battered VW beetle in Eastern direction on Locust Street in Philadelphia's Center City area, is subjected to a traffic stop by Police Officer Daniel Faulkner immediately after the intersection Locust and 13TH Street. He stops his VW directly after the entrance of street number 1234, and the police cruiser stops about one meter behind the VW.

Faulkner is working his shift without a partner that night. As for the reasons for the traffic control, there are only speculations; in Abu-Jamal's murder trial, they are not even addressed.[107] Faulkner communicates the traffic stop via police radio and asks for back-up. In a second radio call, he asks for sending a wagon instead of a simple police car.

After all this, Faulkner gets out of the vehicle, walks up to the driver's side of Cook's VW and tells the driver to get out. Faulkner then walks Cook to the gap between the Volkswagen and the police cruiser and attempts to handcuff him. At first, Cook doesn't offer any resistance, but then he swings around and slaps the police officer in the face. Faulkner pulls his heavy police flashlight from his belt and begins to beat the arrested man.

At that moment, a third man, Abu-Jamal, comes into play. He is driving a cab that night, which he has parked somewhere not far from the intersection of 13TH Street and Locust. He notices the altercation between his brother and the policeman and runs across a parking lot at the corner of the intersection and across Locust towards the scene of the events.

As Faulkner stands facing the entrance of Locust 1234, he cannot see what is happening behind him. Even as he runs, Abu-Jamal draws his revolvers and shoots Faulkner in the back. Taken by surprise, the officer stumbles, but still manages to pull out his service revolver and shoot Abu-Jamal in the chest. But he has lost his balance, and while he is still firing, he falls backwards and falls down to the right of the front wheels of Cook's VW.[108]

Abu-Jamal, though severely wounded himself, continues to pursue him, straddles him, and fires several shots at him at point blank range. One of these hits Faulkner in the head, and as it will later turn out, he dies almost instantaneously. Abu-Jamal himself collapses in front of the front bumper of the VW. When Faulkner's first colleagues arrive at the scene shortly afterwards, this is where they find Abu-Jamal, and behind him, they find Abu-Jamal's brother, Billy Cook, who raises his hands and says: "I had nothing to do with it."[109]

THE EVIDENCE OF THE PROSECUTION

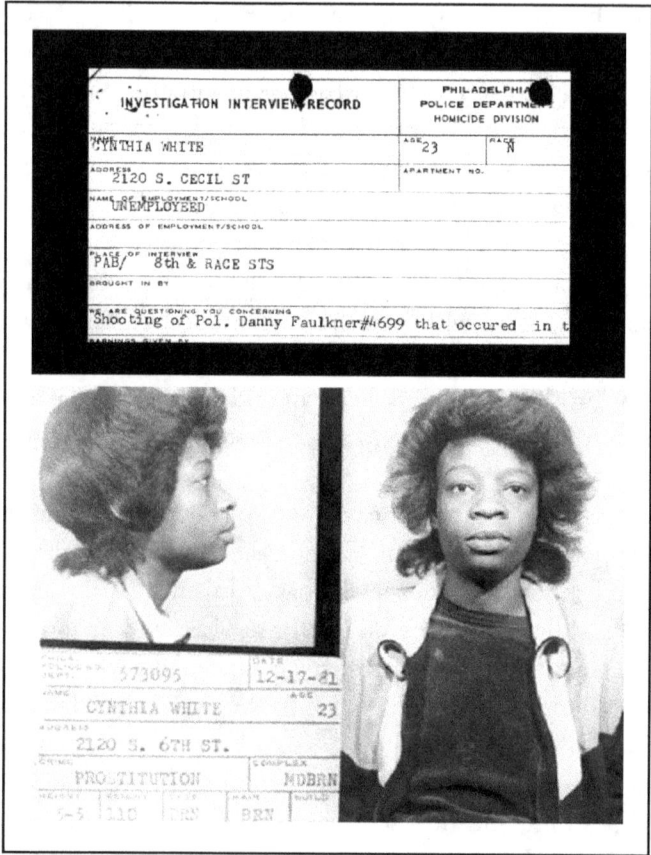

The scenario of the prosecution corresponded to a brutal murder, a shootout in which Abu-Jamal was unequivocally the aggressor. The prosecution's evidence could be divided into three groups: eyewitnesses, ear witnesses, and Abu-Jamal's gun, which had allegedly been found on the sidewalk in close proximity to the killed officer. Here is a summary of the main points of the prosecution's case:[110]

- The eyewitnesses:
    - The street prostitute Cynthia White claimed to have seen the whole scenario from beginning to end—and from very close by. As she also identified Abu-Jamal

as the perpetrator, she was practically the star witness.
  - The cab driver Robert Chobert said his vehicle was parked behind Faulkner's police car when he heard shots. He then saw Abu-Jamal stand on top of the officer and literally execute him.
  - Michael Scanlan was waiting with his car at the intersection. He said a man was running across the street. A shot was fired, and then another one, and Faulkner fell down. Then the man shot Faulkner dead in the manner described above.
  - The pedestrian Albert Magilton saw Abu-Jamal running towards the scene. He crossed Locust Street without paying further attention. Then he heard shots ring out, but he did not see Abu-Jamal again until later, when he was already slumped on the sidewalk, next to the dying Faulkner.

- The ear witnesses:

  - One police officer and former partner of Daniel Faulkner, Gary Bell, testified that Abu-Jamal, while being brought into Jefferson Hospital (which is close to the crime scene), had shouted: "I shot the motherfucker, and I hope he dies!"
  - An (African American) security guard at Jefferson Hospital, Priscilla Durham, corroborated Bell's testimony.

- Abu-Jamal's gun:

  - According to their own testimony, the two officers Robert Shoemaker and James Forbes were the first to arrive at the crime scene. They both said that Abu-Jamal's revolver was lying to his left and was secured by Officer Forbes.

The prosecution could thus field an impressive array of evidence. The jury, which was carefully "cleansed" of African American members, consequently found the defendant guilty, and following the prosecution's portrayal of Abu-Jamal as a "dangerous" Black man prone to violence, they sentenced him to death. The verdict was certainly not inspired by racist motives alone; rather, it was the result of a joint effort on the part of the police, the prosecution and the presiding judge, in combination with a defense whose work had pretty soon all but collapsed.[111] The prosecution's evidence was practically all that the members of the jury ever saw and heard.

MOTIVES BEHIND A ONE-SIDED INVESTIGATION

15:56	4:07:24	Radio: 601	Wakshul, Trombetta: "We got who we believe is the doer in the back of the wagon going to Homicide."
16:17		Radio: Okay, 01 you want to take him over to Jefferson Hospital, that's from CI-1	
16:29		EPW: 601	"Yeah if that's what CI-1 wants, that's what we'll do."

What the jury never heard about was the background that animated the investigations on the part of police and prosecution. The police officers arriving at the scene found a dying colleague, and just next to him, a seriously wounded Black man. To make matters worse, from their perspective the man happened to be a dangerous revolutionary, who in his reports had always irresponsibly agitated against law and order in general, and the police in particular.

Only a knave or a fool could have any doubts about his guilt. As for the police officers present, they didn't permit themselves any such second thoughts, and so they began to mistreat Abu-Jamal right then and there.[112] And what is more, they originally also intended to take Abu-Jamal to the police headquarters instead of hospital, in spite of his critical wounds. 15 minutes after the arrival of the police, the police wagon Abu-

Jamal had been thrown into was still parked just a stone's throw away from the crime scene.

At around this time, his guards in the police wagon had the following dialogue on the police radio: "We got who we believe is the doer in the back of the wagon going to homicide." Radio: "OK, you want to take him over to Jefferson Hospital, that's from CI-1." "Yeah, if that's what CI-1 wants, that's what we'll do."[113] According to the testimony of the attending physician, Abu-Jamal did not arrive at the hospital until another 15 minutes later.

Considering all this, there is hardly any doubt concerning the attitude of the police officers who were at the crime scene and then conducted the investigation.

As far as the prosecution is concerned, at the time there was hardly any major city that displayed a shortcoming of the U.S. judicial system to quite the extent that Philadelphia did, namely the close entanglement of police and prosecution (this hasn't changed much since). Under Mayor Frank Rizzo, the District Attorney's Office was assigned the task to take an aggressive stance against "street crime". According to C. Clark Kissinger, a prominent Leftist activist and Abu-Jamal supporter who studied the trial, this was simply a code word for *"Black"* crime, and both the mayor and the prosecution did not just work very closely with the police, but also routinely condoned and covered up, for the abuses of police officers rampant in those years, ranging from the torture of suspects to outright murder.[114]

In the case of a political opponent already stigmatized as an outcast, the prosecution could thus certainly not be expected to impose any barriers on a police investigation whose one-sidedness even stretched to the fabrication of missing evidence.

We will see in a moment that it would be more appropriate to talk about *alleged* investigations. Practically everything that the police and the prosecution did, first at the crime scene and then afterwards, served the single purpose of nailing Abu-Jamal as the perpetrator. The case of Mumia Abu-Jamal thus has all the properties of a classical *frame-up* in which a crime is attributed to a suspect because he is intended to be or even *has* to be the culprit.

DECONSTRUCTION I: THE TESTIMONY OF THE EYEWITNESSES

The Shot That Killed Faulkner

Much has already been written on the countless contradictions and inconsistencies within and between the statements of the alleged eyewitnesses of the prosecution. They alone are sufficient to raise doubts about the authenticity of these statements.[115] But all of them[116] pale in comparison with a forensic observation which irrefutably proves that the statements of the three alleged witnesses for the lethal shot fired at Faulkner *cannot* possibly be true.

At Abu-Jamal's trial, White, Chobert und Scanlan all testified that the shot in the head that killed Faulkner was fired after he had fallen on his back, onto the sidewalk and to the right of Billy Cook's VW. They all claimed that the shooter was standing directly above the officer and fired several shots,[117] only one of which hit home.

According to this scenario, at least one and up to three shots would have had to have missed Faulkner and hit the sidewalk close to his head, leaving unmistakable marks at the point(s) of impact. But exactly these marks are glaringly absent both on both a police photo taken the night of the crime and on a press photo the day after.

Exactly the same is true of the photographs shot by the only press photographer at the crime scene, Pedro Polakoff, which were taken minutes after the shooting of Faulkner and were rediscovered only in 2006. On all of the seven high-resolution photos showing the site where Faulkner came to lie after he had hit the ground, nothing can be detected but clean, absolutely undamaged concrete[118]—the series of shots fired at point blank range at Faulkner's head by Abu-Jamal, allegedly poised on murder after he had himself been wounded, were thus nothing but a figment of the imagination.

In two conversations in 2005 and 2006, the long-time former director of the ballistics division of the Medical Examiner's Office in Tübingen, to whom I showed all these photographs, explained some important facts to me:

- Pistol—or revolver shots fired at point blank range into a

concrete floor such as the sidewalk in front of 1234 Locust at the time will inevitably leave traces.
- Those traces are always so distinct and obvious that they are impossible to overlook, and are well visible to the naked eye.
- It is unthinkable that trained police officers, let alone several of them, can overlook such traces, even if the latter are, as in this case, possibly at least in part covered in blood.

This leads to three all but inevitable conclusions.

Is it even thinkable that the three key prosecution witnesses[119] purely coincidentally all succumbed to the same hallucination? Hardly! As early as in the morning hours of December 9, 1981, their statements were synchronized in a manner that marked Abu-Jamal as a cold-blooded murderer.

Is it even thinkable that the investigators, who after Faulkner's death meticulously searched every square inch at and around 1234 Locust, did not immediately notice this glaring contradiction between their own results and the statements of the "eyewitnesses"? This, too, is hardly possible. But apparently they did not mind the fact that their colleagues had manufactured false testimony that was incompatible with the results of their own investigation.

And finally: It would also have been impossible for any experienced private investigator to overlook this contradiction. Even the totally overwhelmed defense lawyer Anthony Jackson had asked the court for funds for such investigations—and got a ridiculous *retainer* of $ 150 for the purpose.[120] Had the pre-trial judge, Paul Ribner, granted an even halfway realistic sum for the purpose, the outcome of the Abu-Jamal trial would almost certainly have been very different.

The Shot into Faulkner's Back

The testimony by White, Chobert, and Scanlan concerning the *killing* of Faulkner was thus obviously false and "coached," but what about White's and Scanlan's testimony that a man—according to White, Abu-Jamal—had approached the scene from the parking lot and had maliciously shot the officer in the back? The claim that this is exactly what happened was a central part of the prosecution's charge of murder in the first degree.

Here, too, the police investigators must have realized pretty soon that White's and Scanlan's testimony couldn't be true. A shot fired at Faulkner from behind this way would have had to have left traces on or inside building 1234 Locust, and these traces simply were not there. Apart from a few microscopically small lead fragments, which apparently were old and had nothing to do with Faulkner's death, the only relevant things found there were

- A bullet in the door frame to the entrance of 1234 Locust circa 1 meter above the ground
- The splintered fragment of a copper bullet jacket on the sidewalk in front of the entrance
- And a bullet fragment circa ¼ the size of a bullet, sharply to the right of the entrance, stuck in a wall inside the building and at a distance of 2 meters from the outer wall.[121]

The locus of the bullet in the frame of the entrance door was too low for the bullet that, according to the autopsy report, had hit Faulkner in the upper back and had exited his body directly below the Adam's apple. The fragment of the jacket didn't allow for any conclusions as to its source, nor as to the position from which and in which direction the bullet it came from had been fired.

Only the bullet chip in the vestibule of 1234 Locust could *perhaps* have been fired from the gun of a perpetrator who—like Abu-Jamal—was running to the scene, while Faulkner, at least according to the prosecution, was standing a couple of meters away from the entrance, with his back towards the street.

But upon closer inspection, even this is not possible. Bullets that—as in the case of the shot into Faulkner's back—travel through the body without clashing with a bone, usually do not splinter unless and until they hit a hard obstacle. In front of 1234 Locust, there was just one such obstacle, and that was the no-parking sign pole directly in front of the entrance that is clearly visible on the crime scene photo by the police.

In such a case, the bullet of the attacker would have passed through the body of the victim before shattering on the pole, which would have left the fragment, diverted to the right, as a trace. Thus, Abu-Jamal would have shot the unsuspecting Faulkner in the back.

However—had this been the case, the police investigators would have had to have found more than this single bullet fragment that first ricocheted from the pole, and then ended up in a spot located at an unusually sharp angle away from the supposed original trajectory. Experiments have shown[122] (and the ballistician mentioned above corroborated this) that the main parts of projectiles that splinter on a pole like the one in front of 1234 Locust will generally continue their trajectory without great change.

Thus, where were the other fragments of the bullet that left a small splinter in the vestibule of the building? Certainly not where, according to the prosecution's crime scenario, they would have had to have been, which would be in the entrance area of 1234 Locust.

This is in manifest contradiction with the prosecution witnesses' claims concerning the course of events, and therefore inevitably leads to the conclusion that this part of the prosecution's scenario presented at the 1982 trial is also untrue. Just as in the case of the alleged fatal shot, the police and prosecution could hardly have been unaware of this.[123] And in the case of the witnesses White and Chobert, there is another very simple reason for these inconsistencies.

Cynthia White and Robert Chobert

Even at first glance, the assumption that Cynthia White had even witnessed the events was quite questionable. She worked as a prostitute, which at the time was illegal in Pennsylvania, and had been arrested on 36 occasions in the preceding 18 months, with several open cases still pending. It seems strange that, of all people, she would stay around while a traffic control was being carried out, with the police car's dome lights on.

But to this, something else must be added—namely the fact that no one, not one defense or prosecution witness, testified to have seen White at the crime scene, even though Michael Scanlan, sitting in his car on the other side of the intersection, as well as the pedestrian Albert Magilton were located in immediate proximity to White's own alleged location.

The explanation for this is simple and would also explain the numerous internal contradictions in White's statements: White was simply not there when the shots were fired because she had made herself invisible as soon as possible after the first signs that there would be a traffic stop. This is corroborated by the sworn testimony of two other former prostitutes, Pamela Jenkins and Yvette Williams, in 1997 and 2002,[124] who both say that White had told them that she had actually seen nothing and had been forced by the police to testify against Abu-Jamal.

Things are quite similar with regard to the second most important witness against Abu-Jamal, Robert Chobert. He was driving his cab even though he had lost his license due to a DUI conviction. To make matters worse, he was out of jail on parole following a conviction for arson, and therefore had to fear a long stint in prison if caught red-handed while driving a taxi without a license. Would he really park his taxi right behind a police cruiser?

Of all the prosecution and defense witnesses who testified, only a single one claimed to have seen Chobert's taxicab—Cynthia White. At Abu-Jamal's trial, both Albert Magilton and Michael even explicitly testified that there was *no* car or taxi parked behind Faulkner. In Scanlan's case, he was even virtually forced to assert that Chobert was not there as the cab, had Chobert really been there, would have blocked his view of the events.

Once again, the pictures taken by press photographer Pedro Polakoff tell us a bit more. Just like the police photographs taken a good deal later, his photos do not show any taxi whatsoever: Robert Chobert was plainly and simply not there. Instead, he had parked his cab—as he admitted later to an investigator for the defense in 1995—on 13TH Street, north of the intersection, on the right-hand side of the street, ironically almost exactly opposite Abu-Jamal, who had parked his own vehicle on the other side of the street.[125]

Chobert never went to jail to serve what would have been a long term for violating the terms of his probation. On the contrary, in 1995, during Abu-Jamal's PCRA Hearings, he was still driving his cab without a license, regularly paying fines when caught, which was the worst that ever happened to him.

DECONSTRUCTION II: THE TESTIMONY OF THE EAR-WITNESSES

To evaluate the ear-witnesses against Abu-Jamal, no extensive analyses are necessary, since even the way the respective statements came about shows them as a part of the frame-up Abu-Jamal was subjected to—a part that was presented with particular, and breathtaking, chutzpah.

Right in the night of the shooting, Stephen Trombetta and Gary Wakshul, the two police officers who were assigned the task to transport and guard Abu-Jamal, and who were therefore with him all the time until Abu-Jamal had emergency surgery, stated that the suspect hadn't said anything about the shooting of Faulkner.[126]

The only one who, at that time, mentioned a confession on the part of Abu-Jamal was the highest ranking officer at the scene, Police Inspector Alfonzo Giordano, who had joined Trombetta and Wakshul in the wagon before the two left together with their prisoner. Giordano claimed to have had the following dialogue with Abu-Jamal: "Where is the gun that goes into this holster?" Response: "I dropped the gun on the street after I shot him."[127]

The first point that is interesting here is that even at a date as late as Abu-Jamal's bail hearing in front of Judge Mekel, on January 8, 1982, Giordano's statement about Abu-Jamal's alleged confession, along with White's invented testimony, was the only substantial reason presented by the prosecution to keep Abu-Jamal under arrest.[128]

A second interesting fact is that Trombetta claimed to have heard something quite different from Giordano: According to his testimony, Abu-Jamal had said that his gun *was* in the street—Trombetta did not mention anything about Abu-Jamal saying that he himself had thrown it there,[129] let alone about Abu-Jamal making a confession.

And third, according to *Wakshul's* testimony, he had heard neither the one nor the other, but nothing at all.

Later on however, at the trial, neither Inspector Giordano nor any of his claims played any part—at that time, he was already being investigated on corruption charges. On July 5, 1982, he had to quit his job, and in 1986, he was sentenced to four years in jail on probation, having been found guilty of taking more than $ 50,000 in bribes.[130]

But the story about a confession on the part of Abu-Jamal was still far from dead. Instructed by his client, Abu-Jamal's defense lawyer Jackson had—in February 1982—filed a brutality complaint against the police. The officers who had been present at the scene of the shooting were questioned, and—surprise, surprise!—none of them had seen anything to back up Abu-Jamal's claims.

On the other hand, all of a sudden there started a steady trickle of statements that literally turned out to be the nail in the coffin for Abu-Jamal at his trial. On February 9, 1982, two security guards of Jefferson Hospital, Priscilla Durham and James LeGrand "remembered" that they had heard Abu-Jamal shouting loudly while he was being brought into the vestibule of the hospital: "I shot the motherfucker, and I hope he dies!"

Two days later, Gary Wakshul—the same man who two months previously had stated that Abu-Jamal had been silent the whole time—also "remembered" that he had heard exactly the same thing as Durham and LeGrand. On February 25, Faulkner's former patrol partner, Gary Bell, went on record as saying that these were exactly the words that Abu-Jamal had loudly bellowed. A little more imaginative was a statement by police officer Thomas Bray, according to which Abu-Jamal had shouted: "I'm glad. If you let me go, I will kill all of you cops."[131]

To explain the fact that none of them had reported this incriminating confession to the police (and in the case of the policemen, to their superiors) the hospital guards and police officers variously claimed memory loss or that it simply had not occurred to them, and explanation that should make any comment superfluous. At the trial, even Assistant D.A. Joseph McGill took care not to overstep the mark, and restricted himself to presenting only Durham and Bell to the twelve jurors.

A jury already inflamed by the statements of the two phantom witnesses Chobert and White about the execution-style killing of Faulkner by Abu-Jamal was no longer capable of seeing the obvious, and therefore and swallowed both Bell's and Durham's statements and the absurd subterfuges with which the witnesses and the prosecutor tried to explain away the belated confession reports.

DECONSTRUCTION III: ABU-JAMAL'S GUN AT THE CRIME SCENE

It is uncontested that on the morning of December 9, 1981, Abu-Jamal was carrying a caliber .38 Charter Arms revolver, bought in 1979, in a holster under his left armpit. Today, he says he was bearing this weapon for his own protection after he had been robbed twice as taxi driver, to deter potential attackers, and "not necessarily to use it."[132]

In the United States, there are substantially more firearms than inhabitants, so bearing a firearm is nothing unusual. The question is, of course, whether Abu-Jamal did indeed use the gun on that day and if so, for what purpose.

In retrospect, either the investigators arriving at the scene were strangely disinterested in this issue, or else they did investigate carefully, as one would expect from diligent officers, and even more so when a colleague had been killed, but then did not share the results of their work with the public as the results did not point towards the desired perpetrator.

The first question here is whether the gun had indeed been, as claimed by the police, on the sidewalk next to Abu-Jamal and the dying Faulkner, or whether it had been pulled from Abu-Jamal's holster and placed there "just in case" by the arriving officers. December 9, 1981 was an icy winter night; Abu-Jamal's cab was probably not particularly well heated, and the location where the hole that Faulkner's bullet made into Abu-Jamal's quilted jacket was[133] suggests that the zipper of his jacked was closed. It is unclear whether Abu-Jamal was even able to draw his gun in that situation.

Be that as it may, according to the official reports, none of the officers at the crime scene did the obvious and smelled Abu-Jamal's gun or felt its temperature to determine whether it had recently been fired. If such a test is negative, this alone doesn't exonerate the suspect, but if it is positive, it strongly points towards his guilt—how credible is he claim that, of all cases, it wasn't done in this one?

Another omission, if one believes the police was a routine test usually carried out in all gun-related crimes, i.e., the investigation of the suspect's hands for gunpowder residues.

Allegedly, the primary concern of the police was to deliver the wounded Abu-Jamal to the hospital as quickly as possible, which, given his brutal treatment by the arriving officers and his guards' claim not to have noticed his wound until they arrived at the hospital, is literally grotesque. Moreover, Pedro Polakoff's photos just minutes after the arrival of the police and his comments accompanying them make clear that the Mobile Crime Lab of the police had arrived at the scene long before Abu-Jamal was carted away, so that such a test would easily have been possible.[134]

It is barely imaginable that cops, in the case of a fellow officer, didn't conduct such a test which was standard procedure at the time, and, in this case, all but compulsory.[135] The suspicion expressed by the author of an important book on the case, J. Patrick O'Connor,[136] according to which the test was actually carried out but was subsequently deep-sixed because of its unsatisfactory result, seems much more plausible.

One last indication for the stance "We've got the perpetrator and won't let facts get into the way of this good story" is the photo of Chobert's cab, reproduced to the right of Police Officer James Forbes, who is holding both his dead colleague's gun and the alleged murder weapon in his hand—without wearing gloves! This almost looks like deliberate destruction of evidence—the evidence perhaps being finger prints left by colleagues who pulled out Abu-Jamal's gun from its holster and deposited it next to him on the sidewalk?

At any rate, no connection between Abu-Jamal's .38 Charter Arms revolver and Faulkner's death has ever been proven. To this day, .38 is one of the most common calibers in the U.S., and the prosecution expert who testified at Abu-Jamal's trial stated that the bullet that killed Faulkner was too mangled for comparison and could potentially have been fired from multiple millions of different firearms in the United States.[137]

In 2001, Abu-Jamal's then defense team filed an expert opinion in court that contested the claim that no comparison was possible and unequivocally demanded a renewed testing by the most modern means of the bullet that killed Faulkner to determine whether it could have been fired from Abu-Jamal's gun. Just as all other petitions concerning Abu-Jamal's guilt or innocence, this one was also rejected from the lowest to the highest courts.[138]

Considering all this, Abu-Jamal's ironic commentary, made as early as February 1982, on the measures with which the authorities tried to suppress all his questions concerning the police investigations—"Why do they fear one man so much?"[139]—appears only too justified.

RECONSTRUCTION – HOW IT *COULD* HAVE HAPPENED

We have seen that the prosecution's version of the events is not just "full of holes, like Swiss cheese,"[140] but that it is also based on apparently conscious lies and consciously concocted evidence. At the same time, over the last twenty years or so, enormous amounts of facts and observations have been collected that allow for a sketch that is much more realistic and may perhaps come pretty close to what actually happened.

THE COURSE OF EVENTS

Mumia Abu-Jamal's brother Billy Cook and a passenger who is with him in his car[141] are driving in Eastern direction on Locust Street and are approaching the intersection 13TH and Locust. The light is green, but behind them a police car emerges with its dome lights on and signals them to stop. Cook crosses the intersection and stops immediately after the entrance of 1234 Locust on the right side of the street. The policeman Daniel Faulkner stops approximately one meter behind him. It is 3:51 in the morning on December 9, 1981.

At this point in time, Cynthia White is somewhere near the intersection,[142] looking for customers. She notices the beginning of a traffic check and smells trouble.

Robert Chobert has parked his taxi on 13TH Street North of the intersection 13TH and Locust and at first doesn't pay much attention to what's happening behind him.

Michael Scanlan, a motorist driving not very far behind Faulkner's car, is in the middle lane of Locust Street and stops on the other side of the intersection when the traffic light changes to red.

He will observe the events on the other side of the intersection right until their tragic outcome. However, as he will later admit, he has had a few cocktails; the scene where everything unfolds is more than twenty meters away, and it is dark.

Directly to the right of him, Albert Magilton stands at the corner of the intersection.

3:51:08: Faulkner calls the police radio: "I have just stopped—ah—12, 13TH and Locust." Radio: "Car to back [No.] 612, 13TH and Locust." Faulkner: "On second thought, send me a wagon, 1234 Locust."[143] All of this lasts about 15 seconds. Officer Trombetta, who is quite nearby with his police wagon EPW 601 together with his partner Wakshul, tells radio: "I'll take a ride over."[144]

Meanwhile, Cook has left his car and has walked over to Faulkner. He complains about the unjustified traffic stop. Cook and his passenger jointly run a newsstand which they have just closed for the night, and both have been subjected to permanent police chicanery over the preceding years.[145] Faulkner tells Cook: "Go back in your car, nigger." There is an exchange of words between Cook and Faulkner.[146]

At that moment, Abu-Jamal is parked with his cab 15 to 20 meters north of the intersection 13TH and Locust,[147] in front of the Whispers night bar, within earshot of the events. Quite close to him is Chobert's taxicab, where Chobert still isn't paying any attention to the action behind him. Abu-Jamal exits his car and walks, then runs, diagonally across the parking lot in the direction of 1234 Locust.[148]

Magilton, who has watched the traffic stop without particular interest, sees how Abu-Jamal approaches the scene, but doesn't deem this too important and begins to cross the street.[149]

Faulkner picks his police hat from the passenger seat. Like many Philadelphia cops, he is very proud of his carefully trimmed headdress and does not want to destroy it by wearing the hat. Since the latter is compulsory, and since a superior officer could emerge at any time, even at night, he always keeps his hat within reach.[150]

He now also gets out of his car, follows Cook to his and demands to see the latter's license or ID. He takes his hat with him, holding it in one hand. Both men are now beside the VW. They continue their quarrel, but then Faulkner pushes Cook against the front hood of the VW, takes his flashlight from his belt and hits Cook heavily on the head. Cook has no chance to strike back;[151] when he is arrested later on by Faulkner's arriving colleagues, his neck and shoulder are covered with blood.[152]

Billy Cook gets back into the VW, gets down on his knees on the front seat and scrambles on the backseat to find his paperwork.[153] In the meantime, Faulkner has walked to the other side of the VW and places his hat on the roof of the VW.[154]

Cynthia White has apparently dropped out of sight[155]—but even so, will later state that the passenger in the seat besides Billy Cook also gets out.[156] In itself, and given White's likely absence already at this point, this would not mean much, but there is ample evidence (see below) that a third man, most logically emerging from Cook's car, is first present and runs away after the events. This man almost certainly is Billy Cook's business partner and long-time close friend, Kenneth Freeman. Faulkner demands to see ID, and since Freeman apparently has no documents of his own with him, he hands Faulkner the copy of a license application he has borrowed from a mutual friend.[157] Faulkner puts the document in the pocket of his shirt.[158]

Faulkner now finds himself in a confrontation with two Black men, a weaker one he has just hit on the head, and a bigger, stocky man wearing dreadlocks, like Cook, but different from the latter definitely matching the officer in strength.[159] At that moment, he notices another man with the MOVE-style dreadlocks running towards him: Mumia Abu-Jamal. As a cop grown up and educated in Frank Rizzo's police culture, he now acts according to the maxim: "Shoot first, ask questions later."[160]

He whirls into a shooting position, his right arm extended in a line with his shoulders, turning his back to the passenger of the VW, and shoots, across the back of the VW,[161] at the third Black man, Abu-Jamal.[162] The latter collapses in the street and barely manages to slog along to the sidewalk, where he is found just a bit later in front of his brother's VW by Faulkner's arriving colleagues.[163]

This is the point where Freeman, shocked by the behavior of the officer, pulls his own handgun and in turn fires at Faulkner, whose back is right in front of him. The bullet hits Faulkner's upper back a bit to the right of the spine and exits just beneath the Adam's apple. Faulkner's police tie is sent flying like a projectile towards the intersection 13TH/Locust.[164] The bullet hits the pole of the no-parking sign directly in front of the entrance of 1234 Locust just one yard away from Faulkner.[165]

Hitting the pole, the bullet splinters, and one chip goes through a glass panel in the front door, getting stranded in the wall inside the vestibule. One part of its jacket is later found in front of the door. The rest continues its trajectory in the direction of 13TH Street and is never found, presumably because no one looks for it in that area.

All of those involved are too surprised to act in any organized fashion. Faulkner tries to defend himself against his attacker from behind; they wrestle with each other. At some time during this scuffle, the wounded cop loses his service revolver; the .38 Smith and Wesson falls down on the sidewalk where Faulkner's colleague James Forbes will pick it up a short time later.

During the melee, Freeman fires a second time, but his shot doesn't hit Faulkner but ends up in the frame of the entrance door of the building. Freeman finally manages to throw Faulkner off balance. The officer, facing 13TH Street at that point, falls on his knees,[166] and Freeman fires two more shots at him, one of which rips an entry- and an exit hole into the upper left shoulder of his police jacket without touching his body,[167] while another one hits him close to the nose beneath the left eye socket and kills him almost instantaneously.

Everything happens so fast that Billy Cook hasn't even left the car again by the time everything is already over. He sees his brother running up to the scene from the corner of his eyes, and he hears the shots, but he is unable to see who fires the shots.[168]

Faulkner is now lying on the sidewalk, dying, and just a meter away from him, Abu-Jamal is slumped against the front of his brother's car, with the life-threatening wound he has received from Faulkner.

Cynthia White witnesses none of this.

Robert Chobert has heard the shots behind him, turns around, and sees a person who he will call, only minutes later and by a most natural assumption, "the shooter," running away from the scene.[169]

Michael Scanlan takes a turn to the left into 13TH Street immediately after the shots and turns left again into Walnut Street two blocks later in order to look for a police patrol. Another block down the road, he finds Trombetta and Wakshul and tells them that a policeman has been shot.[170]

Albert Magilton is just beginning to walk across Locust Street when he hears the shots. He hurries to get back to the sidewalk but can only see two men who are apparently shot, lying in front of 1234 Locust.[171]

Kenneth Freeman, the shooter, runs away in the direction of 12TH Street. Five persons—Marc Cannon, Robert Chobert, Dessie Hightower, Debbie Kordansky and William Singletary[172]—see him running in that direction. Billy Cook at first accompanies him but then changes his mind and returns because he doesn't want to abandon his heavily wounded brother.[173] From the corner of 12TH Street, a sixth witness, the prostitute Veronica Jones, observes both men running in her direction, but in her excitement, she doesn't notice how one of them, Cook, returns and runs back.[174]

Thirty minutes later, the first police cars arrive, and when press photographer Pedro Polakoff arrives at the scene, another ten or twelve minutes later, the place is already teeming with cops.

MARKING ABU-JAMAL AS THE PERPETRATOR

```
INVESTIGATION INTERVIEW RECORD          CITY OF PHILADELPHIA
CONTINUATION SHEET                      POLICE DEPARTMENT
Pol. Stephen Trombetta #7324       PAGE 2    CASE NO.

cont.: I entered the van and searched the male with Insp. Giordano.
I discovered and empty shoulder holster, he was wearing it. The only
other thing we found was personnal I.D. I asked him what he did with
the gun and he said it was out on the street. I informed the other
Officers of this and they informed us that it was recovered. We told
to bring the male over here to Homicide by Insp. Giordano, but C.I. - 1
resumed us and told us to go to Jefferson Hospital. We took him into
the hospital and sat in the waiting room at which time we discovered that
the male was bleeding from the chest and head. He was then taken into
one of the treatment rooms and was administered to by the Doctors.
Sgt. Dunleavy then relieved us and told us to bring the suspects
I.D. and papers from his pockets.
Q. Prior to asking the suspect where the gun was did he make any statement to
you at all?
A. Not to me.
Q. While at the hospital did he make any statement to you at all?
A. No.
```

The first two officers to arrive at the scene, James Forbes and Robert Shoemaker, don't ask any questions. They immediately begin to kick Abu-Jamal, who is sitting slumped at the curb.[175] They are soon joined by other officers.

Two of them grab Abu-Jamal by the arms, and instead of carrying him directly to Wakshul's and Trombetta's police wagon EPW 601, which by then has arrived and is parked a little further away in the direction of 12TH Street, they walk in the opposite direction, ram Abu-Jamal's head into the no-parking sign pole in front of 1234 Locust several times and then let him drop face down on the concrete of the sidewalk.[176]

Only then is Abu-Jamal carried towards 12TH Street and thrown into Wakshul's and Trombetta's transport vehicle. About four minutes later, Inspector Alfonzo Giordano emerges on the scene.

In or near the crowd of spectators that has assembled, there are the future witnesses White, Chobert, Scanlan and Magilton. In addition, a number of further witnesses who claim to have witnessed parts of the events are there: a parking lot attendant, a drug addict, and possibly also another woman.[177] They never show up in any witness list.

Somewhere in the chaos, Cynthia White is picked up by police officers and brought to the police HQ as a homicide-witness, where she gives a description of the events that is substantially different from the one given later at the trial, but in which she already identifies the "man who sat on the sidewalk and was then brought to the wagon"[178] as Faulkner's murderer.

Robert Chobert comes forward from the crowd and says he saw the perpetrator run away, the latter being a Black man and a MOVE member: "The hair, the hair!" Giordano has him brought to Trombetta's und Wakshul's wagon, where Chobert identifies Abu-Jamal.[179] Chobert is unable to see much, as the "suspect" lies with his head towards him and his face is gummed with hair and blood,[180] but he can still recognize that the man in front of him has the same kind of dreadlocks as the person he saw running away.

Giordano, however, as a veteran of the fight against radicals, particularly MOVE, has no trouble in recognizing who is in front of him—certainly at the point when he sees Abu-Jamal's press ID.[181] With Giordano's arrival at the scene, Abu-Jamal's fate is sealed. Giordano immediately begins to collect "evidence" against Abu-Jamal and has Chobert brought to homicide without further questioning.

Michael Scanlan, probably still shocked by the deadly shooting he has just observed, is also brought to the police wagon, but in contrast to Chobert he is unable to identify the man in the van as the gunman—he even says the man in the van is the driver of the VW (that is, Billy Cook)! Like Albert Magilton, he is sent to police headquarters to give his testimony.

After this, the doors of the transport vehicle are closed, and like his colleagues before, Giordano starts to beat Abu-Jamal.[182] When he leaves the wagon, he is the one who orders the two policemen guarding Abu-Jamal to bring the heavily wounded man to homicide instead of hospital, an order that is rescinded later on via police radio.[183] Fifteen minutes after the shooting, loud cries and shouting still emanate from Wakshul's and Trombetta's EPW 601.[184]

While the witnesses who have so far been only superficially interviewed are brought to police headquarters, the colleagues of the dead policeman proceed to secure the crime scene and the evidence. The 31 photos by press photographer Pedro Polakoff document the incredible sloppiness with which this is done. In 2006, Polakoff will describe what he observes there as "the worst crime scene investigation I have ever seen."[185]

And the photographs do indeed show curious things.

Two of these pictures display the right side of Locust Street directly behind Faulkner's police car. The space is empty, there is no trace of Chobert's cab, supposedly parked behind Faulkner. On some of the other photos, one can scarcely trust one's eyes: By a time when the police "Mobile Crime Lab" has long arrived, Police Officer James Forbes is still running around with Faulkner's and Abu-Jamal's guns—and he is holding them in his bare hand!

There is nothing to be seen far and wide of any traces on the sidewalk of the gunshots witnesses Chobert and Scanlan[186] will fantasize about only minutes later, at the police precinct. On the other hand, a closer look at the first photos reveals something curious: On the right-hand side of the roof of Billy Cook's VW, there is a police hat, which is quite obviously Faulkner's.

If one believes the later testimony of the three main prosecution witnesses, it is inexplicable how the hat ended up there. None of them places Faulkner ever in a position where his police hat might have even remotely had a chance to land on top of the VW. And in fact, the hat doesn't stay there for long. On Polakoff's later photographs, and on the police photographs (which were all taken after Polakoff's pictures), the hat is on the sidewalk, right next to the spot where the dying Faulkner was found!

At that moment, the police investigators don't want to hear about a third person at the scene: They already have their man, or, as they tell Polakoff, "the 'motherfucker' that did it"![187]

Dessie Hightower, a student who keeps telling the police that they have arrested the wrong person and that he saw the real shooter running away towards 12TH Street very fast, is harassed and abused at the police precinct for hours, but sticks to his testimony.[188] Later at the trial, he will be the only substantial witness to testify in favor of Abu-Jamal. An even worse treatment is meted out to William Singletary, who also declares that a third person, who ran away, had been the perpetrator. The minutes of his statement are torn up in front of his eyes again and again until he gives in and agrees to keep quiet.[189] It is not until 1990 that the defense learns of his very existence.

Debbie Kordansky's testimony about a fleeing man is dutifully taken down, but as in the case of all other witness statements, the address of this witness is withheld from the defense to prevent "potential intimidation." She, too, will not appear at Abu-Jamal's trial.

Veronica Jones makes her statement about two men running towards 12TH Street only six days after the shooting. Before the trial, she is visited by the police. Her visitors demand that she name Abu-Jamal as the perpetrator instead of recounting what she actually saw. As she is involved in several open criminal cases, she is threatened with up to 15 years in jail. Desperate and torn by a bad conscience, at the trial Jones claims not to have seen anything.[190]

Marcus Cannon, who also says he saw a Black man fleeing from the scene, contacts the defense team only in late 1996 and isn't even allowed to testify in court.[191]

And with this overview, we are back to Robert Chobert. After all, he, too, told Giordano right at the beginning that the gunman "ran away."[192] Shortly thereafter, however, he is presented with a man in a police wagon whose treatment on the part of the police has already made clear that, for them, he is the perpetrator. And twenty minutes later at the police precinct, Chobert changes his testimony.

All of a sudden, while Chobert still says that the perpetrator ran away, he now adds that "he didn't get very far, perhaps 30 to 35 steps,"[193] i.e., almost exactly the distance between the scene of the shooting and Wakshul's and Trombetta's EPW 601. Interestingly, his description of the man he saw running away as "stocky" does not fit Abu-Jamal's but Kenneth Freeman instead.[194] At Abu-Jamal's trial, the distance that the "perpetrator" ran from the scene will have shrunk to three meters.

Here, at the police headquarters, Chobert also for the first time talks about the alleged course of the events. Considering the importance of his testimony, his words are curiously unspecific: I heard a shot. [...] I looked up and saw a policeman fall down, and I saw this Black stand over him and shoot him several times more." That is all. How many shots exactly? From what (kind of) gun? Fired with the right hand or the left hand?

The curiosity of the interviewing police officers appears suspiciously limited. The whole transcript is barely three pages long. The transcript of the interview with Michael Scanlans is even shorter still. He is not being asked any questions about his alcohol consumption. And he is also unable to identify Abu-Jamal as the perpetrator. But all the same, he already describes the scenario that the prosecution will later use at the trial.[195]

But all this notwithstanding, Scanlan's testimony is still in square contradiction to the simultaneous testimony of the person who was to become the main prosecution witness, Cynthia White. But with six months to go until the trial, the prosecution witnesses' statements, very laconic at first, become ever more specific, and ever more similar to each other. Scanlan never gets in trouble for DWI, Chobert continues to operate a cab without a driving license and never has his parole revoked, and since her testimony(ies) in December 1981, White can, for the first time ever, work as a prostitute without being molested by the police.

During the same six months, a hopelessly outgunned and underfinanced defense is systematically prevented from even getting close to the unstable but powerful house of cards that police and prosecution have cobbled together from trumped-up or fake evidence and solicited testimony. At the trial, Judge Albert F. Sabo will take care of any residual problems. The rest is history.

A history that in the end will also catch up with Kenneth Freeman. One witness will later claim that in December 1981, Freeman is also investigated, but curiously the investigations are dropped.[196] The day after the police massacre of eleven members of the MOVE family on May 13, 1985,[197] Kenneth Freeman's dead body is found in a parking lot on Theodore Roosevelt Boulevard, naked, with a needle in the arm—and in handcuffs.[198]

1995

Commonwealth of Pennsylvania

Governor's Office

To Martin F. Horn,

Commissioner of Corrections, or your successor in office,

GREETINGS:

WHEREAS, at a Court of Common Pleas held at Philadelphia, in and for the County of Philadelphia as to Information Number 1358 of the Criminal Division in the year A.D. one thousand nine hundred and eighty-two, a certain Mumia Abu-Jamal, a.k.a. Wesley Cook, was tried upon a certain Information charging him with the crime of Murder, and was on the second day of July, A.D. one thousand nine hundred and eighty-two, found guilty of Murder in the First Degree on said Information, and on the third day of July, A.D. one thousand nine hundred and eighty-two, the Court fixed the penalty at death, and was thereupon, to wit, on the twenty-fifth day of May, A.D. one thousand nine hundred and eighty-three, sentenced by the Court to suffer death; and

WHEREAS, the Supreme Court of this Commonwealth of Pennsylvania has reviewed the matter and upheld the constitutionality of the death penalty as well as affirmed its imposition upon said Mumia Abu-Jamal, a.k.a. Wesley Cook, and has thus transmitted to the Governor a full and complete record of the trial, sentencing hearing, imposition of sentence and review by the Supreme Court pursuant to an Act of the General Assembly of this Commonwealth entitled the "JARA Continuation Act of 1980," approved the fifth day of October, A.D. one thousand nine hundred and eighty.

NOW THEREFORE, this is to command, authorize and require you, the said Commissioner of Corrections, or your successor in office, to cause the sentence of said Court of Common Pleas to be executed upon said Mumia Abu-Jamal, a.k.a. Wesley Cook within the week beginning the thirteenth day of August, A.D. one thousand nine hundred and ninety-five, in the manner prescribed by the Act of the General Assembly of the Commonwealth entitled "An Act providing for execution by means of lethal injection;

Commonwealth entitled "An Act providing for execution by means of lethal injection; and making a repeal," approved the twenty-ninth day of November, A.D. one thousand nine hundred and ninety, and for so doing this shall be your sufficient warrant.

GIVEN under my hand and the Great Seal of the State, at the City of Harrisburg, this 1st day of June in the year of our Lord one thousand nine hundred and ninety five, and of the Commonwealth the two hundred and nineteenth.

BY THE GOVERNOR:

Thomas J. Ridge

ATTEST:

Secretary of the Commonwealth

NEWS RELEASE

COMMONWEALTH OF PENNSYLVANIA
Office of the Governor
Commonwealth News Bureau
Room 308, Capitol
Harrisburg, PA 17120

FOR IMMEDIATE RELEASE

CONTACT: Tim Reeves
Press Secretary
(717) 783-1116

GOV. RIDGE SIGNS FOUR EXECUTION WARRANTS

HARRISBURG (June 2) - Gov. Tom Ridge has signed warrants scheduling the execution by lethal injection of four men who were convicted of first degree murder, two in Philadelphia and one each in Lehigh and Montgomery counties.

The governor set for the week of Aug. 13 the execution of:

* Leon Jerome Moser, 52, who pleaded guilty to the March 31, 1985, rifle slaying of his ex-wife, Linda, and their two daughters, Donna, 14, and Joanne, 10. The Palm Sunday killings occurred when Moser went to pick up his daughters at church. Moser has filed no appeals since 1988 when the Pennsylvania Supreme Court affirmed the verdict and sentence on automatic direct review.

* Mumia Abu-Jamal, 41, convicted of the Dec. 9, 1981, fatal shooting of Philadelphia police officer Daniel Faulkner. Faulkner, 25, was shot once in the back and three times in the face and chest after stopping Abu-Jamal's brother for a traffic violation. The officer returned Abu-Jamal's fire, wounding him in the abdomen. The shooting was witnessed by a cab driver and two pedestrians, all of whom identified Abu-Jamal as the killer. Abu-Jamal has filed no appeals since 1991.

Commissioner of Corrections Martin Horn scheduled Moser's execution for 10 p.m. Tuesday, Aug. 15, and Abu-Jamal's execution for 10 p.m. Thursday, Aug. 17.

Abu-Jamal and Moser are among the more than 100 death penalty cases inherited by Ridge when he took office on Jan. 17.

Ridge set for the week of Aug. 27 the execution of:

* Zachary Wilson, 39, convicted of the Aug. 3, 1981, fatal shooting of Jamie Lamb, whom Wilson believed was responsible for

the death of his adopted brother. Wilson shot Lamb four times in a Philadelphia bar.

* Ronald Rompilla, 47, convicted of the Jan. 14, 1988, robbery-slaying of Allentown tavern owner James Scanlon. Rompilla crawled through a window after the tavern closed, stabbed Scanlon to death, set the body on fire and left with $500 to $1,000 from the cash register and the victim's wallet.

The warrants for Rompilla and Wilson are for cases the governor received from the Pennsylvania Supreme Court in March, along with notification that the court had sustained both the guilty verdicts and the death sentences.

A new law, advocated by Ridge and enacted earlier this year, requires the governor to sign warrants in all new death penalty cases within 90 days of receipt of such notification from the high court.

Horn scheduled Wilson's execution for 10 p.m. Tuesday, Aug. 29, and Rompilla's execution for 10 p.m. Thursday, Aug. 31.

All of the executions would occur at Rockview State Correctional Institution in Centre County. Moser and Wilson currently are imprisoned at the Graterford State Correctional Institution (SCI). Abu-Jamal is at the Greene SCI and Rompilla is at the Pittsburgh SCI.

Since taking office in January, Ridge has signed 15 execution warrants under a policy he put in place to ensure that death penalty cases are reviewed "in a fair, thorough and expeditious manner."

One of the Ridge warrants was carried out on May 2 with the execution of convicted murderer Keith Zettlemoyer -- the first execution in Pennsylvania in 33 years. Four of the warrants were stayed by various courts after the prisoners filed new appeals. Two executions are scheduled for June and four in July.

# # #

1995

(Copies of the latest execution warrants signed by Gov. Ridge are attached.)

NNPA Feature Column
Week of June 12, 1995

3200 13th Street, NW
(202) 588-8764

DRUMS IN THE GLOBAL VILLAGE
By Todd Burroughs

MUMIA SPEAKS FROM DEATH ROW AS EXECUTION DATE SET

WASHINGTON (NNPA) - (Pennsylvania Gov. Tom Ridge has set the execution date for Mumia Abu-Jamal, a black journalist-turned-political prisoner.

(Abu-Jamal, 41, a Death Row resident for more than a decade after his first-degree murder conviction for the 1981 fatal shooting of a white Philadelphia police officer, is set to die by lethal injection Aug. 17 at 10 p.m., much to the consternation of anti-death penalty activists worldwide. His lawyers recently filed a petition for post-conviction relief.

(Abu-Jamal's supporters have claimed he was framed in the crime and was the victim of an unfair trial. The radio reporter's controversial case, tried in front of a mostly white jury, emphasized his association with MOVE, a radical black organization, and his teenage membership in the Philadelphia chapter of the Black Panther Party.

(The following are excerpts of a transcript of a telephone interview between Abu-Jamal and a supporter. His supporters say the talk took place June 2, the same day that Abu-Jamal heard the news in his Waynesburg, Pa. cell. - TSB)

***

Abu-Jamal: This is just a fight from another front. You know. Don't panic, folks.

Supporter: My God, the guy signed a warrant for political reasons! He knew you were filing an appeal the next day.

Supporter: What's the advantage for Ridge to sign the warrant today? What does he get out of this?

Abu-Jamal: He says, "I've done it!" He has heeded the call of the people who have been calling for my blood since he became governor.

[Jamal claimed during the interview that the day after Ridge signed his death warrant, the Pennsylvania state Department of Corrections took away all opportunities to work on his appeal.]

Abu-Jamal:.... I don't have a pencil. I don't have a pencil. I have to stop a guard if I want a pencil. And if he, you know, wants to give me a pencil, he gives me a pencil. I write what I need and I must give it back to him as soon as I finish writing....I'm sitting in a naked cell. I mean, maybe if you listen you can hear my voice echo off the walls here.

[Abu-Jamal then claimed that prison officials are restricting from his visitation list anyone with a prison record, effectively eliminating his MOVE visitors and others. He also claimed that prison officials have barred his participation in any news media interviews. No news media are allowed to visit the program while an investigation into "whether I have been conducting a business on the writing" of his book, "Live From Death Row," he tells the caller.]

Supporter: What have they done about your paralegals?

Abu-Jamal: They have denied all paralegals based upon the fact that they have said that they have not graduated from recognized and certified teaching institutions and don't have degrees in paralegal science. They have used that as a pretext to further isolate and restrict people. Understand [that] this is the most isolated prison in the Commonwealth.... So the goal is obviously .... isolation, restriction. Not only that, [but] what we have been finding out is that-- what I have said months ago is absolutely true. They have rifled through legal mail from my paid criminal capital case lawyer and from my legal staff. They have read my legal mail before I have read it. And not only that-- they have sent it throughout the Commonwealth....Isolation of prisoners, you know, for the [EXPLETIVE DELETED] reasons, you know, essentially that is the guiding theme of this jail: To isolate people further, and further, and further away from those they love, from those they need. And to thereby make it easy (to kill people), and for some people, like Keith Zettlemoyer, [create] a desire to leave this life.

I am told I am out of time. Give my love to everyone.

DEATH WATCH

Controversy rages as grass-roots support and the spotlight of celebrities focuses on the case of Mumia Abu-Jamal, who has been sentenced to death for the 1981 killing of a Philadelphia police officer

NEW INTRODUCTION FROM THE AUTHOR, JOE DAVIDSON

Mumia Abu-Jamal was one of Philadelphia's best broadcast journalists.

His rich, melodious voice and his expressive, gripping prose brought life and energy to the most routine story.

That voice was interrupted minutes before 4 a.m. on December 9, 1981. Mumia was found on the scene of a shot-dead police officer, Daniel Faulkner, who had hit Mumia with a bullet to his stomach.

Mumia was arrested and convicted in Faulkner's death.

In addition to being a well-known radio reporter, at the time Mumia also was president of the Philadelphia Association of Black Journalists (PABJ), which had been the key chapter in the formation of the National Association of Black Journalists six years earlier.

Mumia and I were friends. His son, Mazi, would sometimes come by my house on Philadelphia's East Phil-Ellena St. before school. Mumia and I would talk about music, politics and the condition of Black folks. I recall walking with him near City Hall at lunch time, as he cracked on Philly brothers who donned cowboy boots and hats as a fashion statement. "Next year," Mumia joked, "niggers will be astronauts."

Faulkner's tragic death and Mumia's arrest rocked the city and led to collateral damage for Black journalists, whose professional fairness was suddenly suspect. As PABJ president, his apprehension after a police killing wounded PABJ. I was president-elect and took responsibility for the chapter's response.

We issued a press release that did not proclaim his innocence, but did call on the city to remember the presumption of innocence—that in America suspects are considered, theoretically, innocent until proven guilty. PABJ initiated a fund to help with Mumia's expenses and expressed condolences for Faulkner's family, friends and colleagues.

Our actions were too much for some, even in PABJ. We lost members who felt they could not be associated with an organization that in any way supported someone who had been accused in a cop killing. Years later, I testified as a character witness for Mumia at a post-conviction hearing.

The image of Mumia I hold is not one of him as a prisoner at that hearing or the time I visited him in jail shortly after his arrest. It's not an image of a cop killer sitting wounded on a downtown street curb with a dead or dying Daniel Faulkner nearby. It's an image of a principled, dreadlocked brother, with a beaming smile and a rich, robust baritone delivering a news story that made listeners feel like they were on the scene.

That's the Mumia I miss.

—Joe Davidson, August 1, 2020

(Originally published as the November 1995 cover story in *Emerge* magazine)

On Death Row, in a 6-feet-by-10-feet cell of a maximum security prison nearly lost in southwest Pennsylvania, sits Mumia Abu-Jamal, a 41-year-old journalist and convicted cop killer. Incarcerated since the 1981 shooting of Daniel Faulkner, a Philadelphia police officer, Abu-Jamal has become an international *cause celebre*. Thousands of grass-roots folks from New York to London and from England to South Africa have staged spirited rallies and passed out literature in his defense. Among his marquee supporters are Maya Angelou, Paul Newman, Johnnie Cochran, Danny Glover, Jesse Jackson, Alec Baldwin, Cornel West, Oliver Stone, Ed Asner, Norman Mailer, E.L. Doctorow, Ossie Davis, Naomi Campbell, Gloria Steinem, Henry Louis Gates Jr., Norman Lear, bell hooks, Spike Lee and Salman Rushdie.

Nelson Mandela wrote Pennsylvania Gov. Thomas Ridge asking that Abu-Jamal's life be spared "on humanitarian grounds." The president of France and the foreign minister of Germany have made public appeals on his behalf. Even the National Black Police Association has called the celebrated prisoner "a victim of the criminal justice system."

Abu-Jamal has become the first self-described "political prisoner" to be launched into cyberspace on a slick $29.95 CD-ROM produced by Voyager Co. His book, *Live From Death Row,* has gone through four printings for a total of 65,000 copies, according to a spokeswoman for his publishing company, Addison-Wesley. And it's hard to visit any major city in the United States without seeing his face and waist-length dreadlocks adorning posters.

A full-page *New York Times* advertisement—which ran on standby for $19,800 (but normally would run for $62,000) and was paid for by his supporters—said the trial "was full of gross procedural errors and judicial misconduct. There is strong reason to believe....," the ad continues, "Mumia Abu-Jamal has been sentenced to death because of his political beliefs."

Abu-Jamal is a former Black Panther who came under FBI surveillance before he was old enough to drive. His lawyers credit the international political pressure with a major role in winning a stay of the original execution date, Aug. 17, 1995, as they seek a new trial.

Those lawyers, led by Leonard I. Weinglass, whose many famous cases include the Chicago Seven and the Pentagon Papers defense, have raised a series of serious issues concerning the first trial. Taken together, they raise significant problems with the adequacy and fairness of his trial.

Many of the issues that have fueled the swell of support for Abu-Jamal involve witnesses, specifically the exclusion from his trial in 1982 of testimony from an eyewitness who fingered another man as Faulkner's killer. There also are questions about the credibility of and conflicts of interest among three star witnesses for the prosecution. Also, much has been made of the fact that one of the first police officers on the scene, who gave contradictory statements to officials, was conveniently "on vacation" during the trial. Discrepancies in reports about the weapon used in the killing, and the failure of police to conduct routine tests immediately afterward, have also given some pause.

If fully explored in the original trial by a skilled and sufficiently funded defense, these concerns could have produced reasonable doubt about Abu-Jamal's guilt in the mind of at least one juror—enough to have avoided a conviction.

As it was, jurors in a Philadelphia courtroom apparently had little doubt to overcome. They returned a guilty verdict in five hours.

Those who believe Abu-Jamal was fairly tried, convicted and should be executed have not been silent during the incredible public debate about this case. Maureen Faulkner, the officer's widow, hired a plane to fly over the Massachusetts headquarters of the company that published a book of Abu-Jamal commentaries, pulling a banner that said the firm supports convicted cop killers.

Philadelphia Mayor Ed Rendell, who was district attorney when Abu-Jamal was prosecuted, told *CBS Evening News,* "If I were picking a poster child for the death penalty, I wouldn't pick someone who the evidence says overwhelmingly came up behind another human being who happens to be a police officer, shot him in the back and then shot him again when he was lying on the ground. That would not be my first pick for poster boy."

Philadelphia District Attorney Lynne Abraham took the unusual step of writing a commentary for the Sunday *New York Times* during Abu-Jamal's hearing on his request for a new trial. "The truth has taken it on the chin," Abraham wrote, "from a well-oiled, well-financed propaganda machine bent on perverting justice as it subverts the facts of the trial of a convicted cop killer."

All of this attention is a surprise to the soft-spoken Abu-Jamal, who says he cannot explain his worldwide fame. As appreciative as he is of his supporters, he rejects his status as a symbol of oppression to the death penalty or injustices in the criminal justice system.

"I'm a man," he told *The Philadelphia Inquirer.* "To call me a symbol is to dehumanize me." In a promo for a series of radio commentaries he recorded in prison, Abu-Jamal defines himself as "a journalist, a husband, a father, a grandfather and an African-American. I live in the fastest-growing public housing tract in America."

Protestations notwithstanding, a symbol he is. To some supporters, he symbolizes the 3,000-plus people on America's death row, 40 percent of whom are Black, many of whom had an impoverished and shoddy defense—as was Abu-Jamal's. He has become a symbol of a U.S. criminal justice system that moves steadily toward greater use of the death penalty as other industrialized nations continue to condemn it. He has become a symbol of a criminal justice system that responds well to those with money but reacts callousness to those with little. And, ironically, given his work to spotlight the unheralded, his symbol status illustrates how much attention can be given to an individual while others go unnoticed.

Abu-Jamal says, "There are hundreds of Jamals on every death row in every state, whose cases are more egregious, in terms of constitutional violations, than mine."

One of those "Jamals" is Gary Graham, whose scheduled 1993 execution in Texas attracted many of the celebrities now rallying around Abu-Jamal. *[EDITOR'S NOTE: Graham changed his name to Shaka Sankofa, and he was executed in Texas via lethal injection in the year 2000.]* And when the hoopla around the Abu-Jamal case subsides, some supporters wonder whether public interest in their *cause celebre* also will fade.

The Prosecution's Case: On Dec. 9, 1981, Faulkner, a 25-year-old newlywed, stopped a green Volkswagen on Locust Street, a red-light district of nightclubs and bars just a few blocks from Philly's ornate City Hall. Abu-Jamal's brother, William Cook, got out of the car and, subsequently, got into a fight with the uniformed, five-year veteran Faulkner. Abu-Jamal, then president of the Philadelphia Association of Black Journalists who was driving a cab to supplement his income, came upon the struggle and ran toward the officer and shot him in the back. Faulkner spun around, drew his revolver and shot Abu-Jamal in the chest. Though wounded, Abu-Jamal stood over the officer, shot him between the eyes, then collapsed himself.

It was about 3:52 a.m. Responding officers found a dying Faulkner and Abu-Jamal sitting nearby on the curb, in a pool of blood. Abu-Jamal's registered .38-caliber handgun was along side him, with five spent cartridges. Three witnesses identified Abu-Jamal as the killer.

By the time he was taken to Jefferson Hospital, arriving about a half-hour after Faulkner, Abu-Jamal had injuries from a serious beating, apparently by police, in addition to his gunshot wound. During the period between his arrest and the onset of treatment at the hospital, Abu-Jamal cried out, "I shot the motherfucker and I hope the motherfucker dies," according to two prosecution witnesses, Faulkner's partner and a hospital security guard.

But Abu-Jamal's new defense lawyer challenges those witnesses at every turn. Neither prosecution witness reported Abu-Jamal's alleged comment about Faulkner to police until months after the shooting, when police internal affairs officers were investigating Abu-Jamal's charges of brutality, defense lawyers say. The district attorney's office said the guard reported the comment to her boss the same day. But another officer, Gary Wakshul, who had Abu-Jamal in custody immediately after the shooting until doctors began working on him at the hospital, filed a report that said, "during this time, the negro male made no statements," according to documents filed by Abu-Jamal's lawyers. The trial lawyer wanted to call Wakshul but was told he was on vacation and unavailable. Trial judge Albert Sabo refused to delay the trial until Wakshul could testify.

In addition to their attack on the alleged confession, Abu-Jamal's new defense lawyers have sought to discredit other prosecution witnesses. One witness, Cynthia White, was a prostitute with three open cases when she testified that Abu-Jamal was the killer. "Without explanation, bench warrants against her were not prosecuted," says Abu-Jamal's petition for a new trial." "Police told another prostitute, Veronica Jones, that Ms. Jones would be allowed to work with impunity like Ms. White if Ms. Jones would testify against" Abu-Jamal.

Robert Greer, a private investigator who worked for the defense in 1982, said in an affidavit this year that he was unable to interview White before the trial because "there were always two (2) plainclothes men near where she worked her corner on Locust. I waited in vain for them to leave, but they never did."

Joey Grant, former chief of the district attorney's homicide unit, said White "wasn't protected by the police while she was prostituting herself." Furthermore, he added, Greer testified that the two people in the car never prevented him from talking to White and he never saw them talking to her.

Another witness who said Abu-Jamal shot Faulkner was cabdriver Robert Chobert. Chobert, argues the defense petition, "was clearly susceptible to police pressure" because he was on probation after being convicted of throwing a Molotov cocktail at a school for pay. At a recent hearing, Chobert again fingered Abu-Jamal. Sabo did not allow the 1982 jury to hear about Chobert's firebomb conviction, nor Jones' full description of the deal she said had been offered by the police.

At a hearing this past August, the defense produced a witness who said he was so intimidated by police after Faulkner's murder that he left town before Abu-Jamal's trial. William Singletary testified at the hearing that he saw someone else shoot Faulkner. The shooter, according to Singletary, was a passenger with dreadlocks in the car driven by Cook, Abu-Jamal's brother. Singletary told his story to police after the shooting, but his statements were repeatedly discarded until he signed one dictated by a detective. This one denied that he had seen the shooting.

After Singletary's testimony this summer, an assistant district attorney was quoted as saying he "has created a fantasy version" of the truth. The 1982 jury, however, never had an opportunity to evaluate Singletary's testimony—testimony that might have led to a reasonable doubt about Abu-Jamal's guilt.

His chances of acquittal also were heavily damaged by an impoverished, deficient and chaotic defense effort. Abu-Jamal acted as his own lawyer during some of the trial, which he regarded as a political tool of an oppressor state. He lashed out at jurors, only two of whom were Black—a low number that was a result of what his current defense team calls "the prosecution's use of racially biased preemptory challenges." As is his constitutional right, Abu-Jamal never told what occurred when Faulkner was killed. He has proclaimed his innocence, but still refuses to tell interviewers what happened. Also strangely silent is Abu-Jamal's brother, who had dropped out of sight until recently.

But no matter how strictly Abu-Jamal might have conformed to standard courtroom procedures, he still faced a judge with a clear bent for the prosecution. Sabo has been dubbed "the king of death row" by the *Philadelphia Inquirer*. Though he hasn't presided over a capital case since 1991, "Sabo still has sentenced more than twice as many people to death than any other judge in the country," according to the NAACP Legal Defense and Educational Fund. Juries presided over by Sabo have "sentenced 32 people to death—all but two of whom are people of color."

Sabo refused defense requests during the trial for funding to hire experts. He approved just $150 each for an investigator, a photographer, a pathologist and a ballistician. In an affidavit published along with other defense documents in *Race for Justice*, a Common Courage Press book compiled by Leonard I. Weinglass, Anthony Jackson, his 1982 court-appointed lawyer, said Abu-Jamal's case "could not be defended with the limited resources that were available. I presented no expert testimony on ballistics or pathology since no funds were available to retain such experts."

Abu-Jamal's current lawyers argue his trial defense was inadequate for reasons beyond the lack of resources. Sternly, the petition for a new trial says he "received the death penalty as a direct result of defense counsel's wholesale failure to prepare for the penalty phase."

Another area the defense has attacked is the lack of conclusive physical evidence directly linking Abu-Jamal's gun to Faulkner's murder. A report by Paul Hoyer, the assistant medical examiner who did the autopsy on the officer, indicated the murder weapon was a .44-caliber handgun, not a .38. He later said that notation is not something he would defend. Nonetheless, his report, done within hours of the incident, could have produced significant doubt in Abu-Jamal's jurors had they known about it, but the document was not produced during the trial.

A prosecution ballistics expert did testify that the fatal bullet was a "Plus-P" .38 caliber consistent with those fired from Abu-Jamal's gun. Because the bullet's condition prevented a direct match, no connection between Abu-Jamal's gun and the fatal bullet ever was established. Also, no test was done to determine if Abu-Jamal had recently fired a gun. Even the simple test of smelling Abu-Jamal's gun barrel to determine the presence of spent gunpowder was not done.

Through his work as a radio journalist, Abu-Jamal has demonstrated a clear bent for those ignored by the powerful and well-heeled. His writing is vivid. He carries the listener/reader to the scene to feel the joy or pain of the occasion:

> *She sits in utter stillness. Her coffee-brown features as if set in obsidian; as if a mask. Barely perceptible, the tears threaten to overflow that dark, proud, maternal face, a face held still by rage.*
>
> *A warm spring day in North Philadelphia saw her on her way home after her tiring duties as a housekeeper in a West Mount Airy home. On arrival, she was stopped by the police, who told her she could not enter her home of twenty-three years, and that*

it would be torn down as part of a city program against drug dens. "My house ain't no drug den!" the fifty-nine-year-old-grandmother argued. "This is my home!" The cops, strangers to this part of town, could care less.

Mrs. Helen Anthony left the scene to contact her grown children. Two hours later, she returned to an eerie scene straight out of The Twilight Zone. Her home was no more.

A pile of bricks stood amid hills of red dust and twisted debris; a lone wall was standing jagged, a man's suit flapping on a hook, flapping like a flag of surrender, after a war waged by bulldozers and ambitious politicians. Mrs. Anthony received no warning before the jaws of the baleful backhoe bit into the bricks of her life, tearing asunder the gatherings and memories of a life well lived. She was served no notice that the City of Brotherly Love intended to grind her home of twenty-three years into dust because they didn't like her neighbors... Another chapter in the tragicomedy called "The Drug War."

This April 1992 commentary, entitled "A House is not a Home," by Abu-Jamal, is among those in *Live from Death Row*. National Public Radio (NPR) had planned to broadcast a series of his commentaries until, Abu-Jamal supporters contend, political pressure organized by the Fraternal Order of Police forced NPR to change its plans. NPR says the decision was not influenced by outsiders.

Publishing the book did get Abu-Jamal in trouble with prison authorities. They said he violated prison regulations by conducting a business while incarcerated. He was put in disciplinary custody and suffered a loss of privileges because he practiced journalism. The book, however, apparently has helped its author provide for his new defense effort. The Sunday *Patriot-News* in Harrisburg, Pa., estimated Abu-Jamal netted at least $425,000 from the book. Overall, the newspaper said, more than $800,000 has been raised since 1990. Mumia supporters dispute that amount.

Abu-Jamal got his start as a journalist as co-founder and minister of information of the Philadelphia chapter of the Black Panther Party (BPP) when he was 15. It was then that the FBI began collecting data on him.

An October 1969 report in his FBI file says: "In spite of the subject's age (15 years), Philadelphia feels that his continued participation in BPP activits [sic] in the Philadelphia Division, his position in the Philadelphia Branch of BPP, and his past inclination to appear and speak at public gatherings, the subject should be included on the Security Index."

During the phase of the trial when the jury decided Abu-Jamal's sentence, the prosecution used his former membership in the Black Panther Party in a way the defense says violated Abu-Jamal's constitutional rights. Prosecutor Joseph McGill asked Abu-Jamal about an article he wrote as a Black Panther which used the Mao Tse-tung quote: "Political power grows out of the barrel of a gun." The Pennsylvania Supreme Court, however, ruled the Panther evidence admissible.

Whatever the impact of the Panther disclosure on the jury's decision to execute Abu-Jamal, his Panther membership had a significant impact on his craft. Writing for the party's newspaper, he later recalled, "charged my pen with a distinctive anti-authoritarian, and anti-establishment character that survives to this day."

CHAKA FATTAH

Congress of the United States
House of Representatives

June 30, 1995

The Honorable Janet Reno
Attorney General
Department of Justice
10th & Constitution Avenue, NW
Room 5111
Washington, DC 20530

Dear Ms. Reno:

A grave injustice is about to be committed. We are rushing to execute someone in the face of ample evidence that his constitutional rights have been denied, that he did not receive a fair trial and most importantly, that he is in fact, innocent. Passionate and documented racial biases, both personal and societal, surrounded this man's arrest, his trial, his conviction, and his sentencing. Because we understand our history, we understand how we got to this point; but as legislators and as persons concerned with the processes of justice in this country, we cannot sit silently by and allow this travesty of justice to proceed.

Mumia Abu-Jamal is an outstanding African-American journalist from Philadelphia known for his reporting of police brutality in the 1970's and '80's. In 1982 he was sentenced to death for the murder of a white police officer. Testimony of eyewitnesses was suppressed, a witness was bribed to testify against Abu-Jamal, the ballistics evidence did not match the circumstances of the case, there is no physical evidence linking Abu-Jamal to the crime, and tests which could have been done to prove his guilt or innocence were not ordered. At the trial, Mr. Abu-Jamal, a most powerful orator, was denied the right to represent himself. His court-appointed attorney -- a man who was later disbarred on unrelated matters -- failed to object to 11 of 15 preemptory challenges to remove African-American jurors, and consented to the judge's replacing an African-American juror who had been chosen, with an older white male who admitted that he could not be fair to both sides. Abu-Jamal was even denied the right to confront his accuser. The judge used his insistence on his right to represent himself as an excuse to remove him from the trial. No audio transmission of the trial was provided, so Mr. Abu-Jamal did not hear most of the prosecution's case.

It is apparent that these outcomes were not accidental. The presiding Judge, Judge Albert Sabo, has sentenced more people to death than any other Judge in this country, all but two of whom were persons of color. Judge Sabo is a lifetime member of the Fraternal Order of Police ruling in this instance on the killing of a police officer. No fewer than nineteen instances of unconstitutional error and legal impropriety have been documented in the this trial, including the use of Abu-Jamal's political affiliation as evidence in the sentencing phase of the trial. In a case regarding a member of the Aryan Brotherhood complaining of similar prosecutorial improprieties that same year, the Supreme Court ruled that the defendant's First Amendment rights barred the use of his political associations against him in the penalty phase of the trial.

The appeals process through the Pennsylvania Supreme Court was similarly flawed. For example, in his summation, the prosecutor in the Abu-Jamal case insisted to the jury that they were not being "asked to kill anyone", that the defendant would have "appeal after appeal after appeal", incorrectly implying that the responsibility for determining a death sentence does not ultimately rest with the jury. Such implications by the prosecution were determined to be "fatally misleading" by courts in New York, Georgia, California, and other states and by the United States Supreme Court, providing reason to overturn the death sentence. In a 1986 Pennsylvania case prosecuted by the same prosecutor (McNiel), and presided over by the same judge (Sabo), the Pennsylvania Supreme Court ruled that language which "minimized the jury's sense of responsibility for the verdict of death" provided reason to overturn the sentence. Yet in Abu-Jamal's case, the court ruled otherwise. All relief was denied in the appeals process and this decision was made by fewer judges than in any other case in Pennsylvania's history. One of the judges who upheld the death penalty had actually engaged in a direct and bitter verbal exchange with Abu-Jamal, leading some to question his impartiality.

It is clear that the treatment of evidence and the application of justice in this instance have been at best arbitrary and capricious. Even if Mumia Abu-Jamal were guilty, we would deserve to have more solid assurance of that before we put him to death. If he is innocent, to put him to death on the basis of the evidence at hand is to make of us the very murderers against whom we seek relief. Governor Ridge's signing Mr. Abu-Jamal's death warrant on June 1st was particularly ill-timed in view of the fact that his lawyers were scheduled to appear in court on June 5th to file a petition for post-conviction relief.

In light of all we have presented to you, we urge you first, to have Judge Sabo recuse himself from this case. We are convinced that Mumia Abu-Jamal cannot get a fair hearing before Judge Sabo. Further we urge you to do all in your power -- and we feel it is particularly important for you, Attorney General Reno, to become actively involved -- to insure that Mumia Abu-Jamal is not executed on August 17 as is now scheduled, and that he is granted a new trial.

Very truly yours,

Chaka Fattah
Member of Congress

John Conyers, Jr.
Member of Congress

Ronald V. Dellums
Member of Congress

Cynthia A. McKinney
Member of Congress

Maxine Waters
Member of Congress

[Signatures]

Melvin L. Watt
Member of Congress

Earl F. Hilliard
Member of Congress

William Clay
Member of Congress

Sanford Bishop, Jr.
Member of Congress

Bobby Scott
Member of Congress

Eva M. Clayton
Member of Congress

Bennie G. Thompson
Member of Congress

Carrie P. Meek
Member of Congress

Corrine Brown
Member of Congress

Alcee L. Hastings
Member of Congress

Barbara-Rose Collins
Member of Congress

Charles B. Rangel
Member of Congress

Donald M. Payne
Member of Congress

Cardiss Collins
Member of Congress

Walter R. Tucker, III
Member of Congress

Major R. Owens
Member of Congress

Adolphus Towns
Member of Congress

Kweisi Mfume
Member of Congress

BOOK NOTE: MUMIA ABU-JAMAL AND THE "DEATH ROW PHENOMENON"[199]

DANIEL P. BLANK

*"'[W]hat torments do they suffer
That make such bitterness ring through their screams?'*

*He answered, 'I will tell you in few words:
These wretches have no hope of truly dying,
and this blind life they lead is so abject
it makes them envy every other fate."*

—DANTE, INFERNO [200]

The U.S. Supreme Court reestablished capital punishment in 1976 with *Gregg v. Georgia*, only four years after that Court held that imposition of the death penalty constituted cruel and unusual punishment. Since then, more than 300 people had been executed, with the annual toll "rising sharply, from 1 in 1977 to [the 1995] record of 47."[201] Forty U.S. jurisdictions currently have capital punishment statues. Texas leads the nation with 100 executions to date, while Florida ranks second with thirty-four. Currently 3,046 inmates in the country wait on Death Row.

In November 1995 [the month the *Emerge* article came out], Pennsylvania conducted its first execution in 33 years... The Death Row population in Philadelphia County [is the third largest in any American county, close behind Los Angeles County and Harris County in Houston]. In *Live From Death Row*, Mumia Abu-Jamal portrays the intolerable physical conditions to with Death Row inmates are subjected and the dehumanizing administration of death sentences in Philadelphia's Huntington prison....

Pennsylvania, through north of the Mason-Dixon line, has a particularly disproportionate level of African-Americans on Death Row. The NAACP Legal Defense and Education Fund notes that 118 of the 193 total inmates on Death Row in Pennsylvania, over 66 percent, are Black, compared to forty percent nationwide. In fact, Philadelphia's Death Row has the highest percentage of African-Americans in the country. The situation has become so extreme that, in an unprecedented action, a federal judge in Pennsylvania recently ordered the Justice Department to explain why it sought the death penalty against a Black defendant in a particular case. [202]

... Despite the rising criticism of the costs and delays involved in the administration of capital punishment in the United States, the death penalty itself has remained exceedingly popular. Unable to resolve this tension between popularity and infeasibility, the authorities have simply tried to keep critics such as Abu-Jamal quiet. This tactic is, of course, not original. Forty years ago, Albert Camus explained the necessity of silence in administrating the death penalty: "The State disguises executions and keeps silent about these statements and eyewitness accounts. Hence it doesn't believe in the exemplary value of the penalty, except by tradition and because it has never bothered to think about the matter." [203]

... Like Virgil, Mumia Abu-Jamal leads us on a first-hand tour of the Inferno in which he lives. Beyond Abu-Jamal's articulate and terrifying observations, and the resonance of the Death Row phenomenon in domestic and international jurisprudence and politics, the fact that so many are working so hard to keep him quiet demands of us that we hear him.

1996-2019

Photos by Linn Washington, Jr.

MUMIA'S ALL-OR-NOTHING GAMBLE[204]

DAVE LINDORFF

In the spring of 2001, Mumia Abu-Jamal electrified many of his more zealous supporters around the world—and troubled many others—with a series of stunning actions. Firstly, just at a point where William Yohn, a federal district judge in Philadelphia, was in the midst of evaluating a crucial federal *habeas corpus* appeal of his conviction, Abu-Jamal filed a hand-written petition with the court stating that he was firing his entire legal team—including lead attorney Leonard Weinglass—and replacing them with the two largely untested attorneys who between them had little or no federal death penalty experience. Second, Abu-Jamal announced he was filing a lawsuit to block the publication of a book about his case written by one of the key members that defense team: legal strategist and death penalty appeals expert Daniel Williams, who he was dumping along with Weinglass.

Soon after those actions, and perhaps most remarkably, at a poorly and hastily organized curbside press conference in front of the Federal Courthouse in Philadelphia on May 4, 2001, his new attorneys Eliot Grossman and Marlene Kamish released affidavits from both their client Abu-Jamal and his brother William "Billy" Cook. For the first time, the two brothers gave what the new legal duo said were their separate accounts of what happened 20 years earlier on Locust Street. These affidavits were accompanied by an affidavit from Arnold Beverly, a career criminal and self-described mob hit-man whose wild and frankly incredible and easily debunked story was that he was the "real killer" of Philadelphia Police Officer Daniel Faulkner.

Abu-Jamal justified his firing of Weinglass, Williams and the rest of his defense team on the grounds that they had betrayed him. Williams, in particular, was accused of having abused his privileged position as legal counsel to develop inside information for use in writing a book, titled *Executing Justice: An Inside Account of the Case of Mumia Abu-Jamal*, which was published in April 2001 by St. Martin's Press. Williams received a modest $30,000 advance from the publisher, though at one point he had been willing to give the manuscript to a publisher offering him no advance. In the unsuccessful attempt in court to have distribution of the book blocked, Abu-Jamal claimed that Williams had violated legal ethics and breached attorney/client privilege in seeking personal gain from the publication of the book.

Williams says he did not reveal any secrets. He insists that he only used information that was already in the public domain.

That depends upon what one is calling "public domain."

Certainly, when Williams is citing the court record, there is no question that he was not disclosing privileged information. But he also talks in his book about what he and other attorneys on the case were thinking when they made decisions on strategy. Where he seems to be on the most controversial ground ethically is in his revelations about the dispute within the legal team over what to do with the witness Arnold Beverly, and Beverly's claim to have been Faulkner's actual killer. Here Williams asserts that the issue had already been mentioned in 1999 in an article by Philadelphia journalist Buzz Bissinger in *Vanity Fair*. He also claims that because more than just the lawyers were present at discussions of this issue, it was technically public information. Both these claims, while technically and probably legally correct, are a stretch ethically, it seems to me. In the *Vanity Fair* piece, the only thing remotely approaching a reference to Beverly was a mention author Bissinger makes about Weinglass having referred to the possibility the Faulkner shooting was a police-sponsored "hit." There is no mention of a defense witness to support this, nor is there any mention of a conflict within the defense over whether to raise the issue on appeal. As for saying that there were others present at the defense strategy sessions on Beverly, Williams doesn't say who they were. If they were part of the Abu-Jamal support network, and if those people kept the matter quiet, it hardly would seem to justify saying the issue was already in the public eye. In fact, the Beverly revelation did seem to come as a surprise to most of Abu-Jamal's supporters, suggesting that the dispute had been kept quiet, even after Rachel Wolkenstein and Jonathan Pipe (two assisting attorneys working under Weinglass who had been helping on

Mumia's case even before Weinglass was hired) had quit the case over the issue. That had happened more than a year before the release of Williams' book.

It's true that, as Williams claims, Abu-Jamal knew that his attorney was writing a book. But Williams also readily concedes that his client never saw the actual contents of that book until it was already in galleys. It seems highly unlikely that Abu-Jamal was aware of William's astonishing equivocation on the matter of his own client's innocence, as for example when he refers repeatedly to the "ambiguities" of the case while at the same time insisting that he believed him to be innocent. Such a position is entirely appropriate for a writer striving for objectivity or seeking the truth. But it is a peculiar and I would argue ethically improper public stance for a defense lawyer to take regarding his or her client.

Weinglass says in his view Williams had revealed too much about the inner workings of the defense, in particular regarding the discussions over whether to use Beverly as a witness. Weinglass also criticizes Williams for criticizing Abu-Jamal's supporters, as he does in the book. "I don't think a lawyer should attack a support committee of someone who is on death row," he told this author.

Williams for his part argues it was not possible for him to provide a draft of the manuscript for his client while he was working on it because having Abu-Jamal even implicitly endorse what he wrote could have opened Abu-Jamal to a claim by prosecutors that he endorsed all of what the manuscript said. The truth is, Williams openly states that he wrote the book as an effort to "broaden the appeal" of Abu-Jamal's case to a wider audience. He says that in order to do that, he had to criticize "some of the nutty ideas being promoted by some of the more left-wing element of his supporters."

By nutty ideas, he primarily meant the alleged witness Arnold Beverly and his testimony, on which point he was correct. Let's look at what Beverly was saying.

Beverly, at the time of his affidavit statement, was a 51-year-old Black man with a long criminal record who claimed in his statement that he had been a "mob hit-man" and that he had been recruited by other Philly cops worried that Officer Faulkner was ratting on them to the FBI which was said to be investigating corruption in the Center City police district. He claims "another guy" shot Faulkner during his stop of Billy Cook, and that, already himself wounded by a bullet to the shoulder, then came over and "shot Faulkner in the face at close range." He also claimed that "Jamal was shot shortly after that by a uniformed police officer that arrived on the scene. Beverly goes on to say he ran into the nearest subway tunnel interest to meet with a pre-arranged police driver who took him safely away from the scene of the crime.

As I wrote about this wacky fairytale in the first chapter of my book *Killing Time*:

> *There are a number of problems with this mob hit-man scenario. First of all,... how did an allegedly premeditated murder [involving multiple police officers] come to take place during a chance traffic stop [on Locust Street by the intended assassination target Faulkner]?... Anyway, why would Beverley, who [also states in the affidavit that he first] was wounded himself by a gunshot, risk delivering a fatal blow to a wounded target when none might be needed?... Finally, it seems extremely unlikely that a group of corrupt police would choose to execute a colleague in a busy locale where any number of witnesses would be on hand to see and report what happened. It also seems improbable that they would involve so many people in the carrying out of such a heinous plot. Police have killed their own. And there are a couple of cases in Philadelphia of police officers who were talking to federal prosecutors being subsequently shot and killed, But the standard modus operandi for police [fratricide] has been for them to occur in a dark part of a park or alleyway, out of view of anyone—often with the officer's own gun used so as to make it look like a suicide. Beverly's story strains credulity further because of the tale of his escape. Why would such a craven group of corrupt cops, having succeeded in hiring a lowlife mob hit-man to rub out one of their own, actually help him to escape, leaving him to eventually tell his story? How much easier, once he was in the subway tunnel [where he claims to have run for a pre-arranged meet-up with his police getaway driver!], to have shot him, leaving investigators with a nicely tied up tale of a cop killed by a mobster who was then killed by his own people? End of story.*

Williams says he also wanted to head off a potential attack from those same elements which he says he and Weinglass anticipated having to face following the *habeas* petition they had filed for Abu-Jamal in federal court, in the event that they failed to win him a new trial. That attack, says Williams, would likely have come in the form of critics claiming that he and Weinglass had "deep-sixed" a witness—Arnold Beverly—who could have proven Abu-Jamal's innocence. Williams was right about that fear, too, only the attack manifested itself before Yohn even considered the *habeas* appeal.

In any case, though, in 1999 Abu-Jamal had agreed with Williams and Weinglass's advice to omit Beverly and his baroque tale of having been Faulkner's real killer from the *habeas* petition they were drawing up to file in federal court. But in trying to anticipate a future political attack over this advice, Williams produced exactly the result he feared—only worse. His book led to the firing of both himself and Weinglass, and to a full-scale attempt by Abu-Jamal himself and his new attorneys to use Beverly as an argument for absolute innocence.

Williams' book also had the perverse effect of producing exactly the opposite result he had been hoping for with the movement supporting his erstwhile client. He intended to drive away the "left" elements with their "nutty" claims about the case. Instead, by leading to the firing of Weinglass and his replacement by Grossman and Kamish, the book led to the driving away of a significant part of Abu-Jamal's more mainstream support.

Weinglass, who died in 2011, insisted in 2002 that Williams' book was the reason the case, once in the hands of Grossman and Kamish, turned to Beverly and the once soundly rejected "hit-man" theory. "The Beverly strategy had been long dead," he said, in an interview in his New York apartment. "It was killed by Mumia himself in 1999 when he decided to let Wolkenstein and Piper [who had advanced the strategy and 'found' Beverly] quit. And it was not coming back—not as long as I was the lead attorney in the case. It was when I was fired that Mumia's new attorneys got all my files, and that's where they learned about Beverly."

In fact, at their May 4, 2001 curbside press conference, Grossman and Kamish introduced reporters to the Beverly affidavit claiming the had "discovered it" in the files turned over to them by Abu-Jamal's former defense team. Their choice of words suggested, incorrectly, that it was new information that had been hidden away. Clearly their client had known all about it for years, and if Weinglass had wanted to "hide" it, he would have shredded it and been done with it.

Weinglass, who says he feared exactly this kind of thing happening, says that once he had read Williams' book in February on 2001, he tried to get his co-counsel to withdraw it from publication. Williams says that on learning of Weinglass's concerns he wrote his publisher asking if the book could be held back from distribution. But Williams says he was told it was too late: the book was already printed and boxed in warehouses waiting to be shipped to bookstores. Holding it back at that point was impossible. He says he decided then that he would make no further efforts to stop publication. But Weinglass claims stopping it might have been possible: He had a lawyer,—Martin Garbus—ready to take the publisher to court if Wiliams was willing to go that route. He wasn't.

The federal judge in New York hearing Abu-Jamal's case against Williams and his book threw it out and made no effort to criticize Williams or to recommend any investigation or sanction by the bar. In a technical sense, Williams can claim by virtue of this exoneration that there was no ethical violation. But considering the damage the book did by leading Abu-Jamal to fire his legal team in the midst of his critically important *habeas* appeal, and by indirectly leading to the resurrection of the discredited Beverly issue, one has to wonder about the wisdom of Williams' unorthodox project.

Clearly, if Williams had felt the need to challenge elements of Abu-Jamal's support movement, and to write publicly about the defense and the struggles within it, he should have resigned from the case to write his book. That, at least, would have avoided making Weinglass, who to that point had a very close relationship with Abu-Jamal who referred to him fondly as "Grandpa," in any way responsible for what was written. "In retrospect," says Williams, "it does seem like the book produced a perverse result, but I have to say that at the time I was writing it, in 1999 and early 2000, I had no idea it would cause this kind of controversy." As to whether he should have resigned before writing the book, he says, "I always thought of this book as being helpful to the case. I certainly wasn't trying to undermine m own position on the legal team by writing it."

Subsequent to his firing as Abu-Jamal's lead attorney, Weinglass has been accused by Abu-Jamal and his new attorneys and movement supporters (on the basis of little or no evidence) of everything from putting private gain over the interests of his client to failing to pursue a legal strategy of absolute innocence because of unsubstantiated fears of alleged death threats. He has even been accused of failing, because of an alleged fear of angering the Philadelphia Police, to pursue an argument that his client was framed. On their face, these accusations are ludicrous. Weinglass during his career, defended convicted police killers and targets of the federal COINTELPRO program (which really *did* off people). He would hardly seem to be someone who would scare easily. Steven Hawkins, a Black lawyer who as lead attorney with the Washington, DC-based National Coalition to Abolish the Death Penalty, is an expert on death penalty law, and worked as part of the defense team during Abu-Jamal's PCRA hearing in 1995 and in the drawing up of his federal habeas appeal, does fault Williams for publishing his book. He says it improperly disclosed defense strategies, but Hawkins disputes the charge that Weinglass wasn't doing his best to free his client. "Len is an excellent attorney. In the years I've worked with him, I know he has had the highest integrity," he says.

If there is a reason to criticize Weinglass, it is for his apparent inattention to a book that he knew Williams was writing. As the lead attorney in the case, if Weinglass didn't know what was going to be included in that book, and didn't insist in advance on ultimate editorial control over its contents, release time, etc., he was clearly remiss. He clearly should have done a better job of monitoring what Williams was doing, and should have insisted on having final control over what could and could not be revealed and what could be submitted for publication. If he disagreed with some of the information that was being disclosed by Williams, he should have taken steps early on to prevent the work from being published. Weinglass, for his part, admitted to me that he didn't pay much attention while Williams was writing, explaining that "It was inconceivable to me that he would publish something like this before the case was over."

Whatever his thinking during the year that Williams was working on his book project, once Weinglass had read a draft of it and realized it would be published, and once he had failed in his effort to get Williams to stop publication, he attempted to convince Abu-Jamal that the book would be useful in building support for his case. In a letter to Abu-Jamal written only a month and a half before publication, Weinglass wrote:

> *I must report to you on a troubling development. Both of us knew Dan was writing a book about the case. He has a publisher and the book is going into print, to be released on April 11TH or thereabouts. Dan provided me with an early treatment of the opening chapter which I glanced at. There was nothing there that bothered me. On the contrary I liked his approach. He set up the prosecution's case as if it was clearcut and then slowly, methodically demolished it. But I was never given the opportunity to see any of his drafts as the book progressed and didn't really ask. However, Dan always assured me that his treatment of the case would be favorable. I trusted that. Now that it's about to come out, I was given a final galley copy which I read on my flying trips the last 10 days. The book is very favorable to the theme that you should have a new trial—not just on the penalty but the guilt phase as well. It's well written and persuasive. To the reading public it will be convincing of the fact that you have not received justice. There are, however, some aspects that are bothersome.*

Among the things Weinglass says he found "bothersome":

> *First, Dan strongly argues for a new trial, but take a neutral, balanced position on the issue of innocence—distancing himself from segments of your support network who argue that you were framed as a former anther and activist. He posits two extremes as equally off the mark—the FOP and those ardent supporters ... I believe Dan is thoroughly honest in arguing that the book is more credible with the reading public since he argues against those positions and puts himself in the middle. Where I differ, and argued sharply with Dan, is that his role is that of an advocate and he should allow others to occupy the middle ground...*
>
> *Aside from this general, philosophical problem with the book, there are some specifics. Dan gives away Singletary and Pamela Jenkins as not worthy of belief. I don't think a lawyer should*

negatively comment in that fashion on witnesses that his side has put on. (Dan says this is nothing new—it's obvious in the record.) He also, unbelievably, goes into the witness who we blocked from coming forward [Beverly] (I really objected to this since it has not surfaced. Dan thinks it will and this is a pre-emptive strike.)

Weinglass also criticizes the book for "revealing internal discussions and debates," and for "dumping all over Rachel" [Wolkenstein]. But he concludes:

Dan is convinced his book will save your life. And maybe it will. It's powerfully written. I just wanted you to know my own thinking on it.

Weinglass writes in his letter that on Feb. 22, 2001, that after having read the book, he met with Williams, and that in an "acrimonious meeting," was "told that it was too late to change the book to meet my objections. It's coming out."

Abu-Jamal, who after all has a right to know what his lawyers are doing with his case, had good reason to be angry at both Williams and Weinglass over the publication of *Executing Justice*. But his accusations that Weinglass and Williams didn't try to prove his innocence, and that they failed to argue that he was framed, are not supported by the record, from the period leading up to his first PCRA in '95 through their filing of his federal *habeas* petition. They did try to show at the PCRA hearing that another person, most likely Billy Cook's friend and business partner Kenneth Freeman, had been at the scene and might have been the killer and the mysterious fleeing suspect testified to at 1982 trial and at the PCRA by some witnesses. They did try to show, through the testimony of Veronica Jones and other witnesses, that the police and prosecution had tried to frame Abu-Jamal. In any event, it seems highly unlikely that either Weinglass—or Williams—would risk careers and reputation by deliberately sabotaging a case out of fear. Had fear interfered with their duties, a perfectly acceptable alternative existed: resigning and handing the case over to another attorney.

Whether true or baseless, the attacks on Weinglass were predictable, even necessary, given the new strategy of Abu-Jamal and his new legal team. Once Abu-Jamal had decided, in the spring of 2001, to proceed with the once-rejected Beverly-did-it strategy, he and his new defense team had to establish somehow that he had been misled by his attorneys in deciding in 1999 not to introduce evidence of Beverly's confession that he had killed Faulkner. He really had no choice but to attack his attorneys, since under the terms of the 1996 federal Anti-Terrorism and Effective Death Penalty Act, and in accordance with Supreme Court precedent, convicted criminals are barred from using evidence if it had already been available but unused for more than 60 days. His only hope to even attempt to introduce the Beverly evidence therefore lay in convincing a court that he was the victim of an ineffective, or better yet, corrupt attorney. This was especially true since he himself made the decision in 1999 to stick with Weinglass And Williams, who determined that Beverly was not credible, and to lose (through the resignation from the case) attorneys Wolkenstein and Piper, who wanted him to use Beverly in his appeal (Wolkenstein had found Beverly, and Weinstein and Abu-Jamal's later attorney Robert Bryan, hired after Abu-Jamal dropped Grossman and Kamish, both said the believed that Beverly's testimony had been "coached," Bryan calling him "a very troubled person.")

What made this effort to bring Beverly into the case and Abu-Jamal's one shot at the federal level to appeal his conviction so difficult, and what has no doubt made it unsuccessful, was that Abu-Jamal did not reach his 1999 decision regarding Beverly in a vacuum. Once Wolkenstein brought in Beverly as a possible confessor to Faulkner's murder, the pros and cons of using his purported confession were presented to him by two sets of attorneys in both of whom he had a high degree of confidence—Weinglass and Williams on one side and Wolkenstein and Piper on the other. In deciding, back in 1999, to accept the strategy and views of Weinglass and Williams and to ignore Beverly, Abu-Jamal was consciously rejecting the advice offered by Wolkenstein and Piper, two attorneys with whom he had a relationship going back more than a decade. That makes it had to argue that he was simply misled or deceived by Weinglass and Williams. As Philadelphia Common Pleas Judge Pamela Dembe wrote in her decision rejecting Abu-Jamal's request, brought by Grossman and Kamish, for a new PCRA hearing on the Beverly confession and other evidence:

The Beverly confession, which is the lynchpin for all the

> *arguments for reconsidering and reinterpreting the trial evidence, was not rejected behind the Petitioner's back. The debate among counsel was apparently so bitter that one of them [sic] removed herself from further participation in the case. Not only was Petitioner aware of the controversy, it is impossible not to infer that he chose to align himself with the lawyers who refused to call Beverly as a witness: he had a choice, and the fact that he continued to permit Weinglass and Williams to represent him refutes quite effectively any argument that he either did not know of or did not agree with their trial strategy.*

Whatever his reasons, Abu-Jamal's adoption in the spring of 2001 of Beverly's testimony, while energizing a narrow group of activist supporters, has dismayed others. A sharp fall-off in financial support to his defense efforts had become critical by 2002, as evidenced by a letter from his new attorneys which was sent to a group attending a fundraising event at Riverside Church in New York City on May 23, 2002. In it, Grossman, Kamish, J. Michael Farrell and Nick Brown, the four attorneys of record in the case, write that there is "no money left" to pay for Abu-Jamal's defense:

> *We will not dwell on the fact that since we took over Mumia's legal representation over a year ago, we have not been paid one cent for the thousands of hours we have spent on his case—and have had to dig into our own pockets to pay thousands of dollars in litigation expenses.*
>
> *Instead, what we want to tell you about is the $30,000 that we need to restart and complete a stalled investigation which could blast another major hole in the prosecution's case and further expose how the frame-up of Mumia was put together. Our investigators are on the trail of a key witness. But we have no money to pay them to continue the investigation.*

Actually, it was not correct to claim that the new legal team had gotten "not one cent" since taking on the case. Kamish and Grossman did submit bills to the Bill of Rights Foundation, which had continued paying the team's bills, and they were paid for the invoices they submitted until the existing money—reported about $50,000—ran out, sources familiar with the fund say.

Their letter goes on to admit that the attacks on Abu-Jamal's former lead counsel have hurt support for his cause (while perhaps inadvertently letting on that they had to attack the highly respected Weinglass in order to have any chance of introducing Beverly as a witness):

> *We understand that we have been criticized in certain quarters for exposing the truth about how Mumia's previous attorneys Weinglass and Williams suppressed the evidence which proves that he is innocent and otherwise sabotaged his defense. People need to understand that we have no alternative but to tell the truth about what happened, because the courts will not consider this evidence without being given a proper explanation as to why it was not presented in June 1999 when Mumia's previous laywers had it in their hands.*

The new attorneys on the case also express "deep concern" over the disbanding the New York-based Committee to Save Mumia, which was chaired by actor/activists Ossie Davis and Mike Farrell, and which was folded by the two men in 2002. That committee was a major source of funds for the defense because of its high-profile leadership and connections to wealthy donors.

Actor Farrell, an intensely committed activist in the anti-death penalty movement who chairs the California-based organization Death Penalty Focus, expressed dismay at the turn in strategy of the case, which led him and Davis to decide to fold the committee.

"There's always been a kind of tension—a sort of 'more Mumia than thou' attitude—where if you weren't willing to be an uncritical, absolute devotee, there was something wrong with you," he told me in a phone interview from his home. "I was okay with that, in the sense that I was able to ignore it, because I have my own ideas. For some time, I was hearing about political tussles within the self-styled hierarchy of control [n the Free Mumia movement]. I didn't care. But when it came to Len [Weinglass] being ousted, and the attempt by the new attorneys to say he had tried to sabotage the case, I found it highly offensive. I began to raise questions about who was running the show. I wasn't interested in raising funds for attorneys who were saying these things about Len and who were sabotaging all the work he had done."

Still, Farrell says that for a time, while he refused to send out any more letters to the committee's contributor list, he held off about disbanding it because of requests by members of the committee's advisory panel. "Even Len said, 'Don't do anything that would be hurtful to the case,'" he recalls.

"But I did feel strongly that this attempt to control the process was being whipped into shape by forces I wasn't comfortable with. There were always representations that another attorney I would feel more confidence in would be taking the case on, but meanwhile the two people who had insinuated themselves in as the attorneys [Grossman and Kamish] seemed to be the ones who were running things. I finally said that I needed to separate myself form it. Ossie said the same thing. So we agreed to close it down."

There were other examples of flagging support following adoption of the Beverly strategy. Supporting endorsements of Williams' book included a number of long-time Abu-Jamal backers, such as Jesse Jackson, Farrell, and Amnesty International Secretary Piers Bannister (all of whom contributed jacket blurbs for the book, and none of whom has so far come forward to condemn it or to retract their endorsement). Novelist E.L. Doctorow, another long-time Abu-Jamal defender, contributed a foreword. These endorsements of a book that denounces the Beverly strategy suggests that many of Abu-Jamal's celebrity supporters were troubled by the change in defense strategy, and by the Beverly claim. Indeed, in his foreword, Doctorow (whose position had always been that, innocent or not, Abu-Jamal did not get a fair trial) acknowledges his own doubts about the more extreme claims of innocence. "At neither extreme can there be a legal certainty to match the righteousness," he said.

Since neither Abu-Jamal nor his new attorneys were willing to discuss with me the reasoning behind his change of heart about using Beverly as a witness, or behind his decision to finally issue a statement giving his account of what happened on December 9, 1981, we are left to wonder.

There is an argument that if a court had agreed a hearing on the Beverly claim, it might have opened the door to Abu-Jamal's bringing in other witnesses and evidence to bolster Beverly's testimony—evidence which on its own merits might have helped to overturn his conviction. This might explain why the D.A.'s office so strenuously fought to block a hearing on or even a formal deposing of Beverly. As Stuart Taylor, the lawyer/legal writer who covered Abu-Jamal's post-conviction hearing for *The American Trial Lawyer*, observes, "I can only speculate that he knew that his chances of winning *habeas* appeal were slim in any event, and that coming up with an alternative theory could not hurt much and might just help."

I have my own speculation. (And it is only that, since Abu-Jamal also chose not to discuss his case with me in the writing of the book *Killing Time*, from which the original version this chapter was drawn, or with any journalists for that matter, though it is a speculation shared by a number of people who have, like me, for years supported calls for a new trial.) Consider the context. A decision was fast approaching on his *habeas* appeal, which had been in the hands of Judge Yohn since late 1999. Following publication of Williams' book in early 2001, Abu-Jamal had lost confidence in his long-time defense team. Perhaps Abu-Jamal grew worried that he could end up spending the rest of his life in jail with no hope of release. This is, after all, a man who had already spent two decades languishing on death row, much of it spent in hellish conditions of near solitary confinement, and cut off from any physical contact with family, friends, even fellow prisoners. It is not hard to imagine why, particularly after feeling betrayed by his attorneys, he might grow concerned that the likely decision in his case would be exactly what it turned out to be—a kind of splitting of the difference that would leave him stuck in prison for the rest of his life, not facing execution, but with no chance of parole and no more avenue to appeal his conviction.

Abu-Jamal is a very political person and as a radical activist probably felt more at home taking a more aggressively political stand in his appeal. Indeed, he himself states, in a letter read out by his new attorney Marlene Kamish to supporters at that Philadelphia City Hall demonstration mentioned earlier held in May, 2001, that it was his intention to move the case in a more overtly political direction. This direction would challenge the very legality of his arrest he wrote. In the message he acknowledged that he had been criticized by some supporters for adopting a new legal strategy, and for questioning the integrity of his former attorneys, Weinglass and Williams. But to those of his supporters who were unwilling to go along with his new strategy his message was clear: "If you choose not to join me, one simple request: don't get in my way."

A savvy political observer and an incisive analyst of the workings of the racist American judicial system, Abu-Jamal must have realized at that point that for reasons both political and personal, it would take a very courageous judge to overturn the conviction of someone (especially a Black radical and former Black Panther) found guilty of murdering a police officer. Federal judges, like many people, likely harbor hopes of moving to higher office. Yohn, a Republican appointee to the federal bench, while highly regarded by attorneys and jurists of both parties, surely knew that, despite his reputation, were to overturn this particular conviction, his chances of ever being appointed to the Third Circuit appellate bench by a Republican president would be zero. Indeed, Judge Yohn was surely well aware of what happened to a fellow Republican-appointed judge on the bench of the same Third Circuit. Judge Steward Dalzell made an unpopular decision reversing a state court murder conviction in a much less politically charged or well-known case. In 1997, Dalzell had found that the 1992 murder trial of a young woman, Lisa Michelle Lambert, in Lancaster County, had been so blatantly unfair that he threw out her conviction and barred the state from retrying the case. His decision was reversed on appeal on procedural grounds. But before that happened, it had led to an impeachment campaign that garnered 37,000 signatures in Lancaster County. It also led to calls by Lancaster-area congressmen for hearings, and to several death threats against the judge.

Did such career motivations and potential for death threats influence Judge Yohn's ruling? That isn't possible to discern. But it certainly was reasonable for Abu-Jamal to imagine that these might be factors that would deter the judge on his case from overturning his conviction. That in turn could have led Abu-Jamal to craft his strategy with that expectation in mind.

At the same time, it is clear from the record and from the arguments made in Abu-Jamal's *habeas corpus* petition that he did not receive a fair trial, or a fair appeal of his conviction and sentencing, in the court system of the Commonwealth of Pennsylvania. Many fair-minded lawyers—ranging from the Cook County Bar Assn. to the Illinois Association of Criminal Defense Attorneys among many others—have agreed. In view of this, what many observers speculated was that Judge Yohn would split the difference, as he ultimately did, finding fault with the way Abu-Jamal was sentenced, but leaving his conviction standing. This result would have a two-pronged effect. First, it would prevent a gross and irreversible miscarriage of justice: the execution of a man for first-degree murder who had not received a fair trial, and who may well have not committed a premeditated act of murder. Second, it would not so infuriate the law-enforcement establishment and the Republican political establishment in Pennsylvania that the judge's future prospects would be forever foreclosed.

In addition, there were external forces at work back in 1999 and 2000 that were pushing Abu-Jamal towards making a radical shift in his legal strategy. Chief among there was the advice of Marlene Kamish. She had taken up temporary residency in the vicinity of his prison. (She stayed for some time with the nearby Bruderhof Collective, a utopian back-to-the-land group which for years had actively backed Ab-Jamal. There was an apparent falling out with the group, and she was eventually asked to leave.) She reportedly became an unpaid advisor to and one of Abu-Jamal's most frequent visitors. Both Weinglass and Williams say that Kamish soon became an almost constant irritant in their relations with their client, calling their offices all the time and haranguing them about their handling—or in her view their mishandling—of the case each step of the way.

It was not the first time Kamish, an attorney who only earned her law degree in 1990 from the Kent School of Law at the Illinois Institute of Technology, had taken a personal interest in a condemned man. Nor was it the first time she had helped to drive a wedge between a capital defendant and his attorneys.

Kamish was widely billed within the Free Mumia movement as the attorney who helped get death penalty prisoner Manual Salazar off of the Illinois death row in 1995. But attorneys in Chicago familiar with her told me that she actually played a primarily peripheral and outside-of-the-courtroom role in the Salazar case; a case which, in a manner eerily reminiscent of Abu-Jamal's, involved conviction for the fatal shooting of a Joliet police officer. In fact, Andrea Lyon, then Kamish's boss at the Capital Resource Center in Chicago, which was handling Salazar's post-conviction hearing, says she had Kamish removed from his PCRA hearing—the second stage of the appeal of his conviction—and from her full-time position as a unionized attorney with the center. Lyon had her transferred to a part-time position with the State Appellate Defender's office, where she remained for only a few months longer. Lyon, a highly regarded capital defense attorney who headed the Capital Resource Center and who is now a law professor at DePaul University Law School and became director of the Center for Justice and Capital Cases, put it this way: "I took her off the case because I was unhappy with the quality of her investigation that she did, and I had questions about the way she handled witnesses in the case."

"It's a close call whether you are preparing witnesses or whether you are putting words in their mouths," concurs Ron Hayes, another attorney in the Salazar case, "and I think she tried to push the envelope farther than she should have," in preparing witnesses for testimony in the PCRA hearing. She was, in other words, coaching witnesses, not just preparing them, he explained.

Kamish went on to serve as the third member of the legal team that handled Salazar's appeal to the state supreme court. But Charles Hoffman, the lead attorney in that appeal, dismissively said of her role, "Let me put it this way. I wrote the brief in that case. The biggest contribution Marlene made is that she got 500 people down to Springfield for oral arguments, and she also managed to get Salazar's paintings exhibited at a museum across the street from the state supreme court building during the hearing." Those two actions were surely important contributors to the public campaign to free Salazar, and both demonstrated organizing acumen, says Hoffman. But doing PR work and organizing supporters are not the same as arguing a case of life-or-death before state supreme court judges.

A number of the lawyers who worked on the Salazar case with Kamish claim that somewhere along the line she had become emotionally and personally attached to the client to the extent that it may have impaired her objectivity. One of the lead attorneys in the Salazar case said that he had her removed from contact with Salazar after he walked into her office while she was having "phone sex" with the client.

Such a emotional attachment is dangerous in an attorney, as it can affect one's judgement on behalf of the client. For example, in the Salazar case, lead attorney Lyon said that Kamish refused to go along with the legal argument developed by Salazar attorney Hayes, which ultimately led to Salazar's getting a new trial. This once again bears an eerie similarity to the Abu-Jamal case. Salazar ultimately won a new trial on a technicality: a constitutionally flawed guilt-phase jury instruction form that led to the vacating of his first-degree murder conviction. Hayes had noticed that at the time of Salazar's first state appeal, the state supreme court was considering another case that was challenging the jury instruction form used in capital cases. The argument was that the form didn't let jurors know they had the option of convicting someone of manslaughter, rather than just a choice between first-degree murder or nothing. In that case, the state's high court ultimately reversed the conviction it was considering. Hayes realized that because the appellate attorney working for Salazar at that time had neglected to have Salazar's case included in that state appeal, the court didn't extend its decision to include it. By raising this issue again, and citing the new precedent, Hayes and the defense team were confident they could get the state's highest court to also order a new trial for Salazar. Once a new trial was ordered, even if he were not found innocent, they reasoned, he might well get a lesser conviction for manslaughter, which meant no death sentence, and a chance to get out of jail eventually.

Kamish's position at the time was simple but a dangerous crap-shoot. "She didn't want that argument to be used because she said it would lead Salazar facing a manslaughter charge," recalls Lyon. In fact, in his retrial, Salazar *was* indeed convicted of manslaughter. But as Hayes had anticipated, his client was released for time served (11 years on death row). He came out of the courtroom a convicted killer but a free man.

Lyon's account of Kamish's tenure and of her dangerously divisive role in the Salazar case was supported by other lawyers involved in that case, including Karen Shields, now a state associate judge, who at the time of his post-conviction hearing was Salazar's lead appellate attorney. "She blocked our relationship with our own client," says Shields. "For some unknown reason, she didn't trust us and made sure that Salazar didn't trust us either. It was all very odd. I cannot understand why she'd want to cut him off from everyone else who wanted to help." Hayes agreed with Shields' account saying, "It was very difficult to work with her. Some of her actions alienated the client from us, which is not a good idea in such a serious case. She spent an awful lot of time meeting with and talking with the defendant on the telephone, and she drove a wedge between him and us."

Kamish continued to have the confidence of Salazar, who later even named her as godmother of his son. She went on to assist with Salazar's subsequent retrial, and helped arrange to bring in as lead attorney in that case Milton Grimes, the prominent Los Angeles lawyer who had represented LAPD beating victim Rodney King. But even Grimes insists Kamish played no courtroom role in the actual retail of Salazar. Recalls Grimes, "She was obsessed with the case—I'll stay with that word—and she was helpful outside the courtroom in digging things up, but she didn't interview any of the witnesses." Meanwhile, he adds, "In the courtroom, she irritated and aggravated the hell out of the judge, so part of my job was just trying to bring him back down. She almost made herself more of a negative in the case."

Back in May 2001, Grimes issued what may in retrospect have been a prophetic warning. "She had better not start trying to be a trial lawyer in a death penalty case! If he [Abu-Jamal] traded Len [Weinglass] for Marlene [Kamish] he has made a big mistake."

A Lexis legal search of Kamish's name turned up only one record of her significant participation in a math penalty case prior to her becoming one of Abu-Jamal's lead attorneys. That was the Salazar Illinois State Supreme Court appeal, where she was listed as "of counsel," a much more minor role than "counsel of record." Her only other listing on Lexis was for a sexual assault and harassment case in 1992, in which she was one of two lead counsels.

Abu-Jamal's other new lead attorney, Eliot Lee Grossman, was a far more experienced trial litigator than Kamish. But, it turns out, he had even less courtroom experience than she did with legal issues surrounding the death penalty. A graduate of Swarthmore College who earned his law degree from the prestigious University of California Hastings Law School in San Francisco in 1977, Grossman in fact, at the time he was hired by Abu-Jamal, seems to have had no practical background at all in this type of litigation. Attorneys familiar with his legal work say he has some expertise in international law and has handles some anti-discrimination cases, but they claim he has done little or no death penalty work in his home state of California, where he has offices in Alhambra and San Francisco. "I know people who are experts in all different areas of law," says one fellow National Lawyers Guild attorney in California, who asked to remain anonymous. "Eliot is not someone who's name would pop up on any of those lists." A Lexis legal search for Grossman done at the time he was hired by Abu-Jamal turned up no death penalty cases at either the trial or appeals level. However, he is listed, along with Kamish, as filer of a friend-of-the-court brief in the Salazar Illinois Supreme Court appeal, and in the retrial of that case, where both he and Kamish played distinctly minor roles.

As in the case with Kamish, there is not a lot of information available regarding Grossman's political background. Active in far left circles, he has been known to recommend the writings of Russian revolutionary leader Leon Trotsky to acquaintances, but also apparently once volunteered a ringing endorsement of the instruction offered by a right-wing Southern California gun club used in Bakersfield, which used a quote from him in its promotional literature.

Attorneys who know Grossman and Kamish described these two members of the National Lawyers Guild as dedicated and committed progressive attorneys. Kamish, who died in 2008, especially was said to be a passionate opponent of the death penalty and someone who threw herself wholeheartedly into cases she was involved with. But she was also said to have a prickly personality that made it difficult for her to work as part of a team. She was evidently an experienced organizer—and a good self-promoter— who managed to get her name in the paper even on cases like Salazar's where she was not a lead counsel.

Kamish and Grossman first came to public attention in the Abu-Jamal case when, on June 28, 2000, they attempted to file, with the federal court hearing Abu-Jamal's *habeas* petition, a friend-of-the-court petition on behalf of a little-known organization in California called the Chicana/Chicano Studies Foundation. In it they argued that Abu-Jamal had been improperly deprived of his right to be his own lawyer at his trial. The brief, fraught with errors and factually incorrect, was rejected by the court but continued to generate a great deal of controversy within the Free Mumia movement. Abu-Jamal himself, in a message to his supporters, urged everyone to study it carefully.

It is not clear how familiar Abu-Jamal was with Kamish's and Grossman's limited experience with the death penalty at the time, almost a year after the *amicus* brief episode, when he hired them and sacked his prior attorneys. Efforts to find out what he knew, in the form of a Federal Express letter from this author delivered to him at SCI-Greene, went unanswered, though it was reported as delivered by Fedex. Marcus

Redeker, a history professor at the University of Pittsburgh and a close friend of Abu-Jamal's who checked out Kamish for him, told me he was unaware of the criticism leveled against her by her former boss and other attorneys working on the Salazar case. The guidelines of the Illinois Supreme Court (where Salazar's case played out) for death penalty attorneys is that they ought to have participated in trying at least eight capital cases before they act as lead attorney in a death penalty case. For what it is worth, neither Grossman nor Kamish would appear to even approach that standard.

In Pennsylvania at the time, the standards for court-appointed attorneys appealing death penalty cases were fairly low. There needed to be two attorneys on the case, and they were supposed to have filed five legal briefs and to have made oral arguments in criminal cases, as well as to have filed one appellate brief. They were also supposed to have demonstrated, through training *or* experience, a knowledge of the principles of constitutional law as they apply to death penalty cases. Grossman, and possibly also Kamish, would appear to have met these minimal standards, but just barely.

There is, however, good reason to question the basic judgement of both attorneys. In terms of their handling of the media, they have been nothing short of amateurish. On the day Judge Yohn issued his ruling on the Abu-Jamal *habeas* petition, a pivotal moment in the case, reporters found that neither Grossman nor Kamish were returning phone calls. Most stories reporting on this major new development in the case consequently ended up reporting that effort to reach them were unsuccessful. (When I called Grossman's office that day, his answering machine was so full it was no longer recording messages, yet he seemingly made no effort to clear it and answer his press calls.) On the crucial day that the news broke, when most major national news media were giving play to the Mumia story for the first time in a long while, this absence by the defense gave Abu-Jamal's critics, from Philadelphia District Attorney Lynne Abraham to spokespeople for the Fraternal Order of Police and other critics, a largely free hand to spin the story their way. One example was D.A. Lynne Abraham's version. Widely quoted in the national media, she was able to peddle the false claim that Judge Yohn had debunked all the "propaganda" of the defense's claims regarding the trial and earlier appeals. In fact, as even a cursory reading of the ruling clearly showed, the judge had found a number of instances where defense's witnesses seemed credible in challenging the prosecution's version of events, and instances where prosecution witnesses, including star witness Cynthia White, had seemed not credible. Though he felt constrained by Supreme Court precedent from overturning the guilty verdict on the basis of those findings, this is far different from Abraham's claim that the judge had "debunked" the defense's arguments. The judge also specifically opened the door for Abu-Jamal to appeal to the Appellate Court level on the issue of racial bias in jury selection in his case—an opening that if properly handled could have led to a vacating of his conviction and to a new trial.

I was involved in another example of media spin on that day and bad handling of the presentation of the case by Grossman and Kamish. On the morning after Yohn's decision was announced, CNN tried to line up a spokesperson from Abu-Jamal's camp for a lengthy report that also included a voice from the opposing side: Faulkner's widow Maureen. But instead of on e of Abu-Jamal's attorneys, the network was offered rapper Chuckie D, an ardent backer and friend of Abu-Jamal's to be sure, but a guy who admitted he only had limited knowledge of the details of the case. At the last minute, an hour before the "Aaron Brown New Night" show was to air, the show's producer called on me. She sounded frustrated and desperate, and asked me to go on with Faulkner and Chuckie D as someone knowledgeable about the case. She said she was calling me largely because no one with a comparable or better knowledge of the details of the case was being made available from Abu-Jamal's defense team or support group.

Grossman began talking to the press only a day or two later. By then though, the story about Yohn's ruling was old and had ceased to be front-page material either nationally or even locally in Philadelphia. A major opportunity to get Abu-Jamal's side of the story out to a national audience had been pointlessly wasted, except for my having been able to present it on CNN.

Several other important press events in Philadelphia were also badly organized and pulled together at the last minute. These included the release of the statements by Abu-Jamal and his brother Billy concerning the events of December 9, 1981, in which notices to the media were sent out the day of the event. With a case where the local media has been ignoring the story anyway, the last thing the defense should have been doing was giving editors an excuse not to even send a reporter.

Even more seriously, Abu-Jamal's amateurish attorneys also risked jeopardizing the viability of an important defense witness who was prepared to testify in a new PCRA hearing about Judge Sabo's racial bias and his alleged judicial misconduct at Abu-Jamal's trial. This occurred when they asked that witness, who is a court stenographer by training, if she would attend a court proceeding before the Court of Common Pleas Judge Dembe and record it for them! She declined the request, considering such a volunteering of her stenographic skills to the defense to be inappropriate. Had she gone along with their incredibly ill-conceived money-saving request, her usefulness as an unbiased witness in the case (she was about to testify that as the court reporter for the actual jury selection at Abu-Jamal's trial, she had overheard the judge, Albert Sabo, on leaving the courtroom, telling another judge just going in to take over the courtroom for another trial that he would "help than hang the nigger") would have been trashed. Talk about professional malpractice!

On the legal side, Grossman and Kamish have also been sloppy, as for instance when, in their petition for that PCRA hearing before Judge Dembe, they asserted incorrectly that alternate trial juror Edward Courchain, who replaced one of the Black jurors at Abu-Jamal's trial who had been removed by the judge, became jury foreman. Actually, Courchain was never jury foreman. That role went to George Ewalt as Abu-Jamal's attorneys certainly could have easily checked.

Their biggest error, however, was in their original *amicus* brief filed on behalf of the Chicana/Chicano Studies Foundation. In it, they assert that Judge Sabo, in removing Abu-Jamal's self-representation rights at the start of his trial on June 18, 1982, had relied on a conference among judge and attorneys for which there was no record, and from which Abu-Jamal had been excluded. They go on to claim that there is "apparently no written record" of oral arguments before state Supreme Court James T. McDermott concerning the same issue of Abu-Jamal's self-representation right, and "apparently no written record" of the judge's ruling. In fact those records of a morning meeting before McDermott do exist, and both Abu-Jamal and local reporters were present at that session (it was at the June 18 hearing before Judge McDermott that Abu-Jamal made his famous remark to the departing jurist, recalled by McGill during the sentencing phase of the trial: "Where are you going, motherfucker?")

"Kamish and Grossman just didn't know how to use the court index," Weinglass said to me when I asked about this error.

Grossman and Kamish got some help with their appeal to the Third Circuit. Michael Yamamoto, immediate past president of the California Attorneys for Criminal Justice, a specialized bar association of one 2000 California criminal defense attorneys, reportedly helped them with their appeal. He also filed an *amicus* brief himself calling for the panel to consider Abu-Jamal's Beverly-based claim of absolute innocence. It was subsequently rejected by the appeals court. Attorneys with the Philadelphia Federal Defenders' Office are also offered informal advice on their own time. That office also filed an *amicus* brief on Abu-Jamal's *Batson* claim of racial bias in jury selection, "to protect the interests of our clients" in the words of one office source.

But Grossman and Kamish are also being widely criticized in the Philadelphia defense attorney community for failing to seek help from local experts in what is an extremely technically difficult and crucial hearing for their client. In a June 2002 interview, David Zuckerman, the attorney who heads up the capital defense operation of the Philadelphia Public Defender's Office, stated, "They have not been coming around looking for help in our office."

> *I did not shoot Police Officer Daniel Faulkner. I had nothing to do with the killing of Officer Faulkner. I am innocent.*

So begins Abu-Jamal's brief 2001 affidavit about what happened on the morning of December 9, 1981. The statement, taken by Grossman and Kamish and presented as a requested amendment to his *habeas* filing before Judge Yohn, is then somewhat vague as to what had transpired. He claims to have been unconscious for most of the time—in particular during the period of time when Faulkner was allegedly shot by someone else. He explains that he did not come forward with his story before because, at trial, he was "denied all my rights" and "would not be used to make it look like I had a fair trial," and because, at his PCRA hearing in 1995, his then attorney, Weinglass, "specifically told me not to testify." Explaining that, "Now for the first time I have been given the opportunity to tell what happened," he finally tells his story. He recounts that he had just returned to the 13TH and Locust Street area of Philadelphia with his United Cab early on the morning of December 9, having just dropped off a fare in West Philadelphia. He says he was filling out his logbook, when he heard some shouting. He continues:

> *I glanced in my rear-view mirror and saw a flashing dome light of a police cruiser. This wasn't unusual.*
>
> *I continued to fill out buy log/trip sheet when I heard what sounded like gun shots.*
>
> *I looked again into my rear view mirror and I saw people running up and down Locust.*
>
> *As I scanned I recognized my brother standing in he street staggering and dizzy.*
>
> *I immediately exited the cab and ran to his scream.*
>
> *As I came across the street I saw a uniformed cop turn toward me, gun in hand, saw a flash, and went down on my knees.*
>
> *I closed my eyes and sat still trying to breathe.*
>
> *The next thing I remember I felt myself being kicked, hit and being brought out of a stupor.*
>
> *When I opened my eyes, I saw cops all around me.*
>
> *They were hollering and cursing, grabbing and pulling on me. I felt faint finding it hard to talk.*
>
> *As I looked through this cop crowd all around me, I saw my brother, blood running down his neck, and a cop lying on his back on the pavement.*

It had taken 20 years for Abu-Jamal to tell his story. He had long been unfairly criticized for not telling it at the time of his trial. But now that he had finally done it, the question arises: why did he come out with it now, after waiting for so long? There are solid reasons why a defendant should not testify at his own trial—and it has always been cynical in the extreme for Abu-Jamal's critics, detractors and enemies to use his failure to do so at his own trial against him, as if his unwillingness to take the stand and tell his story were proof of his guilt. Once a defendant testifies, he is no longer able to avoid being questioned by the prosecution under oath. Skilled prosecutors (and prosecuting attorney Joseph McGill was certainly a skilled and experienced prosecutor!) are adept at asking questions designed to compel the defendant to get himself in trouble or to "plead the Fifth" and refuse to answer, which looks worse than not testifying at all. Even after a trial is over, it is rare for convicted felons to take the stand under oath in their own defense. Ken Rose is an experienced death penalty defender with the Center for Death Penalty Litigation in North Carolina. He says only some five to ten percent of defendants ever take the stand, even in a post-conviction legal forum, "and then only in limited areas where it is the only way to prove something—for example to testify as to what their trial attorney advised them to do." Rose says that even for a defendant to tell his story outside the courtroom, with the aim of building public support, can be dangerous because there are ways that the prosecution can bring such statements into the courtroom as evidence.

Sean O'Brien is a death penalty specialist at the University of Missouri School of Law in Kansas City. He adds, "There is not much to be gained by a death penalty prisoner telling his story, because basically the courts and the press discount anything they say, knowing that they are desperate to get out of their predicament."

Weinglass and Williams in any case denied that they advised Abu-Jamal not to go public with his story after the PCRA hearing in some public, non-legal forum. In fact Weinglass told me he thought it would be a good idea. Both men said that he himself never wanted to do so. (But since he never expressly told either of attorney what had happened on December 9, it's also true that they were *more* comfortable *not* having him testify in a courtroom run by Judge Sabo. They knew the judge would give the prosecution a free hand cross-examining him, overruling any objections they might make, and they didn't know where his answers would go.)

It is quite possible, however, that Abu-Jamal is telling the truth that he was just following his attorneys' advice not to testify at his post-conviction hearing. Certainly when he was questioned by Judge Sabo about whether or not he wanted to address the court, Abu-Jamal was adamant that he did not, "on advice of counsel." It was a phrase he repeatedly insisted on using, to the consternation of the judge, who was trying to establish for the record whether or not it was the defendant's own decision. Indeed at that point in the hearing, Weinglass did specifically tell his client not to answer the judge. Sabo eventually despaired of getting any different answer. On the record then, Abu-Jamal's decision not to testify, at least at the PCRA hearing, was indeed on his lawyer's advice. Williams and Weinglass, however, both maintained in interviews to this reporter, that they had urged Abu-Jamal to tell his story, *after* the PCRA hearing, to an appropriate media outlet. "I thought he should tell his story to someone who'd be sympathetic, like Ed Bradley of CBS's *60 Minutes*," said Williams. He suggested that such an account would only have helped with Abu-Jamal's public image, yet would not have been usable by the prosecution in court unless he later chose to testify.

In any event, it seems Abu-Jamal could have come out with his story in a forum which would have contributed to a more detailed consideration of his *habeas* appeal. This was because back in 2000, Weinglass and Williams had included his name on the witness list sent to Federal Judge Yohn, who was then deciding whether to hold a hearing on that appeal petition. Ab-Jamal, who for years has signed off on all legal documents in his case, asked to have his name removed from that list.

Whatever the truth of the matter, for better or worse Grossman and Kamish had him tell what purportedly was his story in an affidavit which, together with another one from his brother Billy Cook, both of which were submitted to Judge Yohn as requested amendments to the Weinglass/Williams habeas appeal. They also released those affidavits to the media. Abu-Jamal's story in that affidavit—while is has a gaping hole because he says he was unconscious for much of the time—has the merit of suggesting that he was shot by a policeman, which comports with ballistics evidence that he was shot in the chest by Faulkner's revolver. It also suggests that, if as claimed he was unconscious or semi-conscious, he could not have shot Faulkner. His claim to have been semi-conscious gets some support from the attending physician at Jefferson Hospital, who testified that he was close to passing out from shock and blood loss when police dumped him in the ER. Because of the undeniable trauma he had suffered, both from the loss of blood and from having his head pounded into a lamppost by police during his arrest, this account would also allow him a further plausible claim. Under any tough questioning from prosecutors (should it ever come to that), he could say his memory of events is unreliable.

Whatever the legal pros and cons of his putting his account on the record, whatever the truth as to whether it was Abu-Jamal or his lawyers who had him wait 20 years to tell it, it makes little difference in Abu-Jamal's current legal situation. Judge Yohn refused to consider his and his brother's affidavit as part of the *habeas* appeal.

That doesn't mean we can't or shouldn't examine it, though.

The problem with Abu-Jamal's account is that it flies in the face of much of the testimony at his trial and at the PCRA hearing—testimony which, rightly or wrongly, has already been affirmed by state and federal courts as being credible and unbelievable. The biggest difficulty is that Abu-Jamal's affidavit, taken at face value, has him crossing the street to go to the aid of his brother *after* shots had already been fired. This sequence of events conflicts with the accounts of all the major prosecution witnesses at the trial. But more importantly (given doubts we have already raised concerning the integrity of those witnesses' testimony), it also conflicts with the testimony of key *defense* witnesses. For example, it contradicts the testimony of trial defense witness Dessie Hightower who, if he had looked around the corner after hearing a series of shots as he testified, should by Abu-Jamal's account, have seen him crossing the street. Instead, Hightower says he heard shots and then looked, by which time the incident was over, and there was no more shooting. It conflicts with Michael Scanlan too, who testified that he heard the first shot and saw an accompanying flash of light as a man, Abu-Jamal presumably, was crossing the street. It also conflicts with the testimony of PCRA hearing defense witness Robert Harkins, who testified that he had a clear view of all of 13^(TH) Street, and that he saw someone struggle with, knock down, and eventually shoot Faulkner. But Harkins saw no one get shot in the street in front of him.

Billy Cook's affidavit makes things even more problematic. In it, he states that he was driving his VW beetle with his vending-stand partner Ken "Poppi" Freeman (later found naked, bound and dead in 1985 on the day MOVE's house was bombed by police) as in the passenger seat beside him. He explains that he was stopped by Faulkner, and that outside the car, he got into a verbal dispute with the officer, who then beat him three times with a metal police flashlight, causing him to start bleeding from the head. Then he says that, with Faulkner remaining standing at the front of the VW where he had frisked him, he was allowed to enter his vehicle to search the junk-strewn back seat area of the car for documents. This is a peculiar claim. It seems highly unlikely that any officer who was concerned enough to have frisked a driver, and who had already called for backup, would allow a man he had just been in a fight with and had beaten, to rummage around in the back seat of a car, hands unseen to him. In any event, Cook maintains in his affidavit that once he was inside his car looking around in the back he heard gun shots:

> *... I saw flashes of a gun out of the side of my eye. He [Faulkner] was standing in front of the car but I didn't see him shot. I was facing the back of the car.*
>
> *Out of my peripheral vision I knew, I could feel other people around but I can't say where they were. His car was behind mine and the policeman was standing on the street between my car and whatever car was parked in front of me.*
>
> *When I first saw my brother, he was running. He was feet from me. We hadn't made any plans to meet that night or anything like that and I didn't even realize that he came around that area to pick up fares. He had nothing in his hands. I heard a shot and I saw him stumble. I didn't see who shot him. He was stumbling forward.*

Cook goes on to say that while he was looking in the back seat, his partner Freeman was still sitting in the front passenger seat. But when he looked up after hearing the shots, Freeman was gone:

> *... He had been in the passenger seat and I don't know which way he had gone. He left the area right after this happened.*
>
> *Later, Poppi talked about a plan to kill Faulkner. He told e he was armed on that night and participated in the shooting. He was connected and knew all kinds of people. I used to ask him about it, but he talked but never said much. He wasn't a talker. I didn't see Poppi for a while after that.*

This account, besides seeming improbably in its description of Faulkner's wildly incautious alleged actions, also appears to contradict even Abu-Jamals own affidavit account on one crucial matter: Bill Cook seems to be saying that he saw his brother run across the street and get shot from his vantage point *inside* the car. The first time he mentions getting out of the car is after he says he saw his brother shot and after he notices that Freeman has left the car. (If he were already outside the car by the time his brother Mumia ran across the street, Cook would already have noticed that Freeman had exited the car, and he also would have been in a position to see what Freeman was doing.) As he puts it at that point in his affidavit:

> *I got out. I wanted to run. Maybe I could have gotten away. I even started to run. I did. But I couldn't run because of my brother. Not after I saw my brother down on the ground.*

Abu-Jamal, in his account, claims he was running towards his brother, who was "standing in the street staggering and dizzy." Yet Cook doesn't describe himself as dizzy or staggering following his beating by Faulkner. In fact, he claims he was permitted, and had the presence of mind, to go into his car to search for documents after being struck violently by the officer. But beyond this contradiction with his brother's account, the main problem with Cook's account is that it strains credulity. Is it conceivable that this younger brother, knowing that Freeman had confessed to committing the crime for which his brother had been facing death for two decades, would have waited that long to tell his story? (Remember in 1995, Abu-Jamal came within ten days of execution before having his execution order signed by Gov. Tom Ridge cancelled. Why not come forward at that dangerous moment?) Freeman, after all, at the time these two affidavits had been drawn up, had been dead for 16 years, and so could not be hurt by the truth, nor could he retaliate for being "fingered" by Cook. And the PCRA hearing was underway, where he could have been brought in by the defense to testify under oath. But even before Freeman's slaying in 1985, it's hard to believe Cook wouldn't have come forward to say who the real killer was, at least to his mother or other siblings, or to his brother's attorney, or his own attorney. After all, his own attorney Daniel Alva had an absolute right to keep such information from a client to himself because of lawyer-client "confession," and his replacement of his legal team, for all the upheaval these decisions have caused, have been largely irrelevant to the legal case. Irrelevant that is, unless one accepts the notion that putting forward a claim of innocence based upon the claims of an unbelievable witness—and one whose story undermines the testimony of other defense witnesses—could have soured a judge on the other more credible claims being made in what the all-important pending federal appeal of Abu-Jamal's conviction.

This was precisely what had worried Abu-Jamal's former appellate lawyers Weinglass and Williams about Arnold Beverly and his story. If that is indeed what happened, one can reasonably argue that by pushing the Beverly testimony on judges Dembe and Yohn, Abu-Jamal and his new attorneys Grossman and Kamish undermined their client's chances of winning a new trial on any of the 20 claims so carefully laid out in the *habeas* appeal by Weinglass and Williams.

Only Judge Yohn can say whether that attempt to amend and apply the Beverly, Cook and Abu-Jamal affidavits to the Abu-Jamal appealed and to push forward with the Beverly claim of being the "real killer" of Faulkner negatively impacted his view of the already filed 20 claims regarding his conviction. But Weinglass and Williams both report that as recently as late 2000, when they were still lead attorneys on the case, Judge Yohn was discussing with them a potential schedule for hearings and oral arguments. Once Williams and Weinglass were replaced by Grossman and Kamish, and the Beverly affidavit was filed, Yohn halted those discussions and made his ruling on the *habeas* appeal based solely upon the written appeal petition and the written arguments filed by the two sides.

David Zuckerman, the most experienced homicide expert on the staff of the Philadelphia Public Defenders' Office, thinks that the Beverly strategy sank Abu-Jamal's *habeas* appeal, particularly his effort to raise the issue of racial bias in the selection of his jury. "I think Judge Yohn might have ruled favorably at least on the *Batson* claim, before Abu-Jamal changed lawyers and tried to come in with Beverly as a new witness," he says. Zuckerman also suggests that factual errors and obvious errors of interpretation made by Yohn in his ruling on the *Batson* claim might well have been avoided or cleared up had there been hearings on the claims where issues or confusion could have been clarified by the Abu-Jamal's attorneys. Zuckerman, who participated in gathering the data used in one of the jury selection studies that Yohn misidentified and improperly decided weren't relevant based upon his wrong understanding of the dates of the studies, says, "Yohn was simply wrong. Unfortunately if there had been a hearing held on it, the defense could have demonstrated that to him."

Neither the state court, in the person of Common Pleas Judge Dembe, nor the federal court, in the person of Judge Yohn, were willing to grant a hearing on the Beverly claim, or even to authorize the taking of a sworn deposition from Beverly, Cook or Abu-Jamal. Instead, Dembe denied the entire petition for a new or reopened post-conviction hearing on the case. Judge Yohn just ignored it.

On December 18, 2001, Yohn split the difference, denying all claims for overturning the conviction, but supporting one claim that the sentencing hearing had been unconstitutionally unfair and improper. Yohn concluded, based upon Weinglass's and William's habeas petition, that the sentencing forms used by jury members, and Judge Sabo's instructions to the jury at the end of the sentencing phase of the trial, could have led jurors to a mistaken belief that they had to unanimously agree on any mitigation circumstances for those to be considered as weighing against a death sentence. In fact, in Pennsylvania as in many states, even one juror's finding of a mitigating circumstance means it must be included in the penalty deliberations of the entire jury. Just as even one juror voting against guilt means a defendant is not guilty in a criminal trial, even one juror voting against a death sentence means there can be no death sentence.

And with that ruling by Yohn, Abu-Jamal's death sentence was lifted, a decision later upheld by the Third Circuit Court of Appeals. As a result, Abu-Jamal went from a being condemned sentenced to death and waiting execution in solitary confinement on death row to being a convicted murderer sentenced to life without possibility of parole and confined in an ordinary high-security prison in the company of other convicted felons. With that decision too, and its confirmation by the Third Circuit Court, Yohn's decision affirming Abu-Jamal's guilt, and his rejection of the *Batson* claim of a racially biased jury, also stands, leaving Abu-Jamal with no more avenue of appeal except with for new evidence not previously available to the defendant, such as the current boxes of prosecution documents uncovered in the offices of the Philadelphia District Attorney's Office by the city's new prosecutor Larry Krasner, currently the subject before the state court.

There is a tremendous irony in Judge Yohn's 2001 ruling on Abu-Jamal's *habeas* appeal. In the end, it was the work of Abu-Jamal's fired attorneys, Weinglass ad Williams, which only months after he had sacked them, succeeded in lifting his death sentence. His subsequent attorneys, Grossman and Kamish, now no longer representing him, had not been allowed by Yohn to amend or change the petition at all and so had nothing to do with it, and yet it was likely their efforts to amend the habeas petition that led Yohn to misunderstand the details of the Weinglass/Williams *Batson* appeal, and to reject it because of that misunderstanding.

Marlene Kamish has been dead for over a decade. But Eliot Grossman is still a practicing attorney in California, and is still claiming, falsely, that it was his and Kamish's legal work that got Mumia Abu-Jamal off of death row. (In an article by Grossman published on the *bolshevik.org* website headlined "Pennsylvania's Anti-Mumia Gag Law and the Right to Freedom of Speech" described as an "expanded version" of a speech Grossman delivered in Berkeley, California on Dec. 5, 2014, Grossman describes himself as "a member of Mumia's legal team in 2001 when they convinced a federal judge in Philadelphia to overturn Mumia's death sentence."). Nothing could be further from the truth. The truth is that his and Kamish's attempt to shoehorn Arnold Beverly, a troubled man claiming he was the "real" killer of Officer Faulkner, into a new PCRA hearing for Mumia Abu-Jamal was flatly rejected by that judge, as were two mutually contradictory and poorly drawn up affidavits they submitted, purporting to be the "true"recollections of the Dec. 9 shootings of Abu-Jamal and Faulkner.

If those two attorneys had any impact his case at all, before Abu-Jamal dropped them and switched to another attorney, Robert Bryan, it was sinking his last best shot at a new trial.

GUN TEST SHOWS KEY WITNESSES LIED AT ABU-JAMAL TRIAL

Sidewalk 'Murder' Scene Should Have Displayed Bullet Impacts But There Were None

DAVE LINDORFF AND
LINN WASHINGTON, JR.

During the contentious 1982 murder trial of Philadelphia radio-journalist Mumia Abu-Jamal, a central argument of the prosecution in making its case for the conviction and for imposition of a death penalty was the trial testimony of two key eyewitnesses who claimed to have actually seen Abu-Jamal fire his pistol repeatedly, at virtually point-blank range, into the prone Officer Daniel Faulkner.

This testimony about Abu-Jamal's shooting at the defenseless policeman execution-style solidified the prosecution's portrayal of Abu-Jamal as a cold-blooded assassin.

There was however, always the lingering question, never raised at trial, or even during the subsequent nearly three-decades-long appeals process, of why, if Abu-Jamal had fired four bullets downward at Faulkner, only hitting him once with a bullet between the eyes on the morning of December 9, 1981, there was no evidence in the surface of the sidewalk around the officer's body of the bullets that missed.

Now *ThisCantBeHappening!* has raised further questions about that troubling lack of any evidence of missed shots by doing something that neither defense nor prosecution ever bothered to do, namely conducting a gun test using a similar gun and similar bullets fired from a similar distance into a slab of old concrete sidewalk similar to the sidewalk at the scene of the original shooting on the south side of Locust Street just east of 13TH Street in Center City, Philadelphia.

The test was conducted to replicate conditions at the crime scene. Here reporter Linn Washington, Jr. aims a shot at the concrete slab.

Our test conclusively demonstrated it is impossible to fire such a gun from a standing position into a sidewalk without the bullets leaving prominent, unambiguous and clearly visible marks. Yet, the prosecution's case has Abu-Jamal performing that exact miracle, missing the officer three times without leaving a trace of his bad marksmanship. So where are the missing bullet marks? The police crime-scene photos presented by the prosecution don't show any, and police investigators in their reports don't mention any bullet marks on the sidewalk around the slain officer's body.

The results of this test fundamentally challenge the prosecution's entire case against Abu-Jamal since they contradict both eyewitness testimony and physical evidence presented by the prosecution about the 1981 murder of Officer Faulkner in a seedy section of downtown Philadelphia.

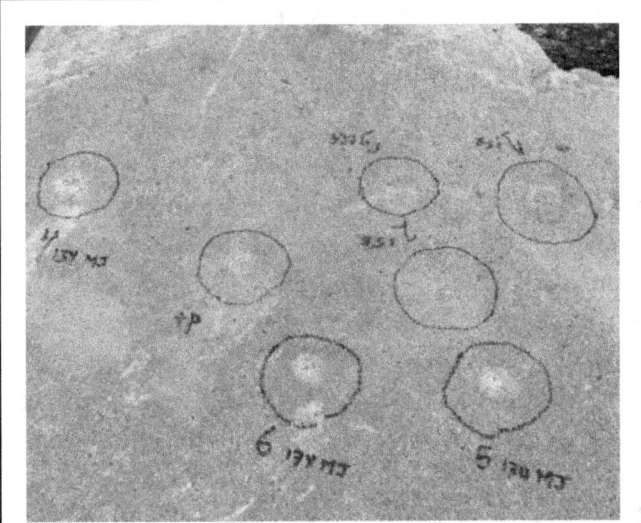

Impact marks in the test are clearly visible, especially for the Plus-P metal-jacketed bullets

Further, this test reignites questions about how police handled and/or mishandled their investigation into the murder of Officer Faulkner, quickly targeting Abu-Jamal as the killer.

For example, police failed to administer the routine gunpowder residue test on Abu-Jamal's hands to determine if he had recently fired a gun. Such a test has long been standard procedure for crimes involving gun shots. Oddly, police did perform this routine residue test on at least two persons initially suspected of being at the crime scene, including one man who fit the description of a man numerous eyewitnesses told police had shot Faulkner and then fled the scene. Police, finding a critically-wounded Abu-Jamal at the crime scene, arrested him immediately, but never bothered to do a test of his hands—or if they did, never reported the results.

While appellate courts—federal and state—have consistently upheld Abu-Jamal's conviction, no court has considered the contradiction between prosecution claims of Abu-Jamal having fired into the sidewalk and the complete lack of any evidence of bullet impacts, or even of an explanation for the missing marks. Last week, the Philadelphia District Attorney's Office curtly dismissed results of this test, which shows such marks would have been impossible to miss, as yet another instance of the "biases and misconceptions" regularly presented by persons who have not "taken the time to review the entirety of the record..."

For this experiment, veteran Philadelphia journalist Linn Washington Jr., who has investigated the Abu-Jamal case since December 1981, obtained a Smith & Wesson revolver with a 2-inch barrel, similar to the 2-inch-barrel, .38-caliber Charter Arms revolver licensed to Abu-Jamal which was marked as evidence at the trial as being the weapon which was used to shoot and kill Officer Faulkner.

Meanwhile, journalist Dave Lindorff, who spent two years researching and writing *Killing Time* (Common Courage Press, 2003), the definitive independent book about this case, procured the concrete test slab, a 200-lb section of old sidewalk, about two feet square, five inches thick and containing a mix of gravel and a steel-reinforcing screen, that had recently been ripped up during construction of a new high school in Upper Dublin, Pennsylvania. He then constructed a protective shield using a wooden frame and a section of galvanized, corrugated-steel roofing material purchased from Home Depot.

A small one-inch-diameter hole was drilled through the steel sheet about 18 inches from ground level, to enable Washington to point the pistol barrel through and fire at the concrete without risk of being injured by flying shrapnel or concrete fragments. Washington also wore shatterproof military-surplus goggles for the experiment, so he could safely aim through the hole. During the test a total of seven bullets, including Plus-P high-velocity projectiles similar to the spent cartridges police reported finding in Abu-Jamal's gun, were fired downward at the sidewalk slab from a standing position, replicating the prosecution's version of the murder. (A Penn State history professor knowledgeable about firearms and ballistics including the construction of bullets, observed the experiment from start to finish.)

After each shot was fired into the concrete, the resulting impact point was labeled with a felt-tipped pen. Still photographs were taken showing all seven bullet impacts.

The entire experiment was also filmed using a broadcast-quality video camera.

What is clear from this experiment is that the bullets fired at close range into the sidewalk sample all left clearly visible marks. The three bullets that had metal jackets produced significant divots in the concrete, one of these about 1/8 of an inch deep, and two shallower, but easily observed visually and easily felt with the fingertip. The other four bullets, lead projectiles only, left smaller indentations, as well as clearly visible gray circular imprints, each over a half inch in diameter, where the lead from the bullets appears to have melted on impact and then solidified on the concrete. Police crime scene reports list investigators recovering fragments of at least two jacketed bullets at the scene (Faulkner's police-issue Smith & Wesson revolver was firing non-jacketed ammunition).

When a photo image of these seven prominent impact sites from the bullets is compared to detailed police crime-scene photos, the absence of similar such marks at the crime scene is obvious. Even the higher-quality photos of the shooting scene that were taken by Pedro Polokoff, a professional news photographer who arrived at the shooting scene within 20 minutes of hearing about it on his police radio scanner (well ahead of the police photographer and crime-scene investigation technicians), show no bullet marks.

The bizarre lack of any sign of other bullets having been fired down at Faulkner raises a grave question about the truthfulness of the two key prosecution witnesses, prostitute Cynthia White and taxi driver Robert Chobert. As recorded in the trial transcript, Prosecutor Joseph McGill made a big point of having Chobert, a young white man, describe during the June 1982 trial exactly what he allegedly saw Abu-Jamal do in shooting Officer Faulkner. He asked, "Now, when the Defendant was standing over the officer, could you show me exactly what motion he was making or what you saw?"

Chobert replied, "I saw him point down and fire some more shots into him."

McGill asked, "Now you're indicating, for the Record, a movement of his right arm with his finger pointed toward the direction of the ground and moving his wrist and hand up and down approximately three, four times, is that right?"

Chobert replied, "Yes."

Cynthia White, for her part, testified that Abu-Jamal "came over and he came on top of the police officer and shot some more times."

If there are no bullet marks around the spot where Faulkner was lying when he was shot in the face, neither of these testimonies by the two prosecution witnesses are remotely credible.

And there is another question. When the protective steel sheet was checked after this gun test, there were deep dents in the metal which were produced by either concrete fragments blown out of the sidewalk or by bullet fragments. Such debris, large and small, would have been embedded in Faulkner's uniform and/or in exposed skin, such as the sides of his head, or underneath his clothes, and yet the coroner's report and a report on the analysis of his police jacket make no mention of concrete, rock or bullet fragments.

One can additionally speculate about why, if there were in fact bullet marks in the sidewalk, police investigators at the scene never identified and marked them off with chalk, and never photographed them, as would be standard procedure in any shooting, not to mention a shooting death of a policeman. Even more curious, investigators did note, and even removed as possible evidence, a bullet fragment found in a door jamb well behind Faulkner's fallen body, as well as gathering up three other minute bullet fragments. These actions show that on the morning of the 1981 shooting investigators were combing the crime scene looking for evidence of bullets. Had there been impact marks in the vicinity of where Faulkner's body was lying, they would surely have noticed them and marked them for evidence.

We provided our gun test result photo, as well as a crime-scene photo showing the spot on the sidewalk where Faulkner's body was found, and where there should have been bullet marks in the pavement, to Robert Nelson, a veteran photo analyst at NASA's Jet Propulsion Laboratory in Pasadena, California who is on the team that enhances and analyzes the photos sent in from the Cassini Saturn probe. Employing the same technology and skill that he uses in working with those photos from deep space, Nelson subjected the Polokoff photo to analysis and compared it to the gun test photo. Nelson offered the following comment:

"When one shoots a bullet into solid concrete, the concrete shatters at the impact point and creates a lot of scattering surfaces. It contains many micro-cracks that scatter the light more and make the impact area appear to be more reflective. This is apparent in the white circular areas in the test image.

"When the police photograph image is brightness adjusted for comparison with the test image, no obvious reflective zones (shatter-zones) are detected in the concrete surrounding the bloodspot. This result is inconsistent with the argument that several gun shots were fired into the concrete at close range, missing the body of the police officer and impacting the concrete. There are no lighter-colored circular areas suggesting shattering in the crime scene image."

Dr. Nelson at JPL found no similar bullet marks like those in the test in a crime-scene photo

Dr. Michael Schiffmann, a University of Heidelberg professor and author of *Wettlauf gegen den Tod. Mumia Abu-Jamal: ein schwarzer Revolutionär im weißen Amerika* (Promedia, Vienna, 2006), a detailed book about Abu-Jamal released in Europe, questioned a number of experts about the missing bullet marks including the longtime head of ballistics in the medical examiner's office in Tübingen, Germany. This medical examiner told Schiffmann that the notion that police investigators might have somehow overlooked the bullet impact sites around Faulkner's body, or might have failed to recognize them as bullet marks, is "absolute nonsense." That medical examiner says the marks would have been evident and identifiable as being caused by bullet impacts even if Faulkner's blood had flowed over them.

There are, moreover, other good reasons to doubt that White and Chobert were telling the truth, or even that either one of them was actually a witness to the shooting.

Chobert claimed at trial to have pulled his taxi up directly behind Officer Faulkner's squad car, which itself was parked directly behind the Volkswagen Beetle owned by Abu-Jamal's younger brother William Cook, whom Faulkner had supposedly stopped for a traffic violation. Though the trial judge, Albert Sabo, withheld this information from the jury, Chobert at the time of the shooting admitted to the court that he was driving his cab illegally on a license that had been suspended following a DUI conviction. He was also serving five year's probation for the crime of felony arson of an elementary school. Under such circumstances, one has to ask if such a driver would have deliberately parked his cab behind a police vehicle, where there was a risk he could have been questioned, arrested by the officer, and possibly even jailed for violating conditions of his probation.

In any event, there also are no crime-scene photos that depict a taxi parked behind Faulkner's squad car. Indeed, the official police crime photos, as well as those taken even earlier by Polokoff, show no taxi behind Faulkner's car. Chobert's cab's absence from crime scene photos raises an inescapable issue: either Chobert did not park behind Faulkner's patrol car as he claimed in sworn trial testimony, or police removed his car less than 20 minutes after arriving on the scene and before investigators and a department photographer had gotten there... an action constituting illegal tampering with the crime scene.

There is no taxi behind the squad car in any photo of the crime scene from the morning of Dec. 9, 1981.

Further raising questions about whether Chobert was actually where he claimed to have been during the shooting, a diagram of the crime scene drawn by Cynthia White, plus a second one drawn by a police artist following her instructions, show no taxi, though they do show, in front of Cook's VW, the extraneous detail of a Ford sedan that played no role at all in the case. No other witness at the trial except for White ever testified to having seen Chobert's taxi. Furthermore, if Chobert had witnessed the shooting while sitting at the wheel of his cab behind Faulkner's squad car, as he testified, his view of the shooting, which took place on the sidewalk on the driver's side of the parked cars, would have been blocked by both Faulkner's and Cook's parked vehicles. Making his alleged view even more problematic, it was dark at the time, Faulkner's tail lights were on, and his glare-producing dome lights were flashing brightly.

As for Cynthia White, though she claimed to have been standing on the sidewalk by the intersection of 13TH and Locust, just feet from the shooting, no witness at the trial, including Chobert, claimed to have seen her there. Furthermore, White's story about the shooting changed dramatically over time, as she was repeatedly picked up for prostitution, and each time, was brought down to the Philadelphia Police Homicide Unit, where she was questioned again and again about what she had seen. In her first interview with detectives, she said she saw Abu-Jamal shoot the officer several times before Faulkner fell to the ground. A week later, she said it had been one or two shots that were fired before the officer fell to the ground. A month later, in January, 1982, she was talking about only one shot being fired before Faulkner was on the ground–the version of her account that she eventually presented at trial.

Given the already problematic nature of both Chobert's and White's sworn testimony, this new gun test evidence demonstrating that there certainly should have been obvious bullet marks located around Faulkner's body if, as both these "eye-witnesses" testified under oath, he had been fired at repeatedly at point blank range by a shooter straddling Faulkner's prone body, the whole prosecution story of an execution-style slaying of the officer by Abu-Jamal would appear to be a prosecution fabrication, complete with coached, perjured witnesses, undermining the integrity and fairness of the entire trial, as well as the subsequent death sentence.

Told about the results of the their gun test, and asked four questions to explain the lack of photographic evidence or testimony about bullet impact marks in the sidewalk around Faulkner's body, the Philadelphia D.A.'s office offered only a non-response, saying, "The murderer has been represented over the past twenty plus years by a multitude of lawyers, many of whom have closely reviewed the evidence for the sole purpose of finding some basis to overturn the conviction. As you know, none has succeeded, and Mr. Abu-Jamal remains what the evidence proved – a murderer."

Robert R. Bryan, lead attorney for Abu-Jamal, informed of the results of the gun test, and shown a copy of the resulting marks on the concrete, said, "Wow. This is extraordinarily important new evidence that establishes clearly that the prosecutor and the Philadelphia Police Department were engaged in presenting knowingly false testimony to a jury in a case involving the life of my client. The evidence not only demonstrates the falsity of the prosecution's story about how the shooting occurred, and of the effort to portray the shooting to the jury as an execution-style slaying. It raises serious questions as to whether either of the two key witnesses actually were witnesses to the shooting."

Courts – federal and state – have over the years rejected all evidentiary challenges and all but one procedural error in the Abu-Jamal case, despite granting legal relief on the same issues as those raised by Abu-Jamal in dozens of other Pennsylvania murder cases–including a few cases involving the murder of police officers.

In contrast to these consistent court rulings declaring Abu-Jamal's trial to have been fair, the respected organization Amnesty International and other entities and legal experts contend Abu-Jamal did not receive a fair trial in part due to improprieties by police and prosecutors. AI's seminal February 2000 investigative report on this case stated, "The politicization of Mumia Abu-Jamal's case may not only have prejudiced his right to a fair trial, but may now be undermining his right to fair and impartial treatment in the appeal courts."

The Abu-Jamal case, which has garnered international attention, is currently back before the federal Third Circuit Court of Appeals after a remand order by the U.S. Supreme Court to re-examine an earlier ruling eliminating Abu-Jamal's death penalty. It is also back in the news with two new documentary films being premiered this Tuesday (9/21) in Philadelphia–one, *The Barrel of a Gun*, which concludes Abu-Jamal is guilty, and another *Justice on Trial: The Case of Mumia Abu-Jamal*, which argues his innocence.

—*This Can't Be Happening*, September 20, 2010

Mumia Protests in Germany
beginning 1990, going on today - until Mumia is free
Annette & Michael Schiffmann

1990: German editor with Atlantik Verlag Bremen Jürgen Heiser is visiting Mumia Abu-Jamal on death row. That's the beginning of the German Mumia movement. Mumia's first book „... live from death row" is being published in German, followed by „death blossoms".

1999: Two activists in Heidelberg in Germany are preparing for their first Mumia event, handing out information to more than 200 celebrities in and around the cities, including the mayor - and getting their public support - names in the blue square.

The event is well attended, with more than 140 people. That very evening the group Freiheit für Mumia Abu-Jamal Heidelberg is being founded, then the „German Network Against the Death Penalty"

To this day Germany has seen countless actions small and big to support Mumia and demand his freedom.

Berlin, Carnival of Cultures, 2004

All over Germany grops large and small start working for Mumia's freedom.
And most of them begin a growing collaboration, no matter which walks of life and political opinion they are coming from.
Here is just a tiny collection of some of the actions.

House front in Weimar, Eastern Germany, 2002

2004 Heidelberg is staging a big public event against the death penalty in general and Mumia's injust incarderation and always pending execution in particular.

2005-06 Michael Schiffmann is writing his resarch project on Mumia's case, imbedded into the history of black life in the US. The group in Heidelberg is organizing a one year long, very successful reading tour all over Germany, Austria, and Switzerland far into 2007.

Mumia,

we wish you another
50 years
in freedom!

We stay on a move for you
and all the others on
death row.

mit 1 euro
freimachen

Mumia Abu-Jamal
AM-8335

SCI Greene
175 Progress Drive
Waynesburg, PA 15370

USA

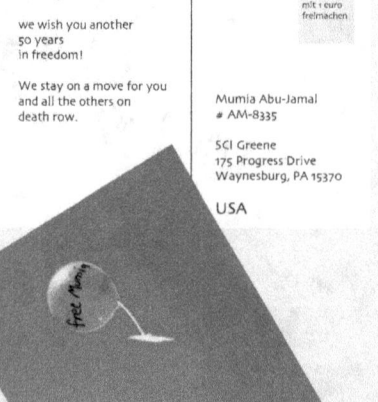

2008-09 series of adversiements in a German liberal newspaper   2007 House in Berlin - one of many!

Netzwerk gegen die Todesstrafe - Network Against The Death Penalty
Haus der Demokratie · Greifswalder Straße 4, 10405 Berlin · GERMANY
0049 - 175 - 844 25 76 · www.hausderdemokratie.de

Supreme Court of the United States
One First Street N.E.
Washington, DC 20543

To the Office of Supreme Court Clerk William K. Suter

for

the Honorable Justices of the United States Supreme Court
Chief Justice John Roberts
Samuel Alito
Stephen Breyer
Ruth Bader Ginsburg
Anthony Kennedy
Antonin Scalia
David Hackett Souter
John Paul Stevens
Clarence Thomas

Berlin, September 21, 2009

Re: Mumia Abu-Jamal v. Jeffrey A. Beard

Dear Clerk William K. Suter,

Herewith we are sending the signatures Nr 4500 - 5000 of the online-petition on behalf of Mr. Mumia Abu-Jamal, and the petition itself.

We would highly appreciate and be very grateful if you could deliver it to all the Justices.

Hoping this is the correct proceedure we remain respectfully,

Sabine Schubert for the German network

Online-Petition on behalf of Mumia Abu-Jamal: www.petitiononline.com/supreme

Bielefeld Germany 2010

Heidelberg 2010 - public event   Happy Birthday Mumia

Heidelberg 2010 - 25 meters of banner

Kaiserslautern - evening event 2010

Frankfurt 2010

Mumia Abu-Jamal, USA
Persecuted author - On death row for nearly 30 years.
We support our colleague.
Free Mumia!
Abolish the death penalty everywhere!
Visit our stand:
LAIKA-Verlag - Hall 3.1 - Stand A 160

Mumia Abu-Jamal is an American citizen, a journalist, a former activist of the Black Panther Party, and the author of six books that have been translated into many languages.

For 30 years, he has lived, in his own ironic words, "in the fastest growing public housing project in America" – the maximum security prisons of the United States – or to be more precise, **on death row in the State of Pennsylvania.**

Arrested in December 1981, he was sentenced to death for the alleged murder of a policeman in July 1982 – by the Albert F. Sabo, a jurist who has sentenced more defendants to death than any other judge in the United States in recent memory and who told his secretary during Abu-Jamal's trial: "Yeah, and I'm going to help them [the prosecution] fry the nigger."

For 30 years, Mumia Abu-Jamal has been fighting for a new trial – and since 30 years, the judicial system has turned him down despite extensive and mounting evidence for his innocence.

His demand for a new trial is supported by amnesty international and countless people worldwide with and without a public name.

His fate is representative for the fate of tens of thousands of other prisoners on death row all over the world, and for the fate of hundreds who are also innocent.

Through his writings and radio columns, he has given a voice to all of them.

Mumia Abu-Jamal - Author & Journalist:
30 Years on Death Row – 30 Years too many!

October 12 to 16 at the Frankfurt Book Fair
Publishers and authors demand the release of Mumia Abu-Jamal and the end of the death penalty

TODAY, Oct. 15: Act-In in front of the Main entrance of the Book Fair
30 Activists in orange prison jump-suits read stories from death row, from the prison-industrial complex, from the courtrooms of the United States and stories about hope against all odds.

JOIN US!

Free Mumia Abu-Jamal!
Abolish the Death Penalty, Is Our Call!

Contact and additional information: www.freiheit-fuer-mumia.de & www.freemumia.com
Write to: Annette Schiffmann - Heidelberg - anna.schiff@t-online.de

Frankfurt Book Fair 2011 READ for MUMIA against the death penalty

BERLIN Rosa Luxemburg Conference 2012: Prof. Johanna Fernandez speaking about Mumia

HEIDELBERG - premiere with the movie we worked together for with Will Francome and Livia Firth

SCI Mahanoy - February 2012 - Dr. Michael Schiffmann - Mumia - Annette Schiffmann - Prof. Linn Washington

★ GENUG IST GENUG ★
FREIHEIT FÜR MUMIA

**DEMO
21.4.2012
BERLIN**

16 UHR
ROSA-LUXEMBURG-PLATZ

ABSCHLUSS
KUNDGEBUNG:
US-BOTSCHAFT

BRANDENBURGER
TOR

GAST AUS
DEN USA:
HAROLD WILSON
"DEM TODESTRAKT
ENTKOMMEN"

BERLIN 2014 - our „Chain gang" & Robert Wilson speaking for Mumia

Time and again: protesting for Mumia in front of the US embassy BERLIN

Prof. Linn Washington in Heidelberg - events with him here plus Frankfurt, Berlin, Tuebingen and Freiburg in 2012 and 2014

Happy Birthday Mumia 2014   Berlin & Heidelberg

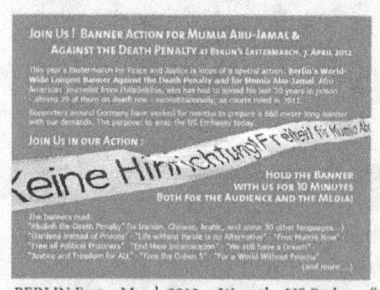

BERLIN Easter March 2013 – „Wrap the US Embassy": 600 meters of banners: Free Mumia - No Death Penalty - Stop Mass Incarceration - Free them All!

Raising awareness in BERLIN 2015 - Mumia is critically ill -DO SOMETHING ABOUT IT !

Action 2015: Postcards for Mumia - in cooperation with Prof. Angela Davis

MOVIES for Mumia - German contributions:

1. Hinter diesen Mauern - Behind these Walls

2. In Prison My Whole Life & organizing a cinema tour in Germany

3. Justice on Trial & event tour in Germany

4. Long Distance Revolutionary & event-and-cinema tour in Germany

All Rosa Luxemburg Conferences in BERLIN since 1999 and counting, until Mumia is free.
With audio messages from Mumia, Video messages from Frances Goldin & Goldie Locks,
with US speakers like Prof. Linn Washington, Mumia's son Jamal Hart, Dan Berger Decarcerate PA, Prof.
Johanna Fernandez, Marylin Zuniga... and guests presenting Mumia's case time and again

And the incredible, exciting story about the discovery of totally unknown photos from the 1981 crime scene

Tainted Evidence and Lying Witnesses

– The Photos in the Mumia Abu-Jamal Case the DA's Office Didn't Want to Know About –

By Michael Schiffmann

An Unexpected Discovery

In 1999, I began research into the case of death row prisoner Mumia Abu-Jamal, sentenced to die in 1982 for the December 1981 shooting death of Police Officer Daniel Faulkner.

Having rolled this work into a highly appraised 2004 Ph.D. thesis, I continued my investigations with a book publication in mind, which materialized when a publisher in Austria got interested and asked me to translate my thesis and whatever new results I had into German.

I had already done most of the work when, in May 2006, I came across a photo of the crime scene on the internet that seemed strange to me because I had not seen them before.

There was no doubt about the photo's authenticity, though.

It clearly showed the battered car of Abu-Jamal's brother whose being stopped by Officer Faulkner had triggered the incident that had led to the officer's death, the whole crime scene including the blood from the slain officer's head all across the sidewalk where he had been shot, as well as a detective investigating the scene.

Despite the apparent triviality of what this new photo showed, I was electrified: The name of the photographer was clearly indicated at the right-hand bottom of the photo, and if he could be found, there was a chance that there would be even more photos showing thing that were less trivial!

A sample of German books on Mumia - translations, a complete edition, the Amnesty Report, own writing...

Mumia Abu-Jamal's Quest for Freedom

This just in: Pennsylvania Supreme Court Puts the Evidentiary Hearing on Hold. Accepts the case under seal and is proceeding in secret!

Pennsylvania Supreme Court 2020

"Justice is being conformable, human and divine; fair, impartial, honest in administering, coordinating and relating with others, no matter what. Not sometimes or most of the time, but at all times be it on trial or appeal."
—Honorable Common Pleas Court Judge Leon Tucker
(when restoring Mumia Abu-Jamal's appellate rights, 3-26-19)

"[T]he Commonwealth does not oppose a remand so that the documents may be presented to the PCRA court.... If the Superior Court granted the remand and if the PCRA court determined that an evidentiary hearing was necessary, the District Attorney's Office plan(s) to present the trial prosecutor, Joseph McGill, Esquire, at that hearing."
—District Attorney of Philadelphia Larry Krasner

Mumia Abu-Jamal is back in court, with a chance for freedom. The Philadelphia District Attorney Larry Krasner agreed with defense counsel this spring that Mumia deserved a new evidentiary hearing based on the revelation of long-suppressed exculpatory evidence. The new documents — buried in the DA's office for 38 years — call into question the entire prosecution case against Mumia Abu-Jamal. Mumia Abu-Jamal's defense attorney Samuel Spital NAACP LDF and Judith Ritter, Esq. and the Philadelphia DA's office have agreed that a remand to hear the new evidence is necessary. This request is pending on appeal before a Superior Court panel. And if successful will be remanded to the Common Pleas court of Philadelphia.

Evidentiary Hearing and New Trial at Stake

Did Assistant District Attorney Joseph McGill actually promise to pay key eyewitness Robert Chobert in cash for his testimony? In a note found in the new files, Chobert demands "his money" from Joe McGill.

Did the prosecution track the race of jurors? The newly released files include a list of potential jurors with notes in the margin indicating the jurors' race. The DA's office has a notorious history of racial bias in jury selection, one only need look at the "Jack McMahon training tapes". See Aug. 19 2020 *Philadelphia*

prisonradio.org

Joseph McGill (Philadelphia ADA on original Abu-Jamal trial) and Maureen Faulkner 4-23-2019 Fraternal Order of Police Lodge Five event

John McNesby, Lodge Five Fraternal Order of Police. 4-23-2019

Voice and John Oliver Aug 2020 news reports. These notes when discussed under oath in court may prove what Mumia's defense has been arguing for 38 years: that the prosecution was racially biased when it struck Black jurors from the case, violating constitutional law under Supreme Court case *Batson v Kentucky.*

Do you see where this train is heading?
Freedom.

"We know that with Larry Krasner as DA we cannot prevent Mumia's release from prison. We are just trying to keep him in prison as long as possible"
—Maureen Faulkner, 4-23-19

But the Fraternal Order of Police (FOP) Lodge Five — Philadelphia's chapter — saw it too. That's why they backed an extraordinary petition by Maureen Faulkner and her attorney George Bochetto asking the Pennsylvania Supreme Court to kick anti-corruption DA Larry Krasner off the case. Because Krasner upheld his oath to turn over exculpatory buried evidence, the FOP wants him gone.

In April 2020, the Pennsylvania Supreme Court reached down from on high and suspended the criminal case. Just stopped it cold. They granted consideration of the Faulkner/Bochetto/FOP-backed Kings Bench extraordinary relief petition. And folks—the process is all under seal. The "special master's report" and the depositions are all being conducted in secret. (Ironically, the seal was at Krasner's request, and was opposed by Bochetto.)

We have to pull back the curtain and look at who is being protected by whom. Larry Krasner ran for Philly D.A. on an anti-corruption platform and was elected by a 74% popular landslide. If the FOP manages to get him kicked off the case, it will be a blow not just to Mumia but to the people of Philadelphia's clear desire to investigate years of illegal conduct by its police officers, former prosecutors and judges.

The ruling from the PA Supreme Court on the King's Bench petition could come down at any time. Join our email listserve for breaking news reports.

Whether the petition is granted or not — whether the prosecution is led by Krasner or Josh Shapiro from the PA Attorney General's office — the new evidentiary hearing and the new trial will not be a cakewalk. Krasner upheld his oath by releasing suppressed evidence, but he's still fighting to uphold all of Philly's old corrupt convictions. It's likely the documents Krasner asked the Supreme Court to put under seal are a pledge that he will work to maintain Mumia's conviction. Stay tuned.

prisonradio.org

PRESS CONFERENCE
FREEDOM & ABOLITION
A CRITICAL MOMENT IN THE FIGHT TO FREE MUMIA ABU-JAMAL

SPEAKERS

- ANGELA DAVIS
- PAM AFRICA
- PROF LINN WASHINGTON, JR
- KWAME AJAMU
- PROF GREGG GONSALVES
- DWAYNE BETTS

MON, NOV 16, 2020
12 PM EST / 9AM PST

REGISTER AT: LINKTR.EE/MUMIA

Co-sponsors: Mobilization 4 Mumia, Black Lives Matter Philadelphia, Black Philly Radical Collective, Black Alliance for Peace, Common Notions Books, Yale Justice Collaboratory, No Cops Union, Yale Green Haven Prison Project, Workers World Party, YLS MLSA, YLS GHJP, NLG, YLS Defender Society, Quinnipiac NLG, Connecticut Bail Fund, YLS Capital Assistance Project, YLS Law and Political Economy, Minority Pre-Law Association (Dartmouth), International Concerned Family & Friends of Mumia Abu-Jamal, FGP, LLSA, JIM

f @MOBILIZATION4MUMIA @BRINGMUMIAHOME

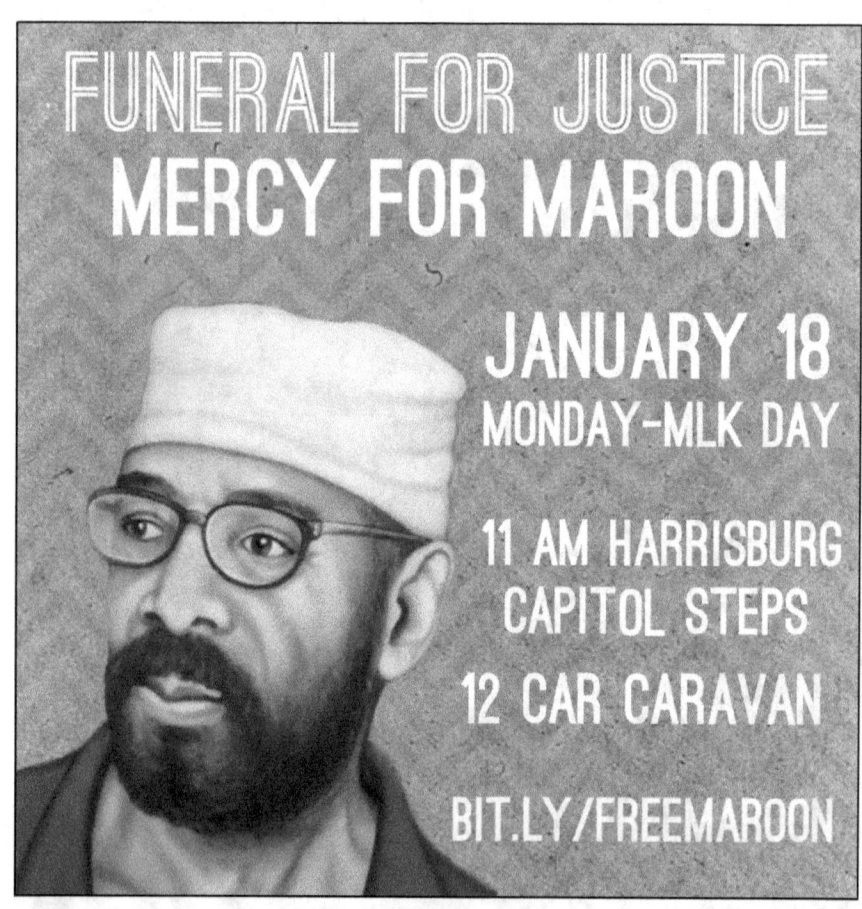

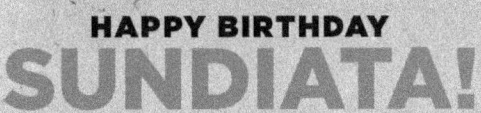

HOW THE INCOMING TIDE FREED MUMIA

JACQUES LEDERER

The author, a fixture of Abu-Jamal protests in Paris. He was part of weekly demonstrations for Abu-Jamal near the U.S. embassy in Paris for at least ten years. Photo by Linn Washington Jr.

How the incoming tide freed Mumia

The sea was very far now, almost invisible, in fact, for Thomas lying flat on his stomach under the beach umbrella, looking at his son Benji galloping towards it a lifebuoy around his waist. A couple of labradors, materialised from out of nowhere, drew immense circles on the sand and their inebriation seemed to have been contagious to the child who, incapable of keeping up with them, ended up however by coming back to his father, breathless, but looking steadfastly at the horizon as if that first attempt at conquest was but put off for the moment. He squatted down, shivering under his bath-towel, looking blankly ahead, musing about what could feed his keen need for possession.

The thought of running as fast, as long as a pair of labradors goading each other on should be discarded, but the idea which suddenly occured to him was a hell of a fantastic idea – and original too!

Thomas lifted an exhausted eyelid and saw his son go back to a place nearby with a spade and a rake, looking very busy, a scene tantamount to twenty minutes' tranquillity – notwithstanding the absence of the pail , which lightly pricked his consciousness before returning to sleep.

Benji stamped the sand to check its consistency and after several tries decided for a spot where it felt both most elastic and most firm. With the handle of his spade he started drawing a rather simple form made up of a number of rectangles fitting together, the greatest of which, containing the others, must have been one hundred square yards large, maybe less. Having done, he abruptly shook his father out fo his siesta:

– Come on, we're going home!

He forced him to rise and briskly took him, not to the car at all, but to where he had been working.

– Look out! Get in through the door! Guess where you stand?

Still unsure of his steps, Thomas staggered around the area, seemingly perplexed and finally slapped his forehead.

– Good gracious! This is the entrance, the lounge, the kitchen, the corridor (a bit swerving, it seems), the closet, the bath-room...

– And here are the toilets, said Benji squatting: This is home, in Paris.

He was laughing like mad at the smallness of the area.

– How is it possible to live in there, he repeated. Look at my bedroom, I kick the ball and it passes right through the wall!

Suiting the action to the word, he kicked the ball in the general direction of the labradors making it evident that an appartment designed for humans is an abode where you can kick the ball away without the referee calling the ball out.

– Pass me the spade.

Thomas walked out of his house through the door, taking care not to slam it and, a little further off, set about tracing a rectangle on tne sand, oh, much smaller, say, the size of his own bath-room.

– You see, this is Mumia's cell.

Once the design of the cot, the table, the washbasin and the toiletseat were traced no room was left.

– Quite impossible, said Benji.

Without waiting for a denial he took the spade from his father's hands and started digging around the cell, hollowing out ditches and with the flat part of his spade packed the dug out sand into low walls. Sitting on the cot Thomas watched him. Four thousand miles away Mumia sat likewise. It was eleven a.m., he had been working for four hours and was indulging in a short break before seeing the guard enter with the lunch-tray. Very likely he was wondering, once more, whether he should absorb that tasteless food laced, he suspected, with psychotropic drugs, or throw away the whole stuff as a starter for a hunger strike. Was he expecting some visit? His lawyer? A parent? Some V;I;P; ? One hour, no more, viciously taken from his personal quota of walking around time. a free hour, fleeing swimmingly, as those in the living world, but which, for that very reason, melted away at full speed, which, you knew it the moment the visitor first appeared, bore within itself its own annihilation, and was therefore a make-believe of the hours the latter was to live the rest of the day. In Human Species, where he narrates his life in a concentration camp, Robert Antelme depicts the haggard vision he had of the piece of bread he was going to pounce upon, which would cease immediately to exist as food to supply him the next day: to eat it or to look at it, you had to choose, and you were denied the choice.

Having finished his work, Benji came back to sit between his father's legs. They were looking at the distant sea, still slack, and at the gulls' tireless whirling flight.
- How can he manage it?

To answer that question is not easy, but Thomas denied himself the shelter of the Inexpressible. That philosophical makeshift, indecent even for grown-ups, becomes unforgivable when one tries to cram it into a eight-year child's head.
- It's a long, endless punishment, he said finally. Take one of these gulls, shut it up in a cage and leave the cage on the beach so that, through the bars, it can see its fellow-seagulls fly about, fish and hop around on the sand.
- But Mumia is not on a beach!
- He is among his memories of sunshine and strong wind. It's the same. For a prisoner memory is like a beach seen through bars; He sees it, smells it, but cannot touch it: it's torture.
- How can he manage, insisted Benji.
- He works, he fights, and Thomas explained what this fight consisted in, how it was possible to resist, by summoning his past life as a militant, for you could not part Man from his ideal. Shutting up his ideal in a separate jail was impossible for the most modern prison and even for the most sophisticated surgery, at most you could knock the prisoner senseless, physically or chemically, make him comatose, but inasmuch as one wanted him to be conscious - and he had to be for the penalty to be felt thoroughly - every time he was awakened his ideal was awakened too: they were one, and that was an unsoluble puzzle for the jailers. Not only had those to put up with an undesirable guest, who spoke loudly, authoritatively, but who, also, introduced a lot of great words: Justice! Freedom!, Truth! And the judges, the policemen, the wardens called him Big Mouth, but however harsh they tried to be, every time he pronounced these words it was as if they found a file in his clothes, a saw-blade under his pallet: the spirit of liberty lived in the prisoner, pushed back his walls, was superactive in his brain - and they were scared, yes, scared stiff. They were scared of the articles, the tracts, the meetings, the demos, the unexpected actions organised on the other side of the ocean, such as putting mourning clothes on the statue of Liberty on Mirabeau Bridge, and it was even laughable to see how a handful of people who had been shouting themselves hoarse, every wednesday, on Place de la Concorde for several years, a handful of peanuts, really, never more than fifty at best, succeeded in scaring the shit out of the whole embassy, which launched forth into angry telephone calls to the headquarters of the police, demanding their arrest, laughable and significant: The American imperialism, the most splendid Tyrannosaurus still alive, incapable of getting rid of a flea! Millions of dollars were spent on building new prisons, prisons which had a sole aim, to put an end to their fear of Blacks, of Indians, of underdogs, of strikers, of the unemployed, but like the ideal, fear did not allow itself to be destroyed. It was part and parcel of the men who had been weak enough to make a pact with it, and it dogged them everywhere, all the time.

All this was not said exactly in these terms: the writer of these lines is no master in the simple art of being understood by children, and, consequently, by grown-ups either, I fear. All the same, after intently listening to his father, Benji remarked:
- Then, if he is not scared, Mumia is better off than a gull.
- He is scared! They want to kill him and he is scared, but not like his jailers and not like the gulls. The jailers' fear is like them, it doesn't amount to much; as for the gull, it dies of fright without knowing what hits it, as, in the like manner, die so many young prisoners, children sometimes, poor little sick ones caught in an incomprehensible machine, not knowing what an ideal is, not even knowing the meaning of the word.
- Me, Benji said abruptly, this afternoon, I mean to have an ideal.

He sat up, put his hand under his brow, visor-like, and scrutinized the horizon:
- You can do what you like, Daddy, but I wont budge from here: not until the sea has freed me.

He looked nasty, the very look he had had, a few years before, when, coming back from nursery school, after a good scolding, he had answered:
— You'd better not, or else I knock your teeth in!
A sentence on hearing which his father had to turn round in order to hide his laughing. This time Thomas did not feel like laughing. The sea was just beginning to set in. It would take four more hours to liberate them, plus two hours to come back: they would not be home before midnight and, whether he phoned or not, there was a row in store for him. To wait such a long time seemed completely unreasonable, but then what would the sermon he had preached him amount to? Thomas opened his mouth wide, then shut it up.

The remaining hours were devoted to looking about for a drink and a nibble, sending off a few calls, trying to read under the last rays of the sun, swimming, wiping himself dry, bathing afresh, running till he was dry again, alone naturally, because, as far as the boy was concerned, he did not move an inch any more, nor unlocked his jaws.

The night, a moon-drenched night, had fallen a long time before the first wavelets set upon the wall behind which Benji waited – Benji and his ideal. The construction was not a fortress and all was done in no time. He had wanted to be left alone for this final instant and, abiding by his decision, Thomas had settled higher up on the dune where, shrinking under a pull-over and smoking a cigarette, he patiently waited for the liberation of his son.

Jacques Lederer
(Translated by Roger Honorat)

2020

A GIANT HAS FALLEN: FRANCES GOLDIN PRESENTE!

NOELLE HANRAHAN

Frances Goldin was ferocious. There is a place on this earth for beautiful, fearless and courageous women. She never once turned her back on a fight. When Robert Moses tried to bulldoze her block in the 50's, the capitalist bully met his match. Frances dove right in and hung on. It took literally 50 years, but her iridescent anger and trenchant love of her friends and her neighborhood saved the East Village of New York City.

Frances and Mumia were made for each other. Brilliant dedicated revolutionary writer on death row meets socialist literary agent and brazen provocateur. What was not to love?

Stephen Vittoria was behind the camera during this interview of Frances for his feature documentary *Mumia: Long Distance Revolutionary* (*www.mumia-themovie.com*).

The transcendent literary career of Mumia Abu-Jamal was built on Frances's belief in his writing, starting with *Live From Death Row*. Mumia got the recognition he deserved, becoming a best-selling author moving beyond pamphlets and protests. With Frances as a lifeline, Mumia garnered an international stage.

Everything begins with a favor. (Although, to hear Terry tell it, it might have been a demand.) In the summer of 1994 I asked Terry Bission to help place *Live From Death Row*, and I asked that he help me find an agent. I knew this book had an audience. It was simply a question of could we reach it. Terry answered that there is one person. And her name is Frances Goldin.

In 1994, NPR's *All Things Considered* had just hired and fired Mumia. Democracy Now was championing him. Mumia's right to speak and the critical value of what he had to say were being hotly contested in the national media and on the Senate floor. It was the perfect time for his first book to be born.

Terry and I traveled to Frances' East Village office/apartment on 11TH St. and made our pitch. She was Frances: bold, brash, and curt. "You do all the prep work and I will write the cover letters and see what happens." Two weeks later Mumia was under contract, had a 30K advance, and a hardcover edition of *Live From Death Row*.

The bond between Mumia and Frances grew. She wrote thousands of letters to him over the last quarter century of her life. Here is just one Frances story: Frances wrote a note on the back of a picture of herself that she sent into the prison. The prison censors went mad. The picture was of Frances, 87, reading a book, nude from the waist up. The picture got Frances banned. Prison Radio launched a campaign on her behalf to reinstate her visiting rights.

It took months of calls and letters, and round after round of with the prison administration, but eventually she was able to visit again. She could now sit side by side with him. Mumia had just gotten off death row and was able for the first time after over 30 years to have regular visits.

I had many visits to Frances' apartment at 305 E. 11TH St. I would stop and bring updates on Mumia's case along with Veniero's cannoli and spumenti.

Thank you, Frances, for championing courageous and moving authors like Mumia, Adrienne Rich, Barbara Kingsolver, and Dorothy Allison Thank you for bringing their words into the world.

One night I was reading a copy of Frances's own book to my son Miles. He reached over and filled in his name. He knew it was for him as well as for me.

Long Live Frances Goldin's spirit and those that dare to follow in her footsteps.

When We Fight, We Win!

THE INVISIBLE SCHOLAR? MUMIA ABU-JAMAL'S IMPACT ON AFRICANA STUDIES

KELLY HARRIS

Mumia Abu-Jamal is rooted in the Black tradition that produced him, [and] he is ready for battle.

—*Cornel West*[205]

When I was asked to write about Mumia Abu-Jamal and his impact on Africana Studies, I struggled in deciding how to approach the topic. Should I talk about what his case represents and how it may have impacted the Africana Studies curriculum? Should I discuss the import of his writings and how it intersects with a variety of movements? After tossing around these ideas, I decided to write about the struggle itself. The arc of Mumia's life encapsulates the story of Black journalism and its impact on serving as a voice for and reporting on Black protest movements; the Counterintelligence program designed to dismantle Black organizations, radical or not; and the Prison Industrial Complex, inclusive of the police and the justice system. As important, Mumia is a recent representative of the organic intellectual tradition, particularly as a historian, that has been invaluable to the formation and development of Africana Studies. Each of these areas are well known and oft-discussed in Africana Studies but rarely serves as key elements in the curriculum of Africana departments. Understanding phenomenon is one thing, and being intentional about teaching it is another. Critically engaging the life and writings of Mumia Abu-Jamal would fill a void in Africana Studies departments.

As a native Philadelphian, it is very easy for me to talk about Mumia Abu-Jamal. Although I was very young when he was arrested in 1982, and for his stint as an on-air journalist for local Black stations (WHAT and

WDAS), I recall hearing him on the radio and my elders being impressed by his melodious voice. But that was it. At least any I was privy to at that age, there was no discussion that considered his politics. There was discussion about MOVE, the 1978 Powelton Village assault, the 1983 Osage avenue bombing, and Frank Rizzo, the racist Mayor and former police commissioner. For some reason, discussing the politics of someone like Mumia was off-limits. This just was not limited to Mumia. My own cousin, Nathan Long, was convicted and sentenced to life for the murder of Daniel Gleason, a Philadelphia police officer. There was zero conversation in my family about Nathan until I did my due diligence detective work as an adult. In like manner, my introduction to Mumia would have to come from the world of Africana Studies.

As I tried to think about discussions of Mumia's case in my African American Studies classes as an undergraduate, I came up empty. My first reaction was, "I must be tripping!" I reached out to my peers who were at Temple University and in African American Studies at the same time as I. To my surprise, no one could recall any discussions about Mumia - at least not in the classroom. However, beyond the classroom, discussions about Mumia were ripe in the activist community. This experience is an apt reminder that if we limit Africana Studies to simply Africana departments, then we are missing the village that Africana Studies encompasses and where Mumia's impact is most evident.

Africana Studies is not and should not simply be relegated to departments at colleges and universities. One could argue that grass-roots organizations and Black bookstores, in many ways, are the blood in the veins of Africana Studies. In Black bookstores in Philadelphia (*Know Thyself Books* and *The Merchant of Alkebulan*), I first encountered Mumia Abu-Jamal . Local study groups, most notably from the All African People's Revolutionary Party, deepened my appreciation for Mumia and attended a meeting of the International Concerned Family and Friends of Mumia Abu-Jamal . These environments provided spaces for studying and critiquing capitalism and the Prison Industrial Complex. More importantly, these spaces understood that learning about Mumia and discussing his case requires one to confront the prison industry, the repression of the police state, and the historic contradictions of capitalism.

Mumia joined the Black Panther Party at the age of 14, and, unbeknownst to him, he was joining an organization that was thoroughly infiltrated by the coercive arms of the state. Not coincidentally, Black Studies, as an academic discipline in universities, was formed during this same period.[206] Importantly, the movement for Black Studies inspired Black social scientists to reject their professional organizations and establish their own. Interestingly, once I finally enrolled at Temple University and majored in Africana Studies, the focus was on African and African diasporan culture from antiquity to the present. Discussions about South Africa, Pan-Africanism, the Black aesthetic, and the like were ever-present. I certainly learned a great deal, but there was a distinct void concerning the Black Radical Tradition, at least for me as an undergraduate.

Joy James raised the question, "what is our relationship to the 'imprisoned intellectual'?" A question that we are forced to confront when interrogating the writings of Mumia. Mumia has served as an authentic organic intellectual contesting the validity and justness of the Prison Industrial Complex. He has achieved this through his many essays in *Live from Death Row, Have Black Lives Ever Mattered, Writing on the Wall: Selected Prison Writings of Mumia Abu-Jamal*, to just name a few.[207] While Joy James is a true activist-scholar in Africana Studies and teaches about incarceration, many Africana Studies departments and programs lack that element. There are a variety of reasons, understaffing, chief among them, certainly being one of the main barriers. But that does not dissolve Africana departments of the responsibility of teaching about incarceration, COINTELPRO, and radical Black journalism.

As we consider the trajectory of Africana Studies, the emergence of Black social science organizations, such as the National Conference of Black Political Scientists, Association of Black Psychologists, Association of Black Social Workers, and the Association of Black Sociologists, have to be interrogated as part of the Black Power/Black Studies zeitgeist. It was during this period, the late '60s to early '70s, that one was most likely to discuss the destructive role of the Federal Bureau of Investigation (FBI) and Black political prisoners. Today that discussion is stronger in activist circles than as constituent elements of the Africana Studies curriculum.

In 1975 the National Conference of Black Political Scientists (NCOBPS) published its first journal. The journal title, reflecting the Black Power/Black Studies zeitgeist, was *The Journal of Political Repression*, which was a joint publication of the NCOBPS and the Commission for Racial Justice (United Church of Christ). The editor of the journal was Mack Jones, founding president of NCOBPS and chair of the political science department at Clark Atlanta University (where Max Stanford of RAM would matriculate as a graduate student). Lewis Myers, movement lawyer and activist, was on the editorial board.[208] In contrast to today, Jones outlines the purpose of *The Journal of Political Repression* in its first issue:

1. To maintain a comprehensive record on both the use of repression against Blacks in the United States and elsewhere, and of reactions to that repression, and
2. To serve as a forum for serious analyses of this repression in all its nuances and dimensions which will help individuals and social formations to understand the relationship between their own biographies and transcendent societal issues. This understanding, in due course, should facilitate the development of incisive prescriptive analyses of what is to be done to move the Black nation from where it is to where we wish to go.[209]

Jones proceeded to discuss a report by Clarence Kelley, director of the FBI in 1974, who acknowledged the formation of COINTELPRO from 1956-1971 against the Communist Party, U.S.A., Socialist Workers Party, White Hate Groups, the New Left, and Black extremists. To be sure, COINTELPRO required serious interrogation by Black social scientists, then and now. Unfortunately, the *Journal of Political Repression* lasted for two volumes. Studying repression was not seen as the best path to tenure (for obvious reasons). The result was that Africana Studies codified in colleges and universities privileged other discussions. There are, of course, outliers and a lot more recent work on the Prison Industrial Complex, the intersections of race class, education related to incarceration. And while much activist work has been done concerning the PIC, particularly around the case of Mumia, Mumia has not been critically studied as a historian in addition to his notoriety as a Prisoner of Conscience.

As an academic discipline in American universities, Africana Studies was birthed in a cauldron of liberation movements, repression, and resistance. If we only took a cursory glance at 1968, one would readily see events worthy of semester-long discussion. Black Studies beginning at San

Francisco State College; Howard University and other HBCUs introducing Gospel Choirs for the first time in their history; the assassination of Dr. King; Tommie Smith and John Carlos protesting at the 1968 Olympics; The Orangeburg massacre where three Black men were killed, and 28 protestors shot; Student protests at campuses across the nation; the Tet offensive; the assassination of Robert Kennedy; and rebellions in over 100 cities in response to the King assassination. 1968 also marks the year Mumia Abu-Jamal joined the Philadelphia chapter of the Black Panther Party. In this manner, Mumia's life represents a perfect case study of the import of the Black Power era and the resulting repression of the police state.

There are many approaches to examining movements, and one way has been to examine an event or era through a participant's life. The lives of Amiri Baraka, Martin Luther King Jr., Malcolm X, Eslanda Robeson, Ella Baker and W.E.B. Du Bois, just to name a few, have all provided grist for expansive biographies by which we can critically examine the civil rights and Black Power movements. The life and writing of Mumia provide an opportunity for scholars in Africana Studies to unpack Black Power and the repressions of Black Power organizations through the lens of a young participant. Mumia's life and work also coincide with the expansion of the prison Industrial Complex. Deindustrialization and repressive conservative government at the local level. While Africana Studies practitioners are familiar with Assata Shakur, George Jackson, Angela Davis, and the Attica Prison rebellion, more work and classes need to be developed deconstructing the post-1968 turn in Black protest movements, the capitalist state, democracy, and the 1970s as a precursor to the Reagan Era.

Where are the voices of the poor, the excluded, the powerless? Absent those voices, absent a recognition of their worth, there can be no true dialogue, and thus no true democracy.

—*Mumia Abu-Jamal*[210]

On June 3, 2020 the statue of Frank Rizzo, former Philadelphia Police Commissioner and Mayor, was removed from City Hall. For years, the legacy of Rizzo loomed large over Philadelphia and has proven to be a contested space. Rizzo not only justified repression – he embraced it with honor and pride. He infamously bragged, "Just wait after November, you'll have a first-row seat because I'm going to make Attila the Hun look like a faggot."[211] This was not empty rhetoric or veiled threats. Under his leadership, the Philadelphia police ran roughshod over the Black community in Philadelphia, particularly its most progressive and revolutionary members. The MOVE Organization, led by John Africa, was the primary target of Mayor Rizzo. However, the assault against MOVE was not an outlier. In response to the protests of the 1960s, Lyndon Johnson and Richard Nixon both embraced repression, under the guise of law and order. Heather Ann Thompson observes that by 1964 federal and state governments "embrace(d) more punitive laws and more aggressive policing."[212] The end result was the dismantling of radical Black organizations, expansion of the prison industrial complex, comingled with deindustrialization, urban blight, and drug epidemic. Scores of Black men, miseducated and undereducated, were shipped off to prisons such as Holmesburg, Graterford, Rikers, Attica, Soledad, Menard, and the like. Mumia would come of age in this atmosphere and honed his journalistic skills documenting the federal assault on Black lives.

In grappling with the significance of any academic discipline, subfield, or topic, one only needs to look at the concepts, terms, and variables being utilized. The prison industrial complex, correctional facilities, rehabilitation, illiteracy and education, brutality, and overcrowding are all intricate components of Mumia's writings. More importantly, the work of Mumia Abu-Jamal highlights at a very personal level the dehumanization perpetrated on incarcerated individuals. The following is a poignant reminder of what is being stripped away behind the wall:

> *In early September 1992, on trial under charges for assault by a life prisoner, a common pleas jury found him not guilty, acquitting him of all charges.... A trial observer said that when the verdict was returned, Brightwell didn't even smile. His mind probably was taken up with a picture of his tormentors, the guards, the well-paid civil servants, who stole all but his very life and who have never been charged with anything.*[213]

It is observations like the above that only Prisoners of Conscience can display. Unfortunately, as forward-thinking as Africana Studies has been, utilizing the work of Mumia and other political prisoners as a means to grapple with the PIC is found wanting. For logical and sound reasons, Africana Studies historically has leaned toward history, psychology, politics, sociology, and the creative and language arts. The failure to prioritize studying the PIC is indicative of understudying the Post-civil rights era.

A cursory glance at texts in Africana Studies—Karenga's *Introduction to Black Studies, Introduction to Africana American Studies: Transdisciplinary Approaches and Implications* by James Stewart and Talmadge Anderson, *Out of the Revolution: The Development of Africana Studies*, edited by Delores P. Aldridge and Carlene Young, *African American Studies Reader* (in two editions) by Nathaniel Norment Jr., and *In the Vineyard: Working in African-American Studies* by Perry Hall—all provide insightful commentaries on the history, paradigms, contours, and epistemologies of Black Studies. But they noticeably overlook the prison industrial complex and fail to interrogate the scholarship of Mumia.[214] And the recent text by Nathaniel Norment Jr., *African American Studies: The Discipline and Its Dimensions*, includes discussion about the prison industry, particularly as it relates to Black males. However, the work of Mumia (nor his case) is not mentioned in any of the texts.

In "What Black Studies is not: Moving from Crisis to Liberation in Africana Intellectual Work," Greg Carr offers a "preliminary" outline of seven areas "to categorize the political impulses of thinkers doing work in the name of Black Studies." Mumia is not listed as an example for any category, though Carr admits that "most of these thinkers, in fact, often spills across categories." While true, that still doesn't solve the problem of where Mumia rests in the Africana Intellectual tradition and if Africana Studies thinkers view him as a part of the tradition. To be fair, Carr comments on "Africana Intellectual Genealogy" and includes "The Black Radical Tradition Approach" as a part of this tradition. He provides examples of representative thinkers, and while Mumia nor the Black Panther Party (Huey Newton or Bobby Seale) are mentioned, one could infer that they would be a part of this tradition. Their absence is curious since Carr begins his work by locating "Africana Studies [as] an academic extension" of the Black Radical Tradition – a tradition that birthed the BPP and Mumia Abu-Jamal.[215] Carr and other Africana Studies scholars undoubtedly embrace the radical roots of their discipline, particularly the role of the Black Panther Party and the Black Power Movement. Student activism is also widely acknowledged and celebrated. However, the experiences of an activist-intellectual such as Mumia, and the context from which he emerged, have not been prioritized in discussions about the history of Africana Studies, conceptual frames of reference, and the future of the discipline.

Abu-Jamal, in many ways, simultaneously extends the tradition of radical Black journalism and socially and politically conscious prison writings while charting new territory in his role as historian, journalist, and his first-person critique of the justice system (in all its aspects) provides a unique lens for interrogating U.S. style democracy, imperialism, state repression, and the like.

To be sure, Mumia's analyses are not run-of-the-mill personal reflections. In *Live from Death Row*, he turns his critical gaze to the most nuanced aspects of the prison industry that only an insider can provide. He reminds us not only of the contradictions and repression embedded in the justice system but of the daily toll being incarcerated has on those imprisoned and their families. One chapter in *Live* describes "Camp Hell" and the inhumane treatment inmates are forced to endure.[216] In what becomes a staple of Mumia's writings, he conceptualizes prisons as criminal enterprises, which is the beauty of his writing. His writing is shorn of the formalities of traditional verbiage of academic writing – in the same manner of Black Studies adherents at its birth.

In *Have Black Lives Ever Mattered?* Mumia offers a trenchant critique of the intersection of race, class, and the PIC:

> *And so the Central Park jogger rape case folds, and it now seems that those boys got raped, by judges, by defense lawyers, by prosecutors, by juries, and by "the white nationalist media," to quote Black novelist Ishmael Reed. The very media that sensationalized and demonized the boys 13 years ago and sold ad space to call for their deaths now make new millions off their exoneration.*[217]

The above quote encapsulates what is often missed about Mumia. Admittedly I have been guilty of reducing him to being a political prisoner and to his critiques of the prison industrial complex. Nevertheless, he is a journalist who was elected as the president of the Association of Black Journalists of Philadelphia (now known as the Philadelphia Association of

Black Journalists) in 1981 – a year before his conviction. His writings always highlight the duplicitous role and function of the media (print and broadcast) in maintaining a white nationalist status quo. While Africana Studies often locates the role of COINTELPRO in negating the Black Power Movement (correctly, I might add), Mumia examines how the profit motive, media, the prison industrial complex, and the coercive arms of the state function as interlocking oppressive forces. Crucially, he shares with readers in his essays and his longer historical works that Geronimo Ji-Jagga, Russell "Maroon" Shoatz, Lynne Stewart, John Africa, MOVE, and other activists and organizations were and are victimized by these interlocking forces. What he produces is not only worthy of study but status as required study for Africana Studies.

The 1972 National Black Political Convention that was held in Gary, Indiana (Gary Convention for short) is often discussed in Africana Studies.[218] The convention represents a watershed moment in African American history that is illustrative of a thrust in the Black liberation struggle to unify around common goals. Less discussed is the 1970 Revolutionary People's Constitutional Convention (RPCC) in Philadelphia that was organized by the Black Panther Party. As David Hillard does in *This Side of Glory*, Mumia offers his first-person account of the RPCC. The RPCC was intended to be a springboard for a multi-racial coalition inclusive of the Gay rights movement, Women's movement, and a variety of other progressive forces. Mumia locates a source of tension that is instructive for understanding why this moment is not often discussed in Africana Studies:

> *The Revolutionary People's Constitutional Convention manifested a distinct tendency within the BPP that distinguished it from its contemporaries and left it, especially within nationalist circles, subject to some criticism. The very framework of the RPCC conflicted with the norm of the more insular nationalist groups of the era. This meant that although the Black Panther Party did not have non-Blacks in its ranks, it did think about and act upon the idea that coalitions across lines of race and ethnicity could prove effective in reaching broader segments of the U.S. and global polity.*[219]

Mumia offered that the failure of the 1970 was more a "a failure of the movement entire" than it was simply of the BPP. The fact that Mumia, as a teenager in the BPP, was a part of this movement at a time when the Black Studies community was expanding (i.e., Institute of the Black World and various groupings) is an important moment to consider.

A little more than fifty years in, the history of the development of Africana Studies has only begun to be written and assessed. It is important to note that it matches the trajectory of Mumia's whole life. He will be accepted into the canon—once the canon catches up to his life and work. That is inevitable because his lifetime of activist and intellectual work will make it irresistible to those Africana scholars looking for organic, radical thought and action. As the discipline grapples with the recent discussions around "racial capitalism," revisiting the works of Harry Haywood, Oliver Cox, Claudia Jones, Cedric Robinson, and the like will be given much attention. Africana Studies scholars would be remiss if they do not calculate the work of Mumia Abu-Jamal into their assessments. In many ways, his life and work are a fitting coda to the first 50-plus years of Black Studies in higher education.

MUMIA SPEAKS

Heartened by Black Lives Matter, imprisoned activist Mumia Abu-Jamal is still fighting the good fight—which now includes a deadly pandemic

KEVIN L. CLARK[220]

We are living in unprecedented times, and Black Americans are feeling it. From the numerous killings of unarmed men, women and children by the police to the White House's failed response to the coronavirus pandemic to violent retaliations by rogue "vigilantes" who infiltrate Black Lives Matter protests, recent events have offered and unending display of how deeply entrenched in the country's social, economic and healthcare systems racism truly is.

Some of the most vulnerable persons affected by the coronavirus crisis reside in jails, prisons and other detention centers across the country. According to a continually updated New York Times study, those places account for the top ten COVID-19 clusters in America. And as cases among the incarcerated climb, prison systems refuse to collect or disclose race data. Without those numbers, public health experts, community organizations and Black families of the imprisoned have an incomplete understanding of the racial disparities in the coronavirus cases that occur behind bars. The dearth of information also limits the effectiveness of health practitioners' responses.

By exposing the huge inconsistencies in health care access for all Americans, COVID-19 has placed the U.S. at the center of a long-overdue conversation. Yet a recent report by the Marshall Project noted that when prison officials from all fifty states and the federal government were asked for the races of the people tested for, diagnosed with or killed by COVID-19, forty-three prison agencies, including the Federal Bureau of Prisons, would not provide the information.

The lack of data is deadly. The coronavirus claimed nearly 200,000 American lives through August 25, 2020—that's an average of about 1,100 deaths *per day.* "There is a bottleneck happening," says Barun Mathema, an epidemiologist at Columbia University. "People of color are being incarcerated at a far higher rate than their counterparts, while neighborhoods that are economically or politically disenfranchised [also] have an accumulation," of health factors that make them more vulnerable to COVID-19.

With their overcrowding and unsanitary conditions, prisons have inflamed the spread of the coronavirus. According to the NAACP Criminal Justice Fact Sheet, Black people are locked up at more than five times the rates of whites, which, when compounded with the systemic racism, makes tackling the coronavirus pandemic a particularly difficult problem to solve.

Mumia Abu-Jamal has an inside perspective on how the pandemic and White terrorism has affected the Black community. The 66-year-old political activist and respected journalist has been incarcerated since his 1982 conviction for killing Philadelphia police officer Daniel Faulkner in a polarizing, racially-charged case. In 2011, prosecutors withdrew the execution case against him because of flawed jury instructions—and in 2018, Philadelphia Common Pleas Judge Leon Tucker reinstated Abu-Jamal's appeal rights. "This is an unheard of legal victory," said Rachel Wolkenstein, a supporter and former Abu-Jamal lawyer.

After spending 39 years in prison—on Death Row since his 1983 sentencing and in general population since 2011, when his sentence was changed to life imprisonment—Abu-Jamal continues to maintain his innocence as he and his attorneys pursue a new review of his case. Over two weeks, he talked with ESSENCE from Pennsylvania's State Correctional Institution Mahanoy about the impact and growth of Black Lives Matter, the organization's character and mission, and how COVID-19 has affected the prison community.

ESSENCE: Black Lives Matter has galvanized the world to address systemic racism and police brutality in this country. What are your thoughts on the movement and how this period will look through the lens of history?

ABU-JAMAL: What I've learned is that the Black Lives Matter has a very keen sense of history. Most of the members are students, I believe. They are certainly reading all the key works, and it shows that they are diligent about making change. Shortly after their emergence around the time of Ferguson, when it became the Movement for Black Lives, they came out with a policy paper that stated their position on various issues of importance to the African-American community. When I read it, I was struck by it. Why? Because it was so similar, not in tone then certainly in spirit, to the Ten-Point Program and Platform of the Black Panther Party.

I don't think that is coincidence. Black Lives Matter members read and studied and took what was valuable from the past and utilized it in their own way. They are not the Black Panther Party, despite what Rudy Giuliani has said publicly. White paranoia and fear have governed his thinking, but Black Lives Matter activists are very informed on the Black Freedom struggle. They arrived at it in light of their own experiences and understanding and belief about what this moment demands.

ESSENCE: As a former member of the Black Panther Party, you've witnessed how different sides of an agenda can react when face to face. With all that's going on outside—from the NFAC [Not F**king Around Coalition] to white militias like the Boogaloo Bois and the 3 Percenters—are we sitting on a powder keg while marching in nonviolent protest? Is there a way to navigate around such a threat?

ABU-JAMAL: The short answer is yes. Yes, there is a powder keg and it has been there for a long time. But the question is, how do you respond to the present threats, to the well-being and safety of the Black community? Young Black people are going to have to answer that, because they're the ones who are going to encounter it head-on.

Speaking of the Black Panther Party, we used to talk about fascism in America. Recently I've come to the understanding that all of us where born in what could be called a protofascist era. After Reconstruction, White power was seized by American fascists, who consciously stripped Black people of political power, of the ability to vote. Proof of that is full voting rights didn't become a reality for African Americans until the sixties. Despite that 100-year period after the Civil War, what is written into constitutions and what is lived in the streets of the country are often two very different things. What does that say about a country that can ignore its constitution for a century? Fascism is an American thing, like the Ku

Klux Klan is an American thing, like the White Citizens' Council was an American thing.

We have to think in those terms. It expands our understanding of what it means to be in this country and what White supremacy really, really means. Once that understanding circulates through the atmosphere, people get new ideas about what's possible and respond with new challenges to the white state.

ESSENCE: We know racial biases affect medical care, whether we are inside or outside of prison. For starters, how is your health. What about the health of your fellow inmates? Is Mahanoy Correctional observing a particular guideline throughout this COVID-19 pandemic?

ABU-JAMAL: Every jail is different. Every prison is different—but it's also the same. What the state has elected to do in Mahanoy Correctional is require every guy to wear a mask when he leaves his cell. Moving throughout the jail has been cut down very, very stringently. Let's say the chow [lunchroom] is on the first tier, which would have maybe 25 people. But then you go to the yard, and the number of people there is similar.

The population is cut down and quartered so much that there isn't mass movement. Coming from Death Row to Gen Pop, I remember looking at all the people and thinking of the Congo River or the Mississippi—except it was a sea of guys wearing their coca brown uniforms. You don't see that kind of movement now. And although everyone is required to wear a mask, I see [at the time of this interview] about a half-dozen guys who are not wearing their masks even though it is required to do so.

This is prison, so people find it necessary to respond in ways they find comfortable. There are some jails, like SCI-Phoenix and SCI-Huntington in Pennsylvania, where the death counts related to COVID are excessively high. But this has not been one of those jails.

ESSENCE: Black inmates are testing positive for COVID-19 at a higher rate than White inmates, according to *The New York Times*—which can leave many frightened and frustrated, because there's no way to social distance in an overcrowded community. Is the prison health care system equipped to fight a pandemic that places large groups of people at risk?

ABU-JAMAL: Sadly, the health care system in prison mirrors the one in society. That is to say, both systems are insufficient for the task. The prison system is woefully inefficient, and therefore we get a devalued system that prioritizes private profit over the health of the imprisoned. I know of this firsthand. I was blessed to have a group of people who cared for me and a young lawyer who was aggressive and fought with us, for us. Absent these two elements, I might not be here to be able to talk to you today, because of my own health crisis. *[Essence Editor's Note: Mumia Abu-Jamal was diagnosed with Hepatitis C in 2012 and spent five years fighting for access to treatment. In July 2019, a federal appeals court upheld his right to sue corrections-department employees for denying him access to lifesaving medications.]*

The racial rifts in American society are hidden and silent during regular times. The same thing may be said of the prison system, except there are no regular times. At all times, the health of the imprisoned is secondary or tertiary. The health of the bottom line to the private corporations that "provide health care" is most important—and COVID-19 really makes that clearer and clearer. In a way, just how these 50 states have 50 different systems, the 30-odd prisons in Pennsylvania have 30-odd different systems because they have different leadership—and are all fractured.

ESSENCE: Elaborate on that, because given this high-risk population and how quickly the coronavirus can spread behind bars, Black and Brown inmates are incredibly vulnerable to this deadly virus.

ABU-JAMAL: In California, I have heard about the warden there in Chino—how they have been sending infected inmates into San Quentin, which really caused an explosion of cases, deaths and sickness. The way the media spins it, it is saying that some people consciously want the virus because they think that is the way out to freedom.

ESSENCE: Do you feel that access to noncontact visitation, certain essential equipment like PPE or free medical visitation by doctors is happening and available where you are?

ABU-JAMAL: Funny you should ask—no. I just came from the infirmary and they were wearing masks cloth masks that are similar to the inmates', which are made of cotton and have an extension you can tie around your head or your neck. There's no special equipment, but again, this is an infirmary, not a hospital. I am looking at two guys right now across the way from me who have masks slid down around their necks; their whole mouths and noses are visible.

ESSENCE: In your book *Have Black Lives Ever Mattered?*, you demonstrate how how white police killings of Black people are not a case of " bad apples" on the police force but a continuation of slavery and the systematic consequences of structural racism. With that said, how do you see the Black Lives Matter movement handling the upcoming challenges, here and abroad?

ABU-JAMAL: I am moved by the reach and depth of this Black Lives Matter movement. I wrote that book as a reflection and tribute to it. I find it a remarkable, brilliant and deeply caring group of young people. I love the people. I think of them as I do [celebrated author and political philosopher] Frantz Fanon, who said, "Each generation must discover its mission and fulfill it or betray it." This generation has been impressive, and I depart from those of my generation by really looking at them with empathy and affection. My generation were the bad boys and girls of the party. Black Lives Matter members are not like that. Instead they are attacking the systemic problems that have not been attacked, with that kind of precise focus from prior generations. I love them!

"THE POWER OF TRUTH IS FINAL"

Publisher's Note for Vol. 3 of Abu-Jamal and Stephen Vittoria's Murder, Incorporated[221]

JENNIFER BLACK AND MIRANDA HANRAHAN BEACH

"Conventional wisdom would have us believe that it is insane to resist this, the mightiest of empires, but what history really shows is that today's empire is tomorrow's ashes; that nothing lasts forever, and that to not resist is to acquiesce in your own oppression. The greatest form of sanity that anyone can exercise is to resist that force that is trying to repress, oppress, and fight down the human spirit."—Mumia Abu-Jamal

As we witness everyday, the brave truth-tellers of the current age are ridiculed, scorned, and marginalized as 'raving lunatics.' Some are eliminated. When the Empire is questioned or undressed, the noise machine beholden to the elite cries 'conspiracy theorist... traitor... apostate'—all of which quickly smears and deprecates this newly crowned 'public enemy,' one who is unafraid to speak the unspeakable truth —Stephen Vittoria

Mumia Abu-Jamal once famously opined, "The state would rather give me an Uzi than a microphone." More than five decades of intense surveillance, harassment, confinement, repression, and torture levelled against him by Frank Rizzo's Philadelphia Police Department, the Federal Bureau of Investigation, and the Pennsylvania Department of Corrections, have graphically illustrated the truth of those words.

The United States government is terrified of what Mumia has to say. And with good reason. See, there is a reason slaves were never supposed to learn to read or write. A reason prisoners are best kept muted, retained hidden behind walls, unheeded. People like us are not supposed to tell these troublesome truths. The truth, Ramona Africa reminds us, is always dangerous to those pushing the lie.

Mumia tells the truth.

He has always told the truth, and he does it again here, writing alongside Stephen Vittoria in this third and final installment of their magnum opus *Murder, Incorporated*.

These three books—*Dreaming of Empire, America's Favorite Pastime, and Perfecting Tyranny*—deconstruct and lay bare the United States experiment in imperialism. Written by a captive rebel living under the hostile eye of the state, this historical trilogy exposes the continuous and deadly hypocrisy of empire.

Murder, Incorporated builds on the work of Howard Zinn's manifesto *A People's History of the United States*. This work aims to expand the telling of the story of the United States from the front-line perspective of those dispossessed and discarded by the treachery of U.S. imperialist expansion.

It is important to recognize and respect the conditions under which this opus was written. Unlike other twenty-first century scholars, Mumia writes, researches, and publishes having no contact to a university library and no access to the Internet. He has never surfed the world wide web and has no quick access to books, essays, journal articles, or interview subjects. He is only permitted to have seven books in his cell at a time; any more than that are considered contraband.

In researching *Murder, Incorporated,* Mumia had to constantly cull his stash of written material, absorbing all he could from each book before getting rid of it to make space for a new one. As has been his process since he first started publishing from prison, he took precise, careful, and scrupulously detailed notes of every book and article he read, along with page numbers and citation information. He wrote as small as possible, to fit as much material as he could into his limited number of notebooks.

At what other time and place has a history of this scope—a thoroughly detailed overview of a nation's crimes of colonization from its inception to the present day—been crafted under such draconian measures? When has such a record of the crimes of a state been created by one of the state's own victims, with every word penned under the state's pretense of control?

Consider the barriers placed in the way of Abu-Jamal's and Vittoria's intellectual collaboration. Mumia's access to visitation is strictly limited, and he can only speak on the telephone for fifteen minutes at a time, once a day. Just one fifteen-minute call, if he can get the guard to put in a slip for it. He is permitted two visits a week, to which he cannot bring even a pencil or piece of paper. He endures a full-body cavity strip search before and after every visit. For nearly a decade he was denied visits and phone calls. For two decades, and the first nine of his books, he wrote everything by hand with the mere cartridge of a ballpoint pen.

All visits are supervised, all phone calls recorded and surveilled, and all his mail is read by prison staff. Letters, books, or papers deemed "inappropriate" by the mailroom censors are discarded before they reach him.

In order to build the intellectual partnership that created *Murder, Incorporated,* Vittoria and Abu-Jamal had to overcome the state's exhaustive efforts to limit Mumia's contact with the outside world. These are some of the constraints under which *Murder, Incorporated* was researched and written. Abu-Jamal and Vittoria's success is a testimony to their will, determination, and bond as writing partners.

The book you hold in your hands today is an act of protest and dissent. Its very existence defies the repression of the state. So does its content. While *Murder, Incorporated* can and should be used in the polished hallways of academia, it is deeply rooted in the proud tradition of American protest literature.

Vittoria and Abu-Jamal seek to advance the interests of the exploited, evicted, imprisoned, and marginalized working class people by telling a history that does not flinch from the truth.

In this project, *Murder, Incorporated* positions itself alongside Eduardo Galeano's *Open Veins of Latin America,* Vincent Harding's *There is a River,* and Robert Fisk's *The Great War for Civilisation* by embracing the historic imperative of truth telling. Like those great works, *Murder, Incorporated* makes an intergenerationally significant contribution to the bank of historical political thought and social movement theory.

It is no accident that *Murder, Incorporated* was co-written by a man in prison, a man who has spent the lion's share of his life on death row. Scholar Joy James suggests that prisons function as political and intellectual sites that are largely hidden from our mainstream discourse. Those warehoused within write with "unique and controversial insights into idealism, warfare, and social justice."

Thus, the prisoner, who is denied access to any of the privileges and protections afforded to citizens of the state, who is subjected instead to indignity and deprivations, is uniquely empowered to criticize the state. Moreover, because the prison writer typically has no access to editors or publishers, and writes with no expectation of receiving remuneration from their writing, they are able to write what they know to be true. Their words are uncompromised.

In this regard the prisoner is free in a way that no one else is free. Mumia has nothing to lose from telling the truth. The state has already done everything in its power to silence him. There are no remaining threats that can be leveled against him. There is no tactic of abuse or control left in the state's arsenal that it not already been inflicted on him. He has withstood beatings, torture, and near-fatal gunshot wounds.

From the time he was fourteen years old, working as a young organizer for the Black Panther Party, he had already earned security index status from J. Edgar Hoover's FBI. He spent his teen years and early twenties under unyielding police surveillance and harassment.

Since his arrest and framing in 1981, he has weathered forty years of incarceration—separated from friends, family, and community. Twenty-eight of those years he spent in solitary confinement with a pending execution.

He survived two death warrants, each of which gave him thirty days to live. He survived a life threatening battle with complications from Hepatitis C, dragging himself back from the brink of death after the prison's vicious and deliberate medical neglect sent him into a coma.

He won court battles to overturn laws written and passed by the Pennsylvania legislature with the express specific purpose of forbidding him from publishing his writing. Censorship was discussed at the federal level, on the Senate floor. None of it has stopped him.

He is perhaps the world's most prolific imprisoned radical. *Perfecting Tyranny* is his twelfth published book, and he has authored thousands of radio commentaries.

Within a month after being shot and arrested in 1981, he was writing essays from Holmesburg Prison. When warrants were issued for his death in 1995 and 1999 while he sat awaiting execution, Mumia still continued to write. Recovering from near death in the prison infirmary in 2015, Mumia continued to write. And why not?

The state has already made up its mind to kill him. He is alive because he, and the movement behind him, have fought the state at every turn, sometimes winning extraordinary victories—like the overturning of his death sentence—and sometimes grinding into a bitter stalemate, but never giving up ground. The state has not refrained from killing Mumia: it has failed to kill Mumia. What possible incentive could he have to flinch from the truth?

Given the forces arrayed against Mumia, it may appear as a miracle that this book—or any of Mumia's eleven previous books—was published at all. It was no miracle. It was the hard work of a movement.

Mumia's relentless courage and resilience, and Stephen Vittoria's triumphant accompaniment, created an intellectual bond that would not be denied. This, combined with the dedication and unswerving solidarity of hundreds of thousands of activists and artists and lawyers across the country and the globe, have forced this book through the bars of the prison into printing presses and into bookstores.

This book is a reminder of our individual and collective power. The great Howard Zinn once remarked that to be hopeful in catastrophic times is not naive. Rather, it reflects an understanding that history is as much about courage and sacrifice as it is about cruelty. Abu-Jamal and Vittoria teach us the same lesson.

Mumia Abu-Jamal, relegated to a carceral underworld, has funneled his harrowing experience of captivity into an extraordinary act of truth-telling that benefits our common survival.

Stephen Vittoria imparts his searing analysis, poignant honesty, and tremendous tenacity to craft this labor of courage and love and get it past the censors so that this vital work could be in our hands.

Mumia cautions us to remember that "What history really shows us is that today's empire is tomorrow's ashes, that nothing lasts forever." It is humbling to be taught this lesson from one of our nation's most famous political prisoners, who is also a scholar, a revolutionary, and an educator.

A gift to us, and a labor of love, this final book in the remarkable trilogy *Murder, Incorporated* is the result of unwavering and courageous commitment. It elevates our human spirits and encourages us to have full faith in our ability to change the world.

Again we recall the wisdom of Ramona Africa: the truth is dangerous to those whose power depends on the lie. This book is dangerous. This is why slaves were never taught to write. This is what happens when prisoners contribute to the bank of political thought.

Empires hold their power through the silence of their victims; by breaking that silence, Mumia deals a devastating blow to the empire that cages him. *Murder, Incorporated* exposes all the dirty, vulgar, shameful actions of the United States—hundreds of pages of the state's blunt secrets revealed, exposing the continuous and deadly hypocrisy of the empire.

This historic collaboration between Stephen Vittoria and Mumia Abu-Jamal stands amid the pantheon of social dissent against tyranny and despotism. Its hope and optimism stand as testimony to the unstoppable resilience of the human spirit.

POST-SCRIPT

An Open Letter to Pennsylvania Governor Tom Wolf

Your Honor, Governor Tom Wolf,
Mumia Abu-Jamal is not well.
But is that surprising given the policy of the Pennsylvania Department of Corrections to keep shifting contaminated prisoners from facility to facility, to leave natural disaster Centers empty and to keep testing for guards on a voluntary basis even though they are the ones who bring in the virus?

Mumia is not well—nor are many others like him who are elders with comorbidities and are susceptible to COVID-19.

But what is being done about it? We, his friends, his supporters, upholders of human rights, his family, we wait.

We thought, we hoped Thanksgiving would be the time to announce the compassionate release of all those who like Mumia ... But Thanksgiving has come and gone—and silence.

Mumia is not well.

On the rare two-minute phone calls he can get out to his loved ones from his reinforced lockdown at SCI Mahanoy, he lets them know his whole body is itching and all he can do is to cover himself with vaseline to calm the fire, that he is blowing up ...

Mumia is unwell and could catch the virus at any moment.

When his spokesperson asks him what he does to protect himself, he replies that he does have his green tea but that's all.

Mumia is at high risk.

His prison has now stopped issuing reports on the number of infections and that is felt to be a sign of mounting chaos.

Mumia could at any second ... even as I write ...

If I may be allowed, Governor Wolf, you are at a historical crossroads.

Pennsylvania is the State that has tipped the electoral scales away from Trump but the analysis is still not sufficiently made that this victory was born of decades of grassroot organizing with many, many human, social justice and prison rights activists to thank - the Mumia generations.

Governor Wolf, your D.A. in Philadelphia, Larry Krasner, has launched a "Truth and Justice" Commission based on the revered "Truth and Reconciliation Commission" that the late President Mandela asked Archbishop Desmond Tutu to set up. By the way both Mr Mandela and Desmond Tutu called for Mumia's right to a fair trial.

The thing to bear in mind here is that the Truth and Reconciliation concept was the brainchild of a former political prisoner, Nelson Mandela.

Mumia Abu-Jamal is our Nelson Mandela.

Would Larry Krasner and you wish to wait for a grassroot liberation movement to secure Mumia's release - as it once did for Mandela?

We are aghast at the number of homicides by shooting in Pennsylvania (up by 40% as compared to last year). But our attention is drawn in particular by the deadly, daily shootings of your youth.

Just one tip-of-the-iceberg example from yesterday, December 4TH, when yet another teen was shot down in Philly. The statistics are over 100 children shot down so far this year. If they are not shot by bullets they are grabbed and used for photographic PR stunts to prove that a discredited police force serves and protects against the "anarchy of chaos."

So there is anger.

What is it these bullets are saying that those in your streets are afraid to voice?

I submit to you that your streets, your youth may be calling out for the very leadership that your police and criminal justice system is maintaining behind bars.

Your police departments offer thousands of dollars of rewards for information on the perpetrators - but since when does money or deals buy the Truth?

The truth is that your streets want their elders back - those who they would accept sane guidance from in the spirit of the African culture we former slaves spring from.

Those elders are today behind your bars at imminent, forefront risk.

Mumia Abu-Jamal's dream would be to open a school and teach. He has written twelve books from his cell, has just finished a trilogy and is soon to have a Ph.D.

Major Tillery, with the blessings of Superintendent Kenneth Eason, has opened and successfully animates a Center for Elders in his Prison.

These and others are role models who could bring amazing grace and spirit back to your war zone streets but you would choose to allow them both—the children and the elders–to die?

How will those very streets react if the news reaches them that Mumia and other lost leaders have tested positive in your jails?

Yours Sincerely,
JULIA WRIGHT
December 5, 2020

ABOUT THE CONTRIBUTORS

ANNETTE SCHIFFMANN is an anti-imperialist activist and photographer from Germany.

KELLY HARRIS, Ph.D., is the Director of the Africana Studies program at Seton Hall University.

ZAYID MUHAMMAD is a humanitarian and an activist with a public commitment of over 35 years! Mentored by the late poetry legends Jayne Cortez and Amiri Baraka, he is considered a People's Artist in their tradition. He is a serious jazz poet and a community-based stage actor.

DAVE LINDORFF is a 2019 winner of an "Izzy" Award for "Outstanding Independent Journalism" from the Ithaca College Park Center for Independent Media. A 1995 graduate of the Columbia University Graduate School of Journalism, he is also the author of the ground-breaking book *Killing Time: An Investigation into the Death-Row Case of Mumia Abu-Jamal* (Common Courage Press, 2003). He is the founding editor of the award-winning collectively-run news site *ThisCantBeHappening.net*.

JULIA WRIGHT is an internationally recognized activist and writer in the tradition of her father, Richard Wright. She wrote the preface to Abu-Jamal's *Death Blossoms: Reflections of a Prisoner of Conscience*. Based in France, she has lobbied for Abu-Jamal across the world and via the United Nations.

COLIN KAEPERNICK is an internationally known human rights activist who lost millions of dollars when he was ousted from the National Football League for his activism.

SANTIAGO ALVAREZ is a student-activist at the University of California at Santa Cruz. He was among many who were instrumental in the

2021 organizing of Abu-Jamal activists after Abu-Jamal got COVID. He helped design many of the flyers in this book.

MICHAEL SCHIFFMANN, PH.D., is an author, translator, professor and scholar in Germany. He is the author of the political biography *Race Against Death: Mumia Abu-Jamal, A Black Revolutionary in White America*, one of the first studies of Abu-Jamal's life and case. He is also an anti-imperialist organizer and has protested for Mumia there for decades.

REGINALD SCHELL (1941-2012) was Defense Captain of the Philadelphia Branch of the Black Panther Party. He was the founder of the Black United Liberation Front, also based in Philadelphia.

DANIEL P. BLANK is the Senior Litigator at the Federal Public Defender for the Northern District of California, where he has tried felony cases for indigent clients since 1999. He also teaches Trial Advocacy at the University of California Hastings College of the Law.

DICK CLUSTER is a writer and translator based in Oakland, California. His original work includes a detective novel series and (with co-author Rafael Hernández) *The History of Havana*, a social history of the Cuban capital. His recent translations include Gabriela Alemán's novel *Poso Wells* and Paula Abramo's poetry book *Fiat Lux*.

JACQUES LEDERER is a French writer and a fixture of Abu-Jamal weekly protests in Paris for at least a decade, starting in the 1990s.

LINN WASHINGTON, JR. is a professor of journalism at Temple University in Philadelphia, Pa. His friendship with Abu-Jamal goes back to their days of being fellow reporters in Philadelphia in the 1970s, and he has written scores of news and opinion articles for four decades about the injustices surrounding Abu-Jamal's case. In addition to journalism, his professional career has included service as Special Assistant to the Chief Justice of the Supreme Court of Pennsylvania. A graduate of the Yale Law Journalism Fellowship Program, he earned a Master in the Study of Law from the Yale Law School.

JOE DAVIDSON was incoming president of the Association of Black Journalists in Philadelphia when Abu-Jamal, the outgoing president, was arrested in 1981. In 1995, he wrote the only major magazine cover story ever produced about Mumia Abu-Jamal for *Emerge* magazine. Davidson is a co-founder of the National Association of Black Journalists.

PAM AFRICA is the Minister of Confrontation for the MOVE Organization. For the past 40 years, she has been instrumental in the movements to free the MOVE 9 and for Mumia Abu-Jamal. An internationally recognized progressive activist, she coordinates the International Concerned Family and Friends of Mumia Abu-Jamal and the revived and online Jamal Journal news source.

ANGELA Y. DAVIS is known internationally for her ongoing work to combat all forms of oppression in the U.S. and abroad. Over the years, she has been active as a student, teacher, writer, scholar, and activist/organizer. She is a living witness to the historical struggles of the contemporary era, from her comrade, imprisoned writer George Jackson in 1970, to imprisoned writer Mumia Abu-Jamal in 2021.

NOELLE HANRAHAN, ESQ., a journalist, lawyer and private investigator, is the founder and director of Prison Radio, a nonprofit journalism organization that is more than 30 years old. A former Pacifica Radio producer and host, she has recorded hundreds of interviews with and commentaries by prisoners across the United States for radio, television and film. She has a B.A. from Stanford University, and an M.A. in Criminal Justice from Boston University. She passed the Pennsylvania Bar in 2001, and received her law degree from Rutgers Law School in 2020.

JOHANNA FERNANDEZ, PH.D., is a professor of history at Baruch College of the City University of New York. She is the author of *The Young Lords: A Radical History* and editor of *Writing on the Wall: Selected Prison Writings of Mumia Abu-Jamal*.

JENNIFER BLACK is a researcher at Prison Radio.

MIRANDA HANRAHAN BEACH is a staffer at Prison Radio.

MUMIA ABU-JAMAL, M.A. is an internationally known author of more than ten books of commentary and history. He recently published *Murder, Incorporated*, a comprehensive three-volume historical meditation about the American empire with his co-author, documentary filmmaker Stephen Vittoria. He is taking graduate studies at the University of California, Santa Cruz, for a Ph.D.

KEVIN L. CLARK is a Brooklyn-based writer.

YAHNÉ NDGO is a singer and writer. She is Chief Visionary Officer of Deep Blu Womyn Company (www.bluwomyn.com), an activist/organizing/training group. She is also an active member of Black Lives Matter Philly and the Outreach Coordinator and a member of the Coordinating Committee for the Black Alliance for Peace and works in partnership with other organizers toward Black and Indigenous solidarity.

BETSEY PIETTE is a journalist for *Worker's World* (*workers.org*), a publication that has constantly written about Mumia Abu-Jamal for more than 25 years. She is also a longtime activist.

GABE BRYANT was among many who were instrumental in the 2021 organizing of Abu-Jamal activists after Abu-Jamal got COVID. He is a Philadelphia-based organizer whose work is centered on ending mass incarceration, political prisoners and building sustainable leadership models for marginalized communities. He is a member of the Philadelphia Community Bail Fund, Campaign to Bring Mumia Home and the Claim Malcolm X Day Committee. He also hosts the internet radio show *Stepping Into Tomorrow*, broadcast on Thursdays at 8:00 p.m. on *www.gtownradio.com*.

JAMAL JOURNAL (*www.JamalJournal.com*) is the official print and online newspaper of the International Concerned Family and Friends of Mumia Abu-Jamal. It was published as a print newspaper in the 1990s and was revived as an online publication and print newspaper in 2021. It contains regularly updated blog posts on the struggle to free Mumia, his current health, and an archive of ICFFMAJ events, articles and interviews.

TODD STEVEN BURROUGHS, PH.D. is an independent researcher and writer based in Newark, N.J. He is the author of *Warrior Princess: a People's Biography of Ida B. Wells*, and *Marvel's Black Panther: A Comic Book Biography, From Stan Lee to Ta-Nehisi Coates*, both published by Diasporic Africa Press. His 2014 audiobook, *Son-Shine on Cracked Sidewalks*, deals with the first mayoral election of Ras Baraka, the son of the late activist and writer Amiri Baraka, in Newark. Before Abu-Jamal's COVID and heart scares, he had finished a draft of the forthcoming *Talk-

ing Drums and Raised Fists: Mumia Abu-Jamal, a Biography of a Voice. He is now working on updating that book.

NOTES

1. Email correspondence to the author from Zayid Muhammad, November 27, 2020, 4:53 p.m.
2. Email correspondence to the author from Julia Wright, Saturday, November 28, 2020, 2:59 p.m.
3. MAJ's "Letter of Thanks" 3/19/21. From Stephen Vittoria's Facebook page, March 22, 2021, *https://m.facebook.com/stephen.vittoria/posts/10220286793268455?_rdr*. Retrieved on March 23, 2021. Vittoria's preface: "As many of you may know, my brother and a unique light in this world, Mumia Abu-Jamal, is now battling COVID-19 as well as a chronic skin disease - and yet he fights on with incredible superhuman strength and spirit, as he's fought for all of us from Amerikkka's gulag over the last 40 years; HERE'S HIS LETTER OF THANKS for all the support he 'feels' and acknowledges — for those who care and fight by his side, hour by hour, day by day. As Prison Radio writes, 'the pandemic has lifted the veil of the prison system's unwritten policy of inhumanity.'

    "Indeed it has - for some. With Mumia in the vanguard, many have been shining a bright light into this wretched darkness for decades - dare I say centuries. But like their guns, and wars, and capitalist sledgehammers, this society loves their Draconian inhuman and unnecessary prisons. 30%-60% of the incarcerated population has been infected by COVID-19. Did you expect anything different with how governors, judges, and DOCs everywhere have embraced the inhumanity of incarceration during a murderous pandemic? In fact, when have they ever acted in any other way that would allow us to expect a humanitarian approach at this juncture? Of course, never.

    "But Mumia fights on, rarely for himself, but for others, for all of us. 40 years mostly on death row and in solitary confinement - for only a short time in the general population before the pandemic. And the absolute horrific tragedy of this entire sad chapter? He is unequivocally an innocent man living his precious life in an absolute hell — which over the last year, somehow, got even worse. The lawyers fight hard against this monolithic monster, as does Noelle Hanrahan and Prison Radio, as does the ever committed and diligent Pam Africa — leading the way with love, unyielding support, and revolutionary righteousness. Like Che said, 'a revolutionary is guided by feelings of love and for love of the people.'

    "If you care, *visit abolitionistlawcenter.org* and *prisonradio.org* — check out their Herculean fight against injustice."
4. The Campaign To Bring Mumia Home, as published in *The Jamal Journal*.
5. For Fernandez's insider account of Abu-Jamal's COVID diagnosis, see "The Only Treatment is Freedom: Mumia Abu-Jamal and COVID," *Verso* Blog, March 28, 2021, *https://www.versobooks.com/blogs/5038-the-only-treatment-is-freedom-mumia-abu-jamal-and-covid*. Retrieved April 23, 2021. For an Abu-Jamal COVID scare—actually a Pennsylvania prison prank from a year earlier—see this editor's "Fantasies vs. Nightmares, Prison Abolition vs. Medical

Genocide: As The 'Free Mumia' Movement Prepares To Celebrate His Birthday, A Cruel, Late April Fool's Joke About Abu-Jamal Possibly Having COVID-19 Symptoms Backfires," *imixwhatilike.org*, April 16, 2020, *https://imixwhatilike.org/2020/04/16/mumiaandnightmares/*. Retrieved April 23, 2021.

6. Schell, Wes Mumia's Black Panther Party Defense Captain, as interviewed and introduced by Dick Cluster in 1979. This interview was originally published in Cluster's edited anthology, *They Should Have Served That Cup of Coffee: Seven Radicals Remember the '60s* (South End Press, 197)].
7. Selma, Alabama, the county seat of Dallas County, had been a focus of SNCC voter registration work since 1963. On Freedom Day—October 7, 1963—more than 350 local Blacks lined up at the courthouse to register; their applications were taken at the rate of only four an hour, and they were denied food and water the entire time they stood in line. The work continued, as did arrests and beatings of activists by county sheriff Jim Clark and his deputies.

   Selma achieved national prominence in February and March of 1965, when Martin Luther King began leading mass demonstrations there demanding the right to vote. Day after day, demonstrators were beaten with clubs and electric cattle prods by the sheriffs posse and Alabama state troopers. John Lewis of SNCC suffered a broken skull. Three people—a local Black man and two northern white supporters—were killed by police and local whites in the course of the demonstrations.
8. In May 1963, mass demonstrations in Birmingham, Alabama, for equal employment and desegregation of restaurants were met with clubs and high-pressure water hoses. On Sunday, September 13, after the demonstrations had ended and some demands had been won, the Ku Klux Klan bombed a Black church which had been a staging area for mass marches. Four Black girls were killed. No one was arrested for the crime until fourteen years later. Recent evidence suggests, however, that an FBI undercover agent inside the Klan knew about the planned bombing before it happened, and he may even have participated.
9. June Hilliard, brother of Panther leader David Hilliard, was the Party's Assistant Chief of Staff.
10. Former police chief Frank Rizzo became mayor of Philadelphia in 1971. He became nationally famous for siccing police dogs on Black public school students who were in the Philadelphia streets in 1968, calling for Black Power and Black Studies. To many Black Philadelphians, Rizzo was the epitome of the blatant white racism and white police brutality they suffered until he left office in 1980, after serving two terms as mayor.
11. Formed in response to militant Black organization and urban riots, the Urban Coalition was a federation of business, government, labor, and religious officials created to funnel money and jobs into poor neighborhoods.
12. H. Rap Brown, chairman of SNCC in 1967-68, urged Blacks to arm themselves for revolution.
13. Rioting by angry Blacks in Harlem (1964) and the Watts section of Los Angeles (1965), was followed by even more serious uprisings in Detroit and Newark in 1967 and in Washington D.C. and many other cities in response to the assassination of Martin Luther King in 1968.
14. Schell recalled: "When we started, they would just round us up, take us down,

photograph us, fingerprint us to get us on file, talk that bullshit, threaten you and all that bullshit, and they let you go on back. We found out there were policemen sleeping right with us, eating with us, selling papers with us.... But there wasn't too much you could do, so if you focused on it, you stopped doing your work. So we just carried on our work. We knew there were agents throughout our situation." Interview with Todd Steven Burroughs, Washington, D.C., April 20, 2002.

In *Still Black, Still Strong: Survivors of the War Against Black Revolutionaries* (Semiotext[e], 1993), Abu-Jamal recalled the following undated stop-and-frisk incident in an essay called "Panther Daze Remembered": "The four passengers of the dark-colored, two-tone sedan glide over a span of steel-girded bridge in Upper-North Philadelphia. All is dark, save for the blurry stars of headlights passing each other like meteors, shooting swiftly by.

"Suddenly, sharp stabs of red-blood light pierce the dark interior, jarring several men out of nods.

"'Aw, shit!', Stretch glowers, a yawn cutting off angry curses.

"A short burst of shrill siren, and a blinding searchlight slices dark irises and bounces painfully off of eight retinas, leaving a garish afterglow shining behind closed lids.

"Mary pulls over the ride and two cops appear at each door, barking at occupants harshly.

"Four men pile out into the false, electronic day, torn by the throbbing rotating red eye atop the car.

"One cop covers, while the other conducts an abrupt pat search.

"'What's this?' he asks, his nervous fingers running over a 'suspicious' bulge in my top left-hand jacket pocket.

"I am sleepy, ornery, and pissed at this intrusion, by the gall of two rednecks stopping, searching and possibly arresting four Black men in the midst of the Black community. I stand, arms outstretched, in scarecrowish silence.

"The cop, hooked now, pops the snap, digs his skinny white fingers into the pocket, and snatches out a worn, dog-eared book, with a red plastic cover.

"His attention distracted, he flips through pages, back towards the title page, and slowly, painstakingly, tries to read writing on a flimsy page.

"'Thee... quin... er, quotations of.... uh, uh—what's zis—Mayo Tessey—Tongue... ?!?'

"It takes a second before it clicks, then, like a flash of lightning—(*Quotations of Mao Tse-Tung!*)—'Jeezus Keerist!'

"'Communists!!!'

"The cop drops the book on the cold, wet ground, whips out his .38 revolver, and places it to the skull of the nearest Black man—me.

"His hand shakes, his skinny white finger clutches trigger, and four Black men are close to death because some pimply-faced white rookie cop is aghast that he has apparently uncovered a nigger-commie-spy ring. 'Freeze!!!' he shrieks, assuming a double-hand combat stance.

"(I mean, whatdafuck did he think we were doing—arms held high in a brisk wind? Hanging up clothes? Playing B-Ball?

"My eyes flick to Reg, the Defense Captain, as I search for direction.

"Hot sweat drips down cold flesh, my underarms watering my sides.

"Reg looks back with the wisdom of a thousand such street searches—and his dark, slanted eyes shoot upwards, as in 'Whatta fuck is he tryna prove?'

"He glances at the other cop, older, heavier, more senior, and cracks up in whinny-ish horse laughter.

"Tension flows from us all as we erupt in laughter, and the rookie, not knowing the butt of the joke, but beginning to suspect it is himself, steps back a pace, and glances at his older partner for direction.

"He, too, looks skyward, then cuts tired blue eyes toward his well-intentioned, but utterly melodramatic junior partner, smirks, walks over to the wind-blown pages of the Red Book, picks it up, slides it into my pocket.

"We stand silent in wintry night, wind whips through Afros and denim jackets, arms stretched out and upwards, like dark, leafless trees.

"The elder whispered to the unbearded youth, a few checks on car radio, a mumbled 'routine traffic check,' and they depart, in silence.

"Two cops had the Defense Captain, Lt. of Security, Lt. of Finance, and Lt. of Information of the Phila. Chapter of the Black Panther Party, the city's chapter leadership, under the gun, and let us go.

"We sat in the back of the car, and laughed anew, at the relief and loss of tension—how close." (193-195).

15. A trash protest was used by another revolutionary nationalist group who modeled themselves after (and learned from the mistakes of) the Black Panther Party: The Young Lords Party, a.k.a. Young Lords Organization: See Johanna Fernandez's book *The Young Lords: A Radical History* (Chapel Hill: University of North Carolina Press, 2020).
16. Chapter 3 from the forthcoming *Talking Drums and Raised Fists: Mumia Abu-Jamal, A Biography Of A Voice* by Todd Steven Burroughs.
17. "Philly Daze: An Impressionistic Memoir," in *Live From Death Row*, 173.
18. Abu-Jamal's FBI file, PH File 157-3937, Vol. 1, summary document, October 24, 1969. Abu-Jamal told an interviewer in 1989 said he was so badly battered—"beaten unrecognizable," that his mother walked by him in the hospital while looking him in the eyes. See "Interview from Death Row," Jim Fletcher, Tanaquil Jones and Sylvere Lotringer (eds.) *Still Black, Still Strong: Survivors of the War Against Black Revolutionaries* (New York: Semiotext[e], 1993), 122.
19. Later, Cook would add an Arabic surname when his first child, Jamal, was born three years later. He explained his name to Noelle Hanrahan during their post-commentary Q+A for *Prison Radio*: "Well, it means Prince. And it is also a name of some freedom fighters during the colonial war against Britain by the Kenyans during the times of Uhuru. So it has historical context but also a literal meaning, and for years, for maybe two or three years, I actually misremembered it and misspelled it. I would write 'Mumsia.' It took me a while to pay attention and go back to my sources and spell it the right way." When asked what his birth name means to him, he answered: "Well, it has a sweet meaning to me, actually. When I think of it, I think of my mother calling me by that name. I did not care for it when I was a teenager because it was during the Black revolution, and the Black Power movement, but you know, when you think of your mother, you think of what she called you and it has a real sweetness, and that is what my father called me before he passed, so I don't have a hang-up about it. A lot of people think they do, but I just laugh when people say that because it reminds me of my

mother. And what could be sweeter than that?" "Question for Mumia: Tell Me About Your Name," Prison Radio, February 7, 2003, http://www.prisonradio.org/maj/maj_2_7_name.html. Retrieved March 6. 2020.
20. *Black Men in Their Own Words,* an anthology edited by *Essence* magazine (New York: Crown, 2002), 28.
21. Matthew Countryman dates the beginning of the Philadelphia BPP at October 1968, when an activist named Terry McHarris publicly announced its formation. *Up South: Civil Rights and Black Power in Philadelphia,* 286. Abu-Jamal states that by 1969, the BPP had more than 40 chapters and branches. *We Want Freedom,* 46.
22. Reginald Schell, "A Way To Fight Back," in Dick Custer's (ed.) *They Should Have Served That Cup of Coffee: Seven Radicals Remember The '60s* (Boston: South End Press, 1979), 41-70; Bisson, *On A Move,* 52-53; *We Want Freedom,* 59-63, and Abu-Jamal's "A Life In The Party: An Historical And Retrospective Examination Of The Projections And Legacies of the Black Panther Party," in Kathleen Cleaver and George Katsiaficas (eds.) *Liberation, Imagination and the Black Panther Party* (England, UK: Routledge / Taylor & Francis Group, 2001), 40-42.
23. Because of blotting out by the FBI concerning two of the participants, it is presumed they were informants. Abu-Jamal's FBI Files, PH File 157-3937, Vol. 1, Memorandum, June 9, 1969.
24. Between 1967 and 1971, 233 of the FBI's admitted 295 counter-intelligence (COINTELPRO) actions against Black nationalist groups were against the Party. In *We Want Freedom,* Abu-Jamal recalls (61) that the group wasn't unaware of the presence of authorities: "Cameras went off like popcorn, but we had no real idea who the mostly white photographers were. We assumed they were the press, but some had the unmistakable air of cops about them. It never dawned on us that some were FBI agents building a file on us. Mostly, it was because, in an age of global revolution, it didn't seem too extraordinary to be a revolutionary, for didn't America come into being by way of the American Revolution?"
25. Mitchell was a New York City Panther leader who had East Coast authority, and Sister Love came from the Panther's national headquarters in Oakland. From *We Want Freedom,* 49; 181. Sister Love apparently stayed on, since news articles would list her as a field lieutenant for the branch.
26. Abu-Jamal's FBI Files, PH File 157-3937, Vol. 1, Memorandum, June 9, 1969. In *We Want Freedom,* Abu-Jamal lists on Page 197 the various offices of the branch as: 1928 West Columbia Avenue and 2935 West Columbia Avenue, both in North Philadelphia; 3625 Wallace Street, and in Germantown, 428 West Queen Lane. He wrote that there were four BPP breakfast programs throughout the city: "across from the main office in North Philadelphia on Columbia Avenue in a storefront next to a supermarket; in West Philadelphia, in a church near Party headquarters; in Germantown; and in a community center in Philadelphia" by the fall of 1970. "Soon, another center would open on Susquehanna Avenue, the second in North Philadelphia. Hundreds of children were fed well, thanks to their elders in the Black Panther Party" (194-195).
27. "City's Poor Children Fed by Panthers," *The Philadelphia Tribune,* July 8, 1969, 1, 2. The breakfast program was endorsed by the city's chapter of the National Association of Social Workers. The group even raised funds for it. Schell said the breakfast program was housed in a nearby building across the street from West Columbia—"a small, little,

raggedly place. But we cleaned it up and fixed it up and turned it into a pretty useful breakfast program." From April 20, 2002 Washington, D.C. interview with author. The Panthers would eventually have two sites for the breakfast program. The second was at the Houston Center, a United Fund agency. City Councilman Thomas Foglietta claimed the BPP has hijacked the center. Schell, denying the branch took over the center and explaining he was just meeting the needs of the people, shot back: "How many children have you fed, [Police Commissioner] Rizzo, Foglietta?" See Joe Adock's "Panther Role At UF Agency Stirs Hassle," *The* (Philadelphia) *Evening Bulletin*, January 16, 1970, 1, 23, and "Panthers Defend Breakfasts At United Fund Agency," *The* (Philadelphia) *Evening Bulletin*, January 17, 1970.

28. Abu-Jamal wrote: "As an officer, it was disconcerting to have older members come to me with Party, and even personal, problems. I had to dispel the suspicion that I was a young snot, that I instead had the confidence of the chapter and Party leadership, and thus had a duty to try to do my level best to help any Panther brother or sister, older or younger, who came for help, and if unable to do so, to refer them to other leaders in the organization." From *We Want Freedom*, 198.

29. Schell said he and Philadelphia Panther Craig Williams initially shared duties as co-captains. He also explained that although Philadelphia was a branch, it functioned like a state chapter, with Schell and other Panthers traveling to other offices around Pennsylvania. Interview with author, April 20, 2002, Washington, D.C. Like Cook, Schell was a working-class Black man who wanted to be more involved in the Movement. He left a foreman job at a sheet metal company in order to be part of the BPP's Philadelphia branch. He recalled how his wife initially thought he lost his mind when he told her his plans to be part of a Panther chapter. "I told her, 'I can't take this shit no more.' Blacks getting killed in the South because they were trying to vote, dogs getting sicced on them. My mind couldn't just compute that." From Kia Gregory's cover story, "The Cats Came Back," *Philadelphia Weekly*, December 17, 2003.

30. In *Death Blossoms*, Abu-Jamal recalled (87): "Without a father, I sought and found father figures like Black Panther Captain Reggie Schell, Party Defense Minister Huey P. Newton, and indeed, the Party itself, which, in a period of utter void, taught me, fed me, and made me part of a vast and militant family of revolutionaries. Many good men and women became my teachers, my mentors, and my examples of a revolutionary ideal—Zayid Malik Shakur, murdered by police when Assata [Shakur] was wounded and taken, and Geronimo ji jaga (a.k.a. Pratt) who commanded the Party's L.A. chapter with distinction and defended it from deadly state attacks until his imprisonment as a victim of frame-up and judicial repression—Geronimo, torn from his family and children and separated from them for a quarter of a century."

31. Interview with author, Washington, D.C., April 20, 2002.

32. He added: "I liked what I saw because of his maturity at such a young age, and being able to withstand the tremendous pressure of police and FBI tagging on him, and probably his mother worrying about him, and the police bothering her about him and his ability to stay so focused throughout that whole situation." Interview with author, Washington, D.C., April 20, 2002.

33. *The Distant Drummer*, an alternative paper of the period, described Cook in an article: "An intense and fairly articulate spokesman, Cook is a young man who has no tolerance for anyone not adhering to the revolutionary line pushed by the Panthers." Alan Oslick,

"Red Flag Flutters For A Day," *The Distant Drummer*, August 22-August 29, 1969, 4. Abu-Jamal has great nostalgia for this period. "I remember—and of course we're talking about decades ago now—but I remember it was probably one of the most exciting and liberational times of my life. Of course, for most people, their teen years are a time of freedom. Mine were a time of ultra, super freedom. It was a tremendous learning experience." From Allan Hougland's "Interview with Mumia," *Death Blossoms*, 126.

34. Bisson points out that Cook read his first copies of *The Guardian* and *Ramparts* magazine there, beginning his political education. He also points out that the bookstore's 13TH Street address is only just three blocks from 13TH and Locust. *On A Move*, 43.
35. Thomas Kearney, identified in the press as a former U.S. Marine who claimed to be an original member of the 1968 gathering, told a House of Representatives internal security committee in August that the membership of the Philadelphia branch was at least 150, police gave a similar number for the total. See McAdams, Leonard J. "Black Panthers Few But Feared, And The Phila. Chapter Is Growing," *The Philadelphia Inquirer*, September 1, 1970. 13.
36. Interview with author, Washington, D.C., April 20, 2002.
37. Schell described what Cook and the other Panthers did this way: "Wes would be going out to [the] community *then*, taking [accounts] from victims and then we would come back and either put a leaflet out or we would jump on a traffic light or do some things." Schell described Cook's job as "keep[ing] information coming in and keep[ing] information flowing out—bring it in from the community [and] get in back out to the community," and to keep communication channels open with the Central Committee. Even though the Party was at "war" with those who would oppress Black people, recalled Schell, "information was always our primary focus—to always get information, keep information flowing in and out of the Party to Black people." From interview with author, Washington, D.C., April 20, 2002.
38. Cook travelled to a variety of places as a Panther. In the fall of 1969, he also travelled to Chicago to assist the BPP with a training session for the Young Lords Party, a Latino revolutionary group founded in Chicago and then New York using the BPP model. For more on the Young Lords Party and the similarities and differences between the two groups, see Johanna Fernandez's *The Young Lords: A Radical History* (Chapel Hill, N.C.: University of North Carolina Press, 2020), 128.
39. Hampton was a leader of the Chicago Panthers and a rising star among them nationally. Chicago police shot him in his bed. *The Philadelphia Inquirer* covered the local memorial service, held at the Church of the Advocate. Fr. Paul Washington, the church's pastor, said at the event that 28 Panthers had been killed since the Party's 1966 founding. "The Rev. Washington introduced the next speaker, West Hook [SIC], who adhered to Panther policy of declining to give his name or address, except to say he was a member of the local chapter. In referring to the Dec. 4 slayings in Chicago of party chairman Fred Hampton and defense captain Mark Clark, both 22, Hook said, 'The only thing on his (Hampton's) bed was blood and a book by Lenin. He was murdered.'" From "Memorial Rites Held For Dead Panthers," *The Philadelphia Inquirer*, December 15, 1969, pg. 6. For more on Father Washington, see "Rev. Paul M. Washington: People's Shepard" (column written October 9, 2002), "Fr. Washington Remembered" (Speech written January 26, 2006) and Washington's book, *Other Sheep I Have: The*

Autobiography of Father Paul M. Washington (Philadelphia: Temple University Press, 1994).

40. The photo would appear on the cover of Abu-Jamal's fifth book, *We Want Freedom: A Life In The Black Panther Party*.
41. Prosecutor Joseph McGill used those comments with great skill and with great consequence in the sentencing phase of Abu-Jamal's 1982 first-degree murder trial.
42. At least one out-of-town Panther, a Marylander named Steve D. McCutchen, saw this. McCutchen (who, at the time, called himself "Chaka Masai" or "Lil' Masai") kept a diary of his Panther activities. Laying low from The Man in Baltimore, McCutchen hung with Schell and the Philadelphia Panthers. McCutchen wrote the following in a June 1970 entry, published in Charles E. Jones (ed.) *The Black Panther Party [Reconsidered]*, (Baltimore: Black Classic Press, 2005) a scholarly anthology: "Impressed with the Ministry of Information here. Wes Cook and his cadre supply sufficient and timely information to the community. I can learn from them" (128). The Philly Panthers' enemies equally appalled him: "[Philadelphia Police Commissioner Frank] Rizzo is a monster. His pigs are even more low-lifed than ours [in Baltimore]. He's deadly and lets anyone and everyone know it. He'll attack his own mother given the urge." (128).
43. Clay Dillion, "Panthers Run for Council," *The Philadelphia Tribune*, September 9, 1969, 1. Schell was quoted in the article as calling for Blacks to register to vote so Blacks could gain "community control" over the police. "The government of this city, the government of this state, and the government of this country has proven through practice that they can no longer serve the interest of the people but that of a few bureaucratic capitalists, profiteering exploiters called pigs... We believe that every man, woman and child in this city, state, country and world deserve the best that human knowledge and technology can produce. We will follow up this belief with concrete action." McGriff and Williams were unsuccessful in their quests for council seats.
44. Clay Dillion, "Black Panthers Call For Formation Of 'People's Army,'" *The Philadelphia Tribune*, November 11, 1969, 1, 2.
45. The Harold Brown Jr. story comes from an author interview with Schell, Washington, D.C., April 20, 2002. In We Want Freedom, Abu-Jamal said the branch grew rapidly as 1969 turned into 1970. "A year after our rally, our branch sold 10,000 Party newspapers a week and had functioning Party offices in West Philadelphia and Germantown. The Party nationally sold nearly 150,000 papers through direct street sales and paid subscriptions per week." From Freedom, 62. Recalled Schell: "I saw the intensity of Mumia [during the Brown incident].... .He was just good at his job.... That's when I really saw how good Mumia was." Schell said Rizzo claimed that the pamphlet was asking for a "hit" to be done on the officers. Interview with author, Washington, D.C., April 20, 2002.
46. Clipped newspaper articles by and about Cook are a constant in his FBI files. The periodicals: *The Militant*, then and now the organ of the Socialist Workers Party; *The Philadelphia Tribune*, then and now the city's leading Black newspaper; *The Temple News*, the student newspaper of Temple University; *The Black Panther; Babylon*, a New York-based newspaper affiliated with Eldridge Cleaver, and *The Distant Drummer*, an alternative paper serving Philadelphia. Together, they delineate an era in which young

people demanded change without asking for permission—and definitely without fearing any political, social, economic, or personal consequences.
47. Author interview with Schell, Washington, D.C., April 20, 2002.
48. Mumia (Abu-Jamal), ".... That Another Hand Reach Out To Pick Up The Gun," *The Black Panther*, April 6, 1970, 17. "Throughout our history, some niggers have refused to bow down and be beaten into the dust. They have risen to destroy our oppressor—Denmark Vesey, Nat Turner, Marcus Garvey, Nat Turner, Marcus Garvey, El Hajj Malik Al Shabazz (Malcolm), and then along came Huey." This article, written during the period of Cook's tenure in the National Office, shows traces of what would become the main theme of Mumia Abu-Jamal's Op-Ed work: the mixing of a radical history ideologically merged with the present.
49. West Cook (Mumia Abu-Jamal), "Meeting the Basic Needs of the People," *The Black Panther*, November 8, 1969, 10.
50. Keeping with the community and health focus, a locally produced supplement carried flyer-formatted information on the dangers of lead paint poisoning, an important issue in inner-city neighborhoods in the late 1960s and early 1970s. Small toddlers were eating chips of lead-based paint falling off of urban walls, forcing a health epidemic in urban Black America.
51. Schell, "A Way To Fight Back," in *Coffee*, 52.
52. News accounts stated police found the gun at the home of Schell's sister. An October 6 report in Abu-Jamal's FBI files stated the M-14 in Schell's possession was stolen from Camp Lejune in North Carolina in July of 1968. Mumia Abu-Jamal's FBI File, PH File 157-3937, report, Vol. 2.
53. "City police, FBI raid Black Panthers' HQ," *The Temple News*, September 25, 1969, 6. Months after the incident, Cook was quoted in *The Philadelphia Inquirer* as saying that the police "would have shot us then [in the headquarters], except we were all out in the community working at the time." See Moore, Acel, "Headquarters Cold, But Issues Are Hot for Black Panthers: Protest Killings By Police," *The Philadelphia Inquirer*, January 4, 1970, 1, 12.
54. Alan Oslick, "Panther Offices Raided: Local CD Squad Aids Hoover Team," *The Distant Drummer*, October 3, 1969, 1, 18. Although Schell would eventually be released, Hearn, the branch's Breakfast Coordinator, was convicted of a 1968 robbery and sentenced from six months to ten years in 1970.
55. Oslick, "Panther Offices Raided." Cook was quoted in the article as saying that the Philadelphia branch had fed 300 children every weekday this past summer. "We had started off with about 50. Then the pressure came on, and we were denied places to set up. We really need locations, like churches, badly. In the next month, we do hope to set up two more locations, to the one we have now at 1916 W. Columbia. I can't tell you where. We don't know yet.", 18.
56. "FBI's Philly Frame-Up," *The Black Panther*, October 4, 1969, 3. The raid just helped solidify the Party's standing within Philadelphia's Black communities, according to Schell: "They understood that the more they attacked the Party, the more Black people came into the Party. And that the more Black people came into the Party, then around the world the more Third World people became conscious of the tremendous surge, the tremendous will that was developing in this Black ethnic group or race here in the U.S. They knew that they couldn't eliminate us, because by the time they really started

escalating the killings of Panthers across the country, the seeds of revolution were already sown in the people." In "A Way to Fight Back," in *Coffee*, 59.
57. Lerone Bennett Jr, *The Shaping of Black America* (New York: Penguin Books, 1993) reprint of 1991 revised ed., 121.
58. Ibid.
59. Bennett, 128. *Freedom's Journal*, he writes, placed six issues into Black public space that have lasted to the present day: "1) Black assertion, 2) defense of the Black image, 3) equal education, 4) economic development, 5) civil and political rights, 6) African renaissance" (129).
60. Benjamin Quarles, *The Negro in the Making of America*, 3RD ed. (New York: Collier Books, 1987), 106-107. He continues: "As in the other phases of the abolitionist movement, Negroes were active participants in newspaper work, owning and managing twenty-four periodicals during the thirty years preceding the Civil War. Generally these Negro-run newspapers were not the official organ of any of the abolitionist societies... but they gave their full support to the crusade. These journals invariably had financial problems, and some of them were issued only a few times. Their common devotion to the principles of freedom and equality is evidenced in some of their titles—*Freedom's Journal, The Rights of All, Mirror of Liberty, Impartial Citizen,* and *Herald of Freedom*."
61. Lionel C. Barrow Jr., "Our Own Cause: *Freedom's Journal* and the Beginnings of The Black Press," in Jean Folkerts (ed.), *Media Voices: An Historical Perspective* (New York: Macmillan, 1992), 59.
62. *David Walker's Appeal*, edited by Peter P. Hinks (University Park: Pennsylvania: University of Pennsylvania Press, 2000), 14.
63. Bennett, 149.
64. This writing of an "open letter" of sorts would be used again and again throughout African-American history. The most prominent 20TH century example of this was Martin Luther King's "Letter From A Birmingham Jail," published in book form in *Why We Can't Wait* (New York: New American Library, 1964). King's letter was initially published in several Black and white mainstream newspapers shortly after it was written.
65. Mumia Abu-Jamal, *We Want Freedom*, 112-113.
66. *Ibid*, 198.
67. *Ibid*. Cook was transferred to New York City at the time of the "Panther 21" case, in which 21 members of the New York chapter were jailed for arson, conspiracy and attempted murder. Authorities charged the cadre was planning to blow up several public sites in the city, including department stores and a botanical garden. The group successfully defended themselves in court and in the public, becoming "political prisoners" in the minds of activist Blacks and the white political left. For more on the "Panther 21" case, see dequi kioni-sadiki and Matt Meyer (eds), *Look for Me in the Whirlwind* (Oakland, California: PM Press, 2017), an anthology of writings by Panthers about the case.
68. Mumia Abu-Jamal, "From Death Row" column: "Babylon's Basement," as published in *The Michigan Citizen*, February 24, 1996, A6.
69. "Conversation with Mumia Abu-Jamal," in Chinosole's (ed.) *Schooling the Generations in the Politics of Prison* (second ed.), (Afrikan/Black Prison Education Fund), 1997, 15.
70. Recalling years later, Abu-Jamal described Douglas thusly: "My boss was a gentle

woman, with a soft, Southern accent, who patiently helped the young Panther from Philadelphia write pieces worthy of the paper. She was a selfless and dedicated teacher." From *We Want Freedom*, 182. He described his Oakland job as "writer, graphic artist, typist, proofreader, and assistant" to Douglas. In "A Life In The Party: An Historical And Retrospective Examination Of The Projections And Legacies Of The Black Panther Party," in Cleaver and Katsiaficas, 47.

71. Abu-Jamal, *We Want Freedom*, 88-93. Cook's mother, Edith, did not know he was in Oakland and was very upset when she found out he was in jail there. After his release, Cook saw Schell, and asked to be transferred back to Philadelphia. Bisson, *On A Move*, 88.

72. "In his public statements, he [Rizzo] seemed unable to distinguish between Black criminals and Black activists who challenged authority on the basis of real grievances," wrote Joseph R. Daughen and Peter Binzen in *The Cop Who Would Be King* (Boston: Little, Brown and Company, 1977), their biography of Rizzo. "In this, he was not unlike those whites who watched with mounting fury the television accounts of Blacks marching in protest, occupying public buildings. Demonstrators were seen as thugs. [In the minds of those whites], there were 'good' Blacks, who obeyed the law behind locked doors in their crime-ridden neighborhoods, and there were 'bad' Blacks, who stabbed and pillaged and defined authority, and encouraged others to do so (132)."

73. Schell recalled what happened that night thusly: "About five o'clock that morning I was asleep [in the Philadelphia BPP headquarters], and somebody woke me up (we used to pull guard duty in the Panthers anyway) and said, 'They're here.' I looked out the window, and they're lined across the street with submachine guns, shotguns; they're in the alley. I saw the head man clearly[:] he had a pistol and a gas mask strapped to his leg. He was bending down, and then all hell broke loose. Finally, we had children in there and the gas got to them too much so we had to come out. Each cop took an individual Panther and placed their pistol up the back of our neck and told us to walk down the street backward. They told us [that] if we stumble or fall, they're gonna kill us. They then lined us up against the wall and a cop with a .45 sub[-machine gun] would fire over our heads so the bricks started falling down. Most of us had been in bed, and they just ripped the goddamn clothes off everybody, women and men. They had the gun, they'd just snatch your pants down and they took pictures of us like that. Then they put us in the wagon and took us down to the police station. We were handcuffed and running down this little driveway; when we got to the other end of it, a cop would come by with a stick and he'd punch us, beat us. Some of us were bleeding; I know I was bleeding, but really I thought it was gonna be a whole lot worse. We had three offices at the time—West Philly[,] where 14 Panthers had barricaded themselves, the North Philly office up here, and a small office in Germantown. They raided them, and they raided everyplace we stayed. When they took the office, they took everything; they even took the rugs off. And I couldn't understand the reason, but they took all the clothes, the machines; they took everything. I mean, I['ve] never seen anything as thorough as that—kitchen tables, kitchen chairs, everything we got, refrigerators; they didn't leave us nothing. When we finally got out we had to pay for suits from the prison. They arrested everyone from the North Philly and West Philly offices, and set the bail at $100,000 apiece. But the support out on the street was really picking up. I think something about them stripping all the clothes off and taking pictures was the s*&t that

backfired. Meanwhile, Rizzo was talking all this s*#t about how he wanted to take us all, one Panther and one cop, and we'd do battle on the street." From Schell, "A Way To Fight Back," in *Coffee*, 65-66.

74. Schell, "A Way to Fight Back," in *Coffee*, 66. The Quakers provided the majority of the bail funds. Philadelphia's community activists, including Sister Falaka Fattah, David Gracie and Muhammad Kenyatta, called for a federal injunction against the police department. See Washington, *Other Fish I Have*, 133, and Countryman, *Up South*, 288.

75. See Pamela Haynes, "Panthers' Meeting Began, Closed on Peaceful Note," *The Philadelphia Tribune*, September 8, 1970, 1, 3. She wrote that Newton referred to Rizzo as "Bozo" in his plenary speech.

76. Abu-Jamal, "Blues for Huey," *Live From Death Row*, 167.

77. Ibid.

78. A typed copy of the speech is in vol. 3 of Abu-Jamal's FBI files. David Hilliard, one of the Party's national leaders, recalled the moment in his autobiography: "The crowd wants to love him—he's the star. But they don't understand anything of his treatise on American history.... Huey's frustration with public speaking builds up.... 'These people have no analytic sense,' he tells me [offstage after his speech], referring to the crowds. 'They're hung up on [BPP Minister of Information] Eldridge [Cleaver]'s slogans and revolutionary talk. They're not used to analytic lecturing.'" From David Hilliard's *This Side Of Glory: The Autobiography Of David Hilliard And The Story Of The Black Panther Party* (Boston: Little, Brown and Company, 1993), 313.

79. Schell described it this way: "Masses of people in this country were beginning to side with the Left wing, both white and Black. But I think the U.S. has got a system that people have got to be very, very conscious of. That is, it projects leaders, and then it breaks leaders. I was out in California that summer when Huey P. Newton got out of jail, and I watched it when people from the community came up and talked with him, congratulated him for coming home and told him how much they missed him and supported him. And I saw that he couldn't talk to them. His conversation was gone[;] he was a million miles away from them. At the [convention's] plenary session what he said just lost people. When he spoke to the people at that session, he spoke to ordinary people in the street way over their head[s], while they were talking about committing themselves to going back to their areas and making some very fundamental changes in people. Internally there were certain things happening that left a lot of people across the country dissatisfied. There was drug use, there were problems at the top; and Bobby Seale was in jail in New Haven, Connecticut, and Eldridge Cleaver was outside the country [in Algiers] and couldn't return. We were hoping that Huey could turn it around, but when he came home we found that he wouldn't or couldn't do it, and the Party just started falling, people just started leaving it. The desire was gone. It's not a question of individuals, really. But the people at the top, the [C]entral [C]ommittee of the Party, they were the ones that we looked up to, the ones that inspired us to do more, and when we couldn't get that inspiration any more, then chapters and branches across the country just started to fall apart." Schell, "A Way to Fight Back," in *Coffee*, 61-62.

80. Ibid., 62.

81. Ibid.

82. Interview with author, Washington, D.C., April 20, 2002.

83. Schell recalled that the Party would remain in Philadelphia until about 1973. That was

the year the Central Committee would order all the chapters and branches to shut themselves down in order for members to move to Oakland to help with the Party's unsuccessful campaigns for local elected office.
84. "Philly Daze," *Live from Death Row*, 176.
85. *Ibid.*, 176, 177. Schell recalled: "As Panthers, we were hoping that there was some kind of way it would be resolved, because we really didn't want to get into to taking size. "We didn't go into with kind of idol worship about Huey over Eldridge. We went in because the Party was to us a symbol of the liberation of Black people. We were hoping that somewhere down the line this thing could get resolved, but as COINTELPRO went on, it got worse." Interview with author, Washington, D.C., April 20, 2002.
86. From the interview "The Prison House of Nations," in Jim Fletcher, Tanaquil Jones and Sylvere Lotringer (eds.) *Still Black, Still Strong: Survivors of the War Against Black Revolutionaries (New York: Semiotext[e], 1993)*, 151. The Philadelphia branch was not immune to the "system's" psychological warfare. In his doctoral dissertation, "War Against the Panthers," Newton detailed how the Philadelphia branch of the FBI sent him phony correspondence from the Philadelphia BPP. The fake message was a cover letter from an anonymous BPP supporter, criticizing the Philadelphia leadership for "slandering" members. Attached to the cover letter was phony documents consisting of local BPP leaders criticizing Newton. The FBI also sent faux anonymous correspondence to the National Office about how the Philadelphia branch was stealing from the Party's community service programs. The FBI report Newton quoted from is dated Aug. 19, 1970—the period the Party was preparing for the convention.
87. Acel Moore and Gerald McKelvey, "Panther Chief Resigns Post, Information Aide Steps Down," *The Philadelphia Inquirer*, Sunday, November 1, 1970, 1.
88. "Students Suspended At Franklin," *The Philadelphia Inquirer*, October 30, 1970, 8. In the article, Benjamin Franklin Principal Leon Bass calls Cook a student of "great potential." The quote was also used in a caption under a picture of him. "He had pleaded with Cook, he said, 'not to let his political views interfere with his education.'"
89. Abu-Jamal's FBI Files, PH File 157-3937, Vol. 3. Vol. 4 would list another high school transfer, to Gratz High School. Abu-Jamal would eventually get his high school diploma by passing the GED exam.
90. The fact that Cook resigned from the Philadelphia BPP branch did not stop the FBI from continuing its surveillance of him. Abu-Jamal's FBI files show that agents attempted to interview Cook on January 19, 1971, months after he had left the Party. He refused to participate. More than 600 sheets of paper would be compiled on Cook from 1969, when he had turned 15, until about 1974, the year of his 20TH birthday. Cook was only a Party member from May 1969 until October 1970—less than two years, but the FBI kept up its tabs on Cook for more than three years after he left the Party. Although he had been arrested more than once for political agitation, the teenage Cook had no criminal record. The bureau acknowledged a grudging respect, of sorts, for its subject. An October 26, 1970 memorandum reads: "Cook has worked in Philadelphia, New York and the BPP national office in Oakland, California, where he was officer of the day and worked on the BPP newspaper. Although he is only 16 years old and has no informant potential, he possesses much intelligence and evidentiary information of great interest if he will talk." Abu-Jamal's FBI Files, PH File 157-3937, BUFILE, 67C, 2. Detailing the FBI's subversive and sinister role in helping to destroy

dissent throughout the 20TH century, Abu-Jamal wrote: "The Bureau used its enormous power, influence, and contacts to intimidate politicians and assassinate people in their beds. It used the omnipresent press to hound people out of their jobs. It sabotaged allegedly free elections. It destroyed marriages. It shattered families. It fomented violence between political and social adversaries. And this is but the tip of the iceberg. If this is a law enforcement agency, one shudders to think what a hate group would do." *We Want Freedom*, 135.
91. *Black Men*, 28.
92. This section is an excerpt from Todd Steven Burroughs, *Talking Drums and Raised Fists: Mumia Abu-Jamal, A Biography Of A Voice* (forthcoming biography).
93. Jesse Jackson, *Legal Lynching: Racism, Injustice and the Death Penalty* (New York: Marlowe & Company, 1997), 146.
94. Mumia Abu-Jamal FBI File, PH File 157-3937, Vol. 4, Philadelphia, Pennsylvania FBI summary document, June 30, 1972.
95. Bisson, 116. The fourth volume of Abu-Jamal's FBI files show the Bureau's repeated, and unsuccessful, attempts to obtain specific information from, and about, Abu-Jamal's experiences at Goddard. The Bureau did have sources and informants in and around the area—particularly the Montpelier, Vermont Police Department—but does not specifically list informants within Goddard. Because of the lack of information about his Goddard activities within the files, it can be surmised that the Bureau did not have any direct Goddard sources and informants.
96. Mumia Abu-Jamal's FBI File, PH File 157-3937, Vol. 4, "Urgent" communication from Acting Director, March 13, 1973.
97. *Ibid.*, memo to Acting Director, March 15, 1973.
98. Contributor's Note: This article is the translated and slightly revised version of my German article "Das alte, abgekartete Spiel. Wie Polizei, Staatsanwaltschaft und Gerichte Mumia Abu-Jamal zum 'Mörder' machten," which first appeared in the volume Mumia Abu-Jamal. Der Kampf gegen die Todesstrafe und für die Freiheit der politischen Gefangenen, Hamburg 2011. My thanks go to Annette Schiffmann for discussing earlier versions of the original article with me, and to my friend Nicholas Williams for helping with the translation.
99. On the frequency of the killing of police officers (and the frequency of the killing of unarmed civilians by cops) in the United States, see Michael Schiffmann, "Der Hintergrund: Polizeikorruption und -brutalität in den USA," in *Free Mumia. Dokumente, Analysen, Hintergrundberichte*, Bremen 2002, pp. 133-51, here pp. 137-38.
100. For a list, see http://www.fop5.org/services/honor.php. In 1981, in Philadelphia two police officers met with a violent death, in 1980, three. The next police officer, Thomas Trench, was killed no earlier than 1985.
101. On July 2 und July 3, 1982, respectively.
102. According to the official statistics for the year 1980.
103. See the statistics of the Death Penalty Information Center in Washington, http://www.deathpenaltyinfo.org/.
104. On these questions, see Loïs Wacquant, *Elend hinter Gittern*, Konstanz 2000; Michelle Alexander, *The New Jim Crow*, New York 2010, and Kyrylo Tkachenko, *Der Fall Mumia Abu-Jamal: Rassismus, strafender Staat und die US-Gefängnisindustrie*, Münster 2012.

105. For the line just quoted, see *Philadelphia Inquirer*, December 10, 1981.
106. See for this inter alia Michael Schiffmann, *Race Against Death*, 2006, chapter 5.
107. As the transcripts of the police radio traffic and testimony by a witness show, the most resilient of these speculations that has Cook driving down 13TH Street (which is a one-way street) in the wrong direction is certainly wrong.
108. As the pool of blood on Pedro P. Polakoff's photo clearly shows.
109. For a summary of the prosecution's version, see the opening statement by prosecutor McGill on June 19, 1982, quoted in Schiffmann, *Race*, p. 113.
110. For a more detailed description, see *ibid.*, pp. 113-19.
111. For all these questions, see the contribution of Linn Washington, Jr. to *MAJ*, and also Amnesty International's 2000 special report on Abu-Jamal.
112. See Abu-Jamal's "A Christmas Cage," in *MAJ*, pp. 97-102. Of course, police and prosecution in Philadelphia to this day deny any form of incorrect treatment of Abu-Jamal, but these denials are both self-serving and unbelievable.
113. Police radio transcript, in the possession of the author.
114. See C. Clark Kissinger, "Philly's Killer Elite," in *Resource Book on the Case of Mumia Abu-Jamal*, p. 20.
115. In the books by Lindorff, O'Connor and Schiffmann; see the bibliography in *MAJ*, pp. 253-54.
116. Which perhaps could be explained away by referring to the fallibility of human memory and the fact that contradictory testimony on the part of witnesses is therefore nothing unusual.
117. The number varied from witness to witness and from statement to statement, but all of them talked about minimally two and maximally four shots. White and Chobert identified Abu-Jamal as the shooter, whereas Scanlan at first falsely named Billy Cook as the shooter and then refused to identify the perpetrator at all.
118. At the behest of journalist Dave Lindorff, one of the Polakoff photos was investigated for potential gunshot traces by a NASA photo specialist, and the result was negative.
119. Albert Magilton didn't have to contribute anything substantial concerning the core of the events, but only stated the uncontested fact that Abu-Jamal had run to the scene before the shots. All the same, he is time and again portrayed as an important "prosecution witness."
120. See Schiffmann, *Race*, p. 128.
121. My sketch here follows Schiffmann, *Race*, pp. 210-18, with a slightly different accent.
122. See for this the book of the leading specialist on the topic, Beat Kneubühl, *Das Abprallen von Geschossen aus forensischer Sicht*, dissertation, Thun 1999, pp. 47-75.
123. At the trial, even Abu-Jamal's totally overwhelmed defense lawyer expressed doubts whether it was even possible that the bullet fragment in 1234 Locust had come from Abu-Jamal's gun. See *Trial Transcripts (TT)*, July 1, 1982, p. 122.
124. On Jenkins, see Schiffmann, *Race*, pp. 177-78; on Williams, see *Free Mumia. Dokumente, Analysen, Hintergrundberichte*, pp. 152-55.
125. See Schiffmann, *Race*, p. 236-37.
126. Investigation Interview Records (IIRs) Trombetta and Wakshul, December 9, 1981, in the possession of the author. Trombetta claimed Abu-Jamal had said that his gun was in the street and was silent afterwards, whereas Wakshul simply stated: "During this time, the Negro male made no comments."

127. IIR Giordano December 9, 1981, in the possession of the author.
128. Joyce Gemperlein/Robert J. Rosenthal, "Abu-Jamal Shot Officer in Back, Witness Says," *Philadelphia Inquirer*, January 9, 82.
129. When questioned on February 12, 1982 because of Abu-Jamal's complaint about violent abuse during his arrest, Trombetta synchronized his testimony with the one of Giordano and claimed Abu-Jamal had responded: "I've thrown it in the street." But Trombetta still didn't mention anything about a confession – and he never did.
130. *Philadelphia Daily News*, March 20, 1986.
131. *TT*, Jun 24, 1982, p. 141 (Bell), *ibid.* p. 124 and July 1, 1982 pp. 173-74 (Durham and LeGrand); Transcript of the PCRA Hearings (*PCRAH*), July 31, 1995, p. 86 (Wakshul), Transcript of the four-day (June 1-4, 1982) Suppression Hearings (*SH*), June 1, 1982, pp. 127-28, 133 (Bray).
132. In the HBO documentary film *Mumia Abu-Jamal – A Case for Reasonable Doubt?*, which is also available in a German and in a French version. In 2007, a bonus edition was published in the U.S. that contained the uncut version of the interview with Abu-Jamal, which was conducted for the film, and in which he says that he did not kill Faulkner.
133. Investigation files by the police, in the possession of the author.
134. Polakoff shot a series of 31 photographs, among them pictures of the police wagon where Abu-Jamal was kept. Polakoff doesn't have the negatives of these last photos (No. 18-22) anymore since he supplied them to the *Daily News* and didn't get them back, but in an e-mail interview with me, Polakoff explicitly stated that pictures 6, 9, 10 and 11, all of which clearly show the Mobile Crime Lab, were taken before Abu-Jamal was transported away from the scene and to hospital.
135. See inter alia Svensson, Wendel, Fisher & Pitchess, *Technique of Crime Investigation*, 3RD edition, New York 1981, at the time a recognized standard work.
136. Among other places, in the (abridged version of the) film *Justice on Trial* in *MAJ*.
137. *TT*, June 23, 1982, p. 169. Even the fact that the five chambers of the cylinder of Abu-Jamal's revolver contained only spent shells doesn't have to mean anything if he, as insinuated in the HBO documentary, carried the gun only as a potential deterrent against attackers.
138. See Schiffmann, *Race*, p. 231.
139. See Abu-Jamal's "A Christmas Cage."
140. These were the words of Linn Washington, Jr. when he described the case to Annette Schiffmann and me during our first meeting with him in September 2001.
141. For the numerous cues for the presence of this passenger as well as for his identity, see below and the film *Justice on Trial* in *MAJ*.
142. Because nobody saw her at this point in time, either at the intersection or elsewhere, it is impossible to say where.
143. Police radio transcript, *ibid*.
144. *Ibid*. EPW is for "Emergency Patrol Wagon."
145. Washington on the Events of December 9, 1981, May 3, 2001 in pages 108-113 in this book.
146. The description in this paragraph follows the one by Cook in the documentary *In Prison My Whole Life*, DVD in *MAJ*.

147. See "Suspect's Brother 'Only Heard Shots, Didn't See Shooting,' Attorney Says," *Philadelphia Bulletin*, December 12, 1981.
148. This is one of the few uncontroversial points in this case.
149. IIR Albert Magilton, December 17, 1981.
150. I owe the fascinating information about the habits of the Philadelphia street cops at the time to a conversation with Dave Lindorff. Of course, we don't *know* that this is what happened in Faulkner's case. It would, however, be the best explanation for the curious location of Faulkner's hat on the roof of Billy Cook's VW where it was later found.
151. According to all available descriptions, Faulkner was about twenty centimeters bigger and much heavier than Cook; on the lacking credibility of the testimony by White and Scanlan who claimed that Cook hit Faulkner first see Michael Schiffmann, "The Forgotten Trial: Spurious Witnesses, Impossible Events," *www.abu-jamal-news.com*. Cook has denied right from the start that he ever hit Faulkner; see *In Prison*.
152. Billy Cook's coat, sweater and shirt all had blood there; see Laboratory Division, Criminalistics Unit [of the Philadelphia Police Department], "Investigation of the Shooting Death of Pol. Faulkner," July 1, 1982, p. 2, in the possession of the author.
153. "Suspect's Brother," also "Declaration by William Cook," April 29, 2001, in *Free Mumia*, p. 58.
154. As we will see, this is also where it was when the first police officers arrived.
155. This would explain the bizarre contradictions in her statements about the shooting, and the curious fact that her first two statements didn't even mention the altercation between Cook and Faulkner.
156. During Billy Cook's trial for aggravated assault at the end of March 1982, she testified against Cook and had the following dialogue with prosecutor McGill: "When the officer went up to the car, which side of the car did the officer go up to?" White: "The driver side." McGill: "The driver side?" White: "Yes." McGill: "What did the *passenger* do?" White: "He had got out." My emphasis, see the transcript of Billy Cook's trial, p. 33, in the possession of the author; also see Schiffmann, "The Forgotten Trial," pp. 4-5, and Johanna Fernandez in *MAJ*, pp. 205-221. Given White's probable total absence from the scene, this may simply have been a slip of the tongue by McGill.
157. See Schiffmann, *Race*, pp. 142, 176, 219-20 and the questioning of that friend, Arnold Howard, during Abu-Jamal's PCRA Hearings 1995, *PCRAH*, August 9, 1995, pp. 4-109.
158. See Schiffmann, *Race*, p. 221 and the contribution of Johanna Fernandez to *MAJ*.
159. The description of Freeman is by Linn Washington, Jr., who knew him well.
160. See Linn Washington, Jr., "The Reign of Frank Rizzo: Brutality Explodes," in *Resource Book*, pp. 16-18.
161. At the trial, it was claimed that the shots that hit Abu-Jamal and Faulkner had to have been fired from a very short distance. In the HBO film *A Case for Reasonable Doubt?*, expert McDonnell demonstrates that this is not true.
162. The bullet channel on the wound in Abu-Jamal's chest had a 30-grade downward angle and thus suggests that the latter was bent over in a forward direction, typical for a runner, when he was hit and that the shooter's position was higher than his.
163. At least if one wants to believe the officers James Forbes and Robert Shoemaker who, according to their own testimony, were the first cops to arrive at the scene.
164. See Schiffmann, *Race*, pp. 218-19.

165. For this and the following paragraph, see the attempt at a ballistic analysis in Schiffmann, *Race*, pp. 220-21 und 230.
166. The pitched left knee and the corresponding rift in Faulkner's trousers are documented in the police files. See Schiffmann, *Race*, p. 224.
167. This shot would then have been fired in the direction of 12TH Street, which would explain why the bullet was never found.
168. Reconstructed from the sparse statements Billy Cook has made in the course of the years and that are, in part, contradictory, but consistent with regard to this major statement. What Cook would say in an actual courtroom remains to be seen.
169. According to his first statement to Inspector Giordano (IIR Giordano, December 9, 1981).
170. IIR Michael Scanlan, December 9, 1981 and police radio transcript.
171. IIR Albert Magilton, December 9 and 17, 1981.
172. Only two of these five, Chobert und Hightower, testified at Abu-Jamal's trial. Of course, at that point in time Chobert had altered his testimony quite substantially. See Schiffmann, *Race*, p. 211.
173. See "Declaration of William Cook," *Free Mumia*, p. 60.
174. IIR Veronica Jones, December 15, 1981.
175. See Abu-Jamal, "A Christmas Cage." Even Forbes and Shoemaker have never claimed to have questioned Abu-Jamal.
176. See *ibid.*; the explanations of the officers in question can only be seen as self-serving declarations.
177. Pedro P. Polakoff, personal communication, also see Schiffmann, *Race*, p. 235.
178. *SH*, June 2, 1982, p. 21.
179. IIR Giordano, December 9, 1981.
180. A point that even Giordano himself had to concede in various statements.
181. Documented in defense petitions in 2001, in the possession of the author.
182. See Abu-Jamal, "A Christmas Cage."
183. Later on, Giordano will claim that he was the one who ordered this via police radio, even though he had been in *direct* contact with Wakshul und Trombetta right at the scene.
184. Pedro P. Polakoff, personal communication.
185. Pedro P. Polakoff, personal communication.
186. As for the prosecution's later "star witness," Cynthia White, during her first interview, she didn't mention anything about Abu-Jamal firing at Faulkner as the latter already lay on the ground, but rather said: "He fired at the Police Officer about four or five times. *Then* [my emphasis] the Police Officer fell to the ground. I started screaming." She also didn't mention the altercation between Cook and Faulkner, either because she didn't want to anger her interlocutors by a description of Faulkner's brutal behavior, or because she had disappeared from the scene too early to observe even this. Only after she was arrested two more times for prostitution, she synchronized her testimony with the testimonies by Chobert and Scanlan.
187. See Schiffmann, *Race*, p. 234.
188. See Schiffmann, *Race*, p. 143 and the HBO-Film *A Case for Reasonable Doubt?*.
189. See *A Case for Reasonable Doubt?*.
190. See *A Case for Reasonable Doubt?*, and also Schiffmann, *Race*, pp. 143-44 and 177.

191. On Marcus Cannon see *Free Mumia*, p. 123.
192. IIR Giordano, December 9, 1981; also Giordano's testimony at the Suppression Hearing, June 1, 1982, *SH*, p. 70.
193. IIR Chobert, December 9, 1981. In the film *Justice on Trial*, J. Patrick O'Connor erroneously talks about thirty feet (circa 9 meters), but in his statement, Chobert unequivocally talks about "steps."
194. This is even truer three days later when he estimated the weight of the man as around 220-25 pounds; see IIR Chobert, December 12, 1981. Freeman's appearance in 1981 (stocky, heavy, dreadlocks like Abu-Jamal) was described to me several times by Linn Washington, Jr. According to Chobert's own estimate on June 2, 1982 at the suppression hearing, Abu-Jamal s weight at that time was „about 170, 180 pounds"; see *SH*, pp. 68-69.
195. IIS Scanlan, December 9, 1981.
196. The witness in question is Arnold Howard. According to Howard, who had an alibi for the time of the shooting, the police learned through questioning him that had lent a copy of his license application to Freeman, upon which they proceeded to bring in the latter also in to homicide for interrogation. See *PCRAH*, August 9, 1995, pp. 9-23. Howard also claimed that Freeman was repeatedly identified by a Black woman as having been present at the scene. All of this was vigorously denied by the prosecution during its cross examination of Howard, and there is no independent source that could verify the claims of either side.

    What is not in doubt, however, is the fact that the Howard document was found on Faulkner, nor does anyone deny that the prosecution failed to inform the defense about that fact before the trial. Moreover, it hardly needs Howard's testimony to be convinced that the police did indeed investigate Freeman, since this was simply a no-brainer. At that point, Cook and Freeman had operated a street vending business in Center City for a number of years, were known by everyone who knew them to be extremely close to each other, and had been repeatedly and violently harassed by the police on account of their vending business. This very close relationship also makes it highly likely that the third man at the scene observed by as many as six independent witnesses was indeed Kenneth Freeman.
197. See the contribution by Alice Walker in *MAJ*.
198. Howard (*PCRAH*, August, 9, 1995, pp. 21-22) says that this was then common understanding in North Philadelphia, and this claim *is* corroborated by other, independent sources, among them Philadelphia journalist Linn Washington, Jr., who additionally says that he then approached Freeman's family with an offer to further investigate, but that the family, not wanting to get into further trouble, declined (Linn Washington, Jr., personal communication).
199. Excerpted from the full article in *The Stanford Law Review*, 1625, 1995-1996.
200. Dante Alighieri, *Inferno*, Canto III, lines 43-48 (Mark Musa ed. and translated, 1995).
201. Kenneth B. Noble, "As Executions Increase, Appeals Go to the Public," *The New York Times*, December 12, 1995, pp. 1, 10.
202. Steven A. Holmes, "U.S. Ordered to Tell How It Decides to Seek Executions," *The New York Times,* May 11, 1994, A18.
203. Albert Camus, "Reflections on the Guillotine," in *Resistance, Rebellion and Death: Essays* (New York: Knopf, 1960; First Vintage International Edition, 1995), p. 182.

204. Contributor's Note: This is a 2021 updated version of Chapter 9 of Lindorff's book *Killing Time* (Common Courage Press, 2003) with thanks from both author and editor to Common Courage editor/publisher Greg Bates for allowing permission.
205. Mumia Abu-Jamal, *Writings on the Wall: Selected Prison Writings of Mumia Abu-Jamal*, edited by Johanna Fernandez (City Light books, 2015), xv. This quote is from the foreword written by West.
206. Most works on the history of Black Studies discusses the student protest movements of the 1960s as an important thrust for Black Studies. Merritt College, attended by Huey Newton and Bobby Seale, was one important site for the advocacy of Black Studies. The Black Panther Party, SNCC, and the Revolutionary Action Movement (RAM) members were integral to the movement. *From Black Power to Black Studies* by Fabio Rojas provides a good account of this period.
207. As Todd Steven Burroughs has pointed out in his most current book reviews of Mumia Abu-Jamal's work at *imixwhatilike.org*, the journalist has morphed into a historian. Abu-Jamal has produced a history of the Black Panther Party, a small book on the history of Black religion and has co-written a three-volume work, *Murder, Incorporated*, about the abuses of the American empire. His work as a historian has gone virtually uncommented on by scholars in Africana Studies.
208. Lew Myers was one of Assata Shakur's attorneys, was a movement lawyer in Mississippi, and went on to represent Louis Farrakhan, Jesse Jackson, Larry Hoover, Geronimo Pratt, and countless incarcerated individuals.
209. Mack Jones, ed., *The Journal on Political Repression*, June 1976 vol. 1, No.1. (A Joint publication of the National Conference of Black Political Scientists and the Commission for Racial Justice, United Church of Christ): 6.
210. Mumia Abu-Jamal, *Death Blossoms: Reflections from a Prisoner of Conscience* (City Lights Publishers; Expanded Edition, 2019), 94.
211. *Time* magazine, October 24, 1977.
212. Heather Ann Thompson, *Blood in the Water: The Attica Prison Uprising of 1971 and Its Legacy* (New York: Vintage Books, 2017), 19.
213. *Live from Death Row*, 46.
214. To be fair, many of these works were published in the early 2000s, before Abu-Jamal's arc as a historian fully blossomed.
215. Greg Carr, "What Black Studies is Not: Moving from Crisis to Liberation in Africana Intellectual Work," *Socialism and Democracy*, 25:1, 2011, 178-191.
216. *Live from Death Row*, 62-64.
217. Mumia Abu-Jamal, *Have Black Lives Ever Mattered?* Kindle edition (City Lights Publishers, 2017), location 752-757.
218. Kelly Harris and Kim Dulaney, "The Devil is in the Details: The 1972 Gary Convention as an Activist Learning Model for Africana Studies," *International Journal of Africana Studies* (Winter, 2016).
219. Mumia Abu-Jamal, *We Want Freedom: A Life in the Black Panther Party* (2008), 80.
220. Originally Published in November/December 2020 *Essence* magazine.
221. From Prison Radio. For more information, please visit: *www.murder-incorporated.org*.

www.ingramcontent.com/pod-product-compliance
Lightning Source LLC
Chambersburg PA
CBHW062032120526
44592CB00036B/1874